MARNIX WEL

HÉGUANZÎ

THE DAO OF UNITY

in the Birth

of the Chinese Empire

Pheasant Cap Master, Grand Unity

and the

Nine Augustans,

Linking Politics and Philosophy

to

Religion

in

Ancient China

To order additional copies of this book, contact:
Xlibris
UK TFN: 0800 0148620 (Toll Free inside the UK)
UK Local: (02) 0369 56328 (+44 20 3695 6328 from outside the UK)
www.Xlibrispublishing.co.uk
Orders@Xlibrispublishing.co.uk
768518

鶡冠子

Dedication

To my parents Edward Preston 'Hawkeye Bill' and Mary Dorothea; daughter Sarah; helper and beloved soul-mate Joyce; honorary proofreaders Angus Macindoe and Lillian Chia; my teachers at Oxford University's Oriental Institute, 1964-1967: professor David Hawkes, lecturers Raymond Dawson, Glen Dudbridge, then PhD candidate Wong Siu-kit; and at London University, School of Oriental and African Studies, 1993-2001: my PhD supervisor Paul Thompson.

I would also like to acknowledge a debt of gratitude to all pioneers of *Héguanzî* studies, in particular professors Angus C. Graham (1919-1991), Huáng Huáixìn in China, Carine Defoort in Belgium, and Jean Lévi in France. Last buy not least, to my IT guru Sikander Qasemi.

Prologue

This is the tale of a nation, Zhào (Shanxi), on the eve of destruction. It reflects the last stand of one of six independent kingdoms against imperial Qín, with a novel vision of an egalitarian world order. Yet we also see here the emergent blueprint of a centralised bureaucracy under a messianic ruler, shortly to be implemented by Qín in the draconian person of its 'First Augustan Emperor', Qín Shîhuángdì.

Like Rome's Emperor Augustus, and China's subsequent emperors, he adopted celestial status as if an astral incarnation. This work, which fuses ideas of Lâo Zî's 'Way' with 'Law', Dào with Fâ, is ascribed to Héguan Zî, the 'Pheasant Cap Master', the enigmatic figure who features in its dialogues. Its antiquity has been authenticated by parallels with 'Yellow Emperor' scrolls only recently recovered from a 168 BC tomb of the early Hàn dynasty.

Uniquely, the work speaks frankly of contemporary events together with prophecies of a messiah-like figure, an 'Augustan' who will unite the world. A double ninefold schema, with a messianic revelation of Nine Augustans and Grand Unity, centered on three core chapters (ix-xi), encapsulates the book's plan:

i. Wide Selection, ii. Manifest Hope, iii. The Night Walker,
iv. Heaven's Model, v. Circular Flow, vi. The Way's Governance,
vii. Nearing Collapse, viii. Saving Myriads,
ix. Royal Axe, x. Grand Expanse, xi. Grand Record,
xii. Generations of Arms, xiii. Prepared Knowledge, xiv. Armed Campaigns,
xv. Study Problems, xvi. Generations of Worthies,
Heaven's Balance, xviii. Enabling Heaven, xix. King Wûlíng.

The first half, *i-ix*, outlines hopes for a new order in the face of defeat by Qín with revelation of a divine plan; followed, in *x*, by an inter gods dialogue between Grand Unity and Grand Augustan; ending in the second half, *xii-xix*, with ideas on armed struggle and tactics to save the day.

Abstract

Héguanzî, compiled under the alibi meaning 'Pheasant Cap Master', furnishes us with fertile topics for soul searching in our modern world, fast approaching humanitarian world unity or catastrophe. Written in desperate days of China's Warring States in the third century BC *Héguanzî* opens a window into the thought-processes preceding one of the most momentous events in world history.

It gives the most comprehensive exposition of Lâo Zî's concept of the unity of opposites in the Way (*Dào*), *qì* energy, *shì* dynamics and dialectical return, with blueprints for a unified world foreshadowing Qín First Emperor's 221 BC unification of six warring states, while voicing fundamental opposition to inhumane legislation.

It urges creation of a meritocracy, to replace hereditary privilege. It has no doubts about the existence of a cosmic plan and presents the first explicit account of messianic futurism in China. Its philosophy of reconciling the universality of the Way with the clarity of law finds multitudinous echoes in the 'Yellow Emperor' silk scrolls recovered only in 1973 from an early Hàn dynasty grave.

Key words: cosmic, Dao, dialectic, dynamic, Emperor, energy, futurism, humanitarian, messianic, Qin, unity, Way.

Contents

BOTTOM SCROLL

List of Plates and Figures

Plates, 1-25

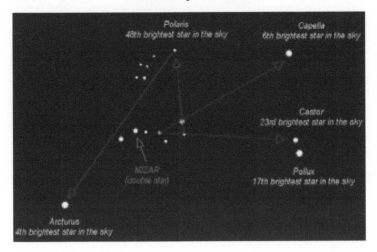

Plate 1. The seven stars of the Dipper, or 'Plough' in the Great Bear, seem to circle the Pole. Daoism identifies the latter as Grand Unity (Tàiyī) and the Dipper as Nine Augustan gods. *Héguānzǐ* makes up the nine with Horn and Halberd, likely Arcturus ('Bear Guard') and Capella, on left and right, bestriding the sky. (*see Introduction 8, 11. Chapter iv-a*) Image: Tom King 2013.

Plate 2. The two extra Dipper 'guardian' stars, nos. eight and nine, from Daoist *North Dipper Extension of Life-span Sûtra*. They are 'Cavern Brilliance, Outer Assistant' and 'Hidden Light, Inner Deputy', both wearing official caps while their companion seven stars are bare-headed. (*Beǐdǒu Yánsheng Jing Zhùjiê* 北斗延生注解 in *Dàozàng Jíyào* 道藏集要, Dôují 斗集 II)

Plate 3. The outline of the 'Big Dipper's Nine Stars' depicted by jars buried in the five-thousand year central Chinese capital at Shuanghuaíshù, Gôngyì, Hénán. Note that the two 'guardian' stars, nos. 8 and 9, are paired on opposite sides of the seven stars (not at their tail), as described by *Héguanzí* (iv-a), but cannot, for reasons of space, be shown spread out across the whole sky as Arcturus and Capella in Plate 1, above. (Ref. Dr Gù Wànfâ, Zhèngzhou Institute of Archaeology. Photo: Li An/ Xinhua)

Plate 4. The Golden Pheasant (*héniâo*) is a courageous bird. Its tail feathers are worn as headdress in martial operas by heroes and heroines. Héguan Zî, the 'Pheasant Cap Master', made it his pseudonym. Shânxi city Bâoji, 'Precious Cock', supposed birthplace of Yellow Emperor, was probably named from it. Photo: Bjorn Christian Torrissen, Kuala Lumpur Bird Park, 31.12.2011, Wikipedia.

Plate 5. Fierce horned god-head mask, with feathered headdress, in sandstone carving on Upper Citadel Wall, ca. 2,000 BC, Shímâochéng, Shânxi. Photo: Ben Sherlock, National Geographic. Childs-Johnson, July 2020, Fig. 3, 4-8. (*see Introduction 1*).

Plate 6. Lú Lèngjia (fl. 730-760) painted a Daoist priest with pheasant-feather cap burning incense to Buddha's tiger-subduing Arhat. (Beĭjing Palace Museum)

Plate 7. Qín army officers, of the First Emperor's Terracotta Warriors, wear a forked 'Pheasant Hat' (*héguan*) said to resemble pheasant tails. (Xi'an Museum)

Plate 8. Taìyi, Grand Unity, or Great One, is the ultimate principle of the Way (*Dào*), and God in human form at the Pole. The earliest labelled depiction of Grand Unity is on this small repainted and tattered banner (43.5 x 4.5 cm) from Mâwángdui tomb no.3, sealed 168 BC.

The banner shows an awesome figure of Grand Unity between Thunder Lord and Rain Master, above four demonic guardians with spears and sabres, and two dragons at bottom. A protective charm advises its owner to follow the direction of the Dipper, shown here perhaps as Grand Unity's nine companions. (see *Introduction* 11; chapters x-a, xi-a) Chángsha Museum, Húnán.

Plate 9. Grand Unity as Saviour of the Distressed (Tàiyi Jiùkû Tianzun), like Manjûsri the Buddhist bodhisattva of wisdom with sword drawn riding a lion, at White Cloud Monastery (Baíyúnguan) founded for Qiu Chûji's Quánzhen 'Complete Truth' Daoism by the Jurchen Jin dynasty in twelfth century Beîjing. Photo: Getty Images.

Plate 10. Daoist monk Master Xû Weihán performs 'Grand Unity, Five Agent Boxing' (Taìyi Wûxíng Quán) at the shrine to True Warrior god (Zhenwû) on Mt Wûdang, Húbeî. He follows the trajectories of Pacing the Dipper in the ancient Luò River Diagram sequence as if in flight. Youtube: 04/07/2015, Wudang Xuan Wu. (*see Introduction 11*)

Plate 11. 'Ten Great Monads' in bottom file, at the Primal Golden Matriarch's right hand, in 'Complete Truth' Daoism's Yuán dynasty Chúnyáng Temple, completed 1358, now relocated from its dam-submerged site near Yônglè, Shanxi, by the Yellow River. I count nine whiskered 'monads', and conclude they are the nine Dipper stars. The second from right, checking alignments, must be an astronomer. The seventh and eighth, wearing pheasant-feather caps, stand next to a swarthy bearded thunder-god (holding miniature drum-wheel). Picture in Liao Ping ed. 1985: 53.

Plate 12. Southern Sòng painting ca. 1250 of the Dipper's seven stars in priestly white robes with two mustachioed 'guardian' stars in red with high black caps behind, all bearing tablets of office, and two female immortals in front. Chikubushima Hogonji, Nagahama, Shiga Prefecture, Japan. Photo: Alamy Stock.

Plate 13. Dipper Mother in Dipper Mother Palace (Dôumû Gong) of Yùquánguan Daoist monastery, at Tianshuî 'Heavenly Water' (Gansù) in the ancient kingdom of Qín and cradle of Chinese civilslisation. A monastery inscription is dated 1281, second year of Kublai Khan's conquest of all China. Photos: MSJW, 23.09.2015.

Plate 14. Dipper Mother with Nine Augustan Star Lords in Dipper Mother Palace (Dôumû Gong) of Yùquánguan Daoist monastery, at Tianshuî 'Heavenly Water' (Gansù). Cf. Appendix II.

Plate 15. Dipper Mother as eight-armed Hindu-Buddhist goddess Marici who rides on a chariot drawn by seven pigs in a nearby shrine.

Plate 16. Giant bamboo banner (*zhújing*) erected to hang nine lanterns at Chui Tui Taobokeng temple for the Vegetarian Festival in honour of the Nine Augustans on Phuket, Thailand in the ninth lunar month, 2015. (*see Introduction: 19*) Photos: MSJW, October 2015.

Plate 17. Nine Augustan banner at Chui Tui temple, Phuket.

Plate 18. A lady devotee of Heaven on High's Holy Mother (Tianshàng Shèngmû) parades in Nine Augustans festival procession. October 2015.

Plate 19. Bronze statue of Ninth Heaven's Holy Mother (Jiû-Tian Shèngmû) in
Phuket's Dipper Mother Temple.

Plate 20. A Nine Augustan altar, Phuket. No Nine Augustan images are used. In front, stands a statue of boy warrior god Nézhà, emblematic of mediums and self-sacrifice, from Buddhist mythology, holding his fiery wheel. (*see Introduction: 4*)

Plate 21. Five Spike-Head gods, coloured blue, black, white, yellow and red, are used in self- piercing trance rituals. (*see Introduction: 19*)

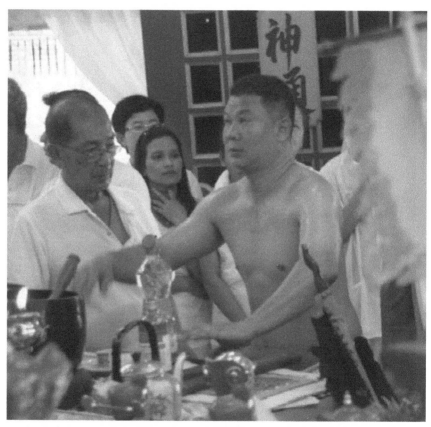

Plate 22. Medium in trance during Phuket's Vegetarian Festival. Flesh piercing and self-flagellation is practiced during the festival. (*see Introduction: 19*)

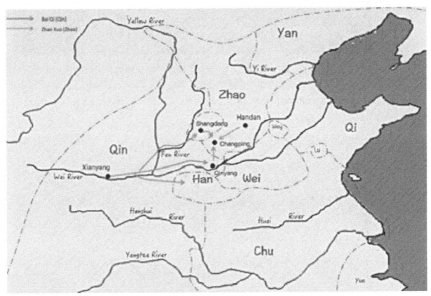

Plate 23. Map of Warring States China, showing battle of Chángpíng, 260 BC, between Qín and Zhào. Wikipedia 2018. (*see Chapter vii*)

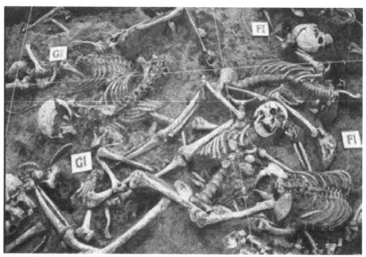

Plate 24. Bone pit of the 260 BC Chángpíng massacre, chilling evidence of Qín ruthless expansionism, was discovered on 2nd November, 1995. Photo: Qin Hongyu/panet.org.cn. Excavations at Nánwàngzhuang, Gaopíng are continuing. (*see Chapter vii*)

Plate 25. Chángpíng Shrine, near the battlefield (Gaopíng, Shanxi), dedicated to defeated Zhào general Zhào Kuò, his spouse and the fallen slaughtered by Qín general Baí Qî in 260 BC. The temple was originally built by Táng emperor Xuánzong (r. 713-755) to house skeletons newly uncovered from the massacre, as depicted in the mural behind the statues, and became known as the Skeleton King Temple (Kulóu Wáng Miào 骷髏王廟. *See Chapter vii*) Photo: Tóutiáo hào, Jìnchéngtong 2018.

Introduction

1. Yellow Emperor, Lâo Zî and Qín

In Chinese mythology, the Yellow Emperor (Huángdì) was the prehistoric ancestor of the Chinese race. His vast reputed pyramid survives near to Xi'an, not far from that of the First Emperor. With supernatural help, he is said to have defeated the demonic Chiyóu in a cosmic battle at Zhuólù (Hébeî).

In 2012, amazing archaeological finds were made in excavations at the unlikely site of Shímâochéng (石峁城) by the Great Wall, near the northern border of Shânxi with Inner Mongolia. Here, not in the central plains, were found China's earliest stone-built palace, town wall, stepped- pyramid and bronze casting. It flourished from around 2,300 to 1,800 BC. Its East Gate, expertly crafted and aligned to sunrise at the summer solstice, was a ritual centre for human sacrifice thought linked to the god 'Grand Unity' Taìyi, Dipper and Pole star. (Childs-Johnson 2020; Sun Zhouyong 2013; 2017; Lyu Yufei et al. 2018: 520-521; Jaang 2018)

Jade axes and sceptre, ferocious stone masks carved with glaring eyes that anticipate the *taotiè* of Shang bronzes (*Plate 5*), and sacrificial skull pits, show that this was no time of peaceful co-existence. The sway of this mutton-eating culture extended south into the central-plains heartland. Was Shímâo, perchance, home to Chiyóu, accredited 'inventor of the five weapons'? (Bodde 1975: 120-125) *Guânzî* (XIV-41, 10a, b) claims Chiyóu, who understood Heaven's ways, had been Yellow Emperor's first minister in charge of calendar.

Texts, written on silk, featuring the person of the legendary Yellow Emperor, were discovered in 1973, together with two of the mystic Lâo Zî, from an 168 BC water-logged tomb at Mâwángdui (Húnán). The former centres on the topic of rulership, and in particular the unification of China, for which the Yellow Emperor serves as figurehead. Most remarkable are the coincidences between these long-lost Yellow Emperor writings and *Héguanzî* whose authenticity had hitherto been questioned. (Li Xueqin 1983: 51-56. Cf. Appendix I, 261ff, below)

Taken together, the publication of these manuscripts heralds the recovery of an ideology, long lost, called the 'Way's Law' (Dàofâ). This hybrid school of thought amalgamated Lâo Zî's vision of the mystic 'Way' (Dào) with the concept of penal 'law' (fâ), ascribed to the primaeval Yellow Emperor. Hence it was also named 'Yellow-Old', Huáng-Lâo, after the Yellow Emperor and 'Old Boy' Lâo Zî. Following the fall of Qín in 206 BC, it was dominant during the first fifty years of Hàn rule before replacement by state Confucianism.

1

Lâo Zî (ca. 450 BC), legendary author of *Dàodé Jing*, the iconic *'Way and Virtue Classic'* of Daoism on his way west, reputedly had it committed it to writing, on the request of Qín's pass-keeper at Lóuguantaí.[1] This tradition suggests a link with Qín in its dissemination. The work, *Lâozî* for short, has sixty occurrences of 'Virtue' *dé*, its practical side, to the same number of the 'Way'. (Star 2001: 326) *Héguanzî's* ratio is fifty-five to eighty-one.

Legalist philosopher Hán Fei Zî wrote the first two commentaries to explain how its ideas might be applied to universal rulership.[2] In 233 he travelled to present these ideas to Qín where the future First Emperor, with his interest in the occult, was reportedly keen to meet him. Unfortunately, premier Lî Si, Hán Fei's ex-fellow student under Confucian Xúnzî, had him executed first.[3]

It might be imagined that Qín, notorious for harsh legalism and rejection of Confucianism, had scarce room for Dào. Archaeology tells a different story. Qín, gateway to the west and entrance to the Silk Road, was the birthplace of early dynasties. A giant pyramid, north of Xi'an, is claimed to be of the Yellow Emperor, who was born at nearby Chéncang (Bâoji), also home to Qín's state cult of the cock-pheasant god. (*Shîjì I, dì-2b; XXVIII dì-222b.*) (*Plate 4*)

As early as 626 BC, the Yellow Emperor was credited in Qín with creation of "Ritual music and Law's degrees."[4] Its legal tradition was further developed by reformer Shang Yang (ca. 390-338) who, citing the Yellow Emperor, codified rewards and punishments[5] to curb the power of a nobility who eventually had him murdered. Codified law was anathema to Confucius (541-478) who preached rule by moral example. Equally abhorrent to Confucians was the person of the Yellow Emperor, conspicuously absent from the Confucian canon.

Mò Zî (fl. 470-391), philosopher of 'universal love', who as a strong critic of Confucius and a strong proponent of law, had an established following in Qín.[6] Concepts of harsh penal law and a mystic Way were evidently both amenable to the radical agenda of the First Emperor.

N.B. Chapters in works cited are numbered by capital Roman numerals (e.g. I, II, III etc), while those of *Héguanzî* are numbered by small numerals (e.g. i, ii, iii etc).

---

[1] *Shîjì* (LXIII, Lièzhuàn 3, Lâo Zî) dì-355b. Traditional site of composition, Lóuguantaí, is near Xi'an.

[2] *Hánfeizî* (XX, Jiê Lâo; XXI, Yù Lâo).

[3] *Shîjì* (LXII, Lièzhuàn 3, Hán Fei). *Hánfeizî* (I, Chujiàn Qín). Schipper 2000: 38-39: argues Hán Fei Zî "used the *Dàodé Jing* as a guide for the political unification of China."

[4] *Shîjì* (V, Bênjì) dì-33a, Qín's Duke Móu 34th year: Lîyuè Fâdù 禮樂法度.

[5] *Shang jun Shu* (XVIII, Huàcè) 64.

Héguanzî contains elements of both systems. Though he condemns 'savage laws' (*mêngfâ*), his blueprint for recruitment and centralised 'bureaucrative' rule (ix-c) has points in common with that implemented by Qín. Héguan Zî's philosophy of divinely inspired law raises the question whether this represented a Chinese 'foundational' or natural law, the basis of scientific thought. (Needham 1956: 547; Peerenboom 1993: 333, n57; Defoort 2015: 300-301)

The Yellow Emperor texts from Mâwángdui, like *Héguanzî*, are centered on the theme of 'unity', spiritual and political, share affinities with the Qín First Emperor's thinking and programs. The succeeding Hàn dynasty, while succeeding to Qín's unified imperial system, came to downplay such writings, and instead reverenced the Yellow Emperor's archenemy, Chiyóu, as divine architect of their victory over Qín and made him their god of war.[7]

China's golden age of philosophy, that of the 'hundred schools', coincided like that of ancient Greece and India with one of warring states. The subject of war is inevitably in the background of debates. The subject is particularly pronounced in the above mentioned Mâwángdui tomb scrolls several of which feature the mythic Yellow Emperor as protagonist. *Héguanzî* by contrast makes only one reference to the Yellow Emperor and his foe Chiyóu (xii-a).

One whole couplet is shared almost verbatim between *Héguanzî* and a Yellow Emperor scroll:[8]
So, he will promulgate the Five Governances
to serve the Five Luminaries.
(*Gù bù Wû-zhèng yî si Wû-Míng.* 故布五正[=政] 以司五明)

Context determines whether 'governance' *zhèng* (正=政), or *zheng* (正=征) 'campaign', is the intended sense. *Héguanzî* (viii-d), analyses each of these forms of government in detail and to combine them. This Yellow Emperor scroll speaks rather of campaigning and self-purification in its preparation. Yet the two strands are connected in that both are forms of 'correction', civil or military. Qin's First Emperor will embody both, and this same word Zhèng was his first given name.

---

[6] *Shîjì* (LXIII, Lièzhuàn 3, Lâo Zî) dì-355c. *Lyûshì Chunqiu* (Mèngchun I-5 Wúsi 11a) on Mohist Grand Master Fù Chun in Qín who insisted on executing his only son for murder despite King Huì (r. 337-311)'s pardon. Cook 2002: 307-345. Sellmann 1999: 193-218.

[7] Lewis 1990: 184, SMQ 1378. *Shîjì* (XXVIII Fengshàn Shu) dì-225-a.

[8] *MWD* (Wû-Zheng): The Five Governances having been promulgated to serve the Five Luminaries, *Wû-Zhèng jì bù yî si Wû-Míng*, 五正既布以司五明. Levi 2009/2111: 138-139 fn. *Guánzî* (XIV-40) 5b-8a has fours sets of seasonal ordinances, each of 'Five Governanaces' (Wû-Zhèng 五政).

2. Zhào Zhèng, prince of destiny

Prince Zhào Zhèng (259-210) of Qín, future First Emperor, had been born and reared as a hostage with his royal father in Zhào, a rival kingdom to Qín, hence his surname Zhào. There his mother had earlier been concubine to millionaire epicurean Lyû Bùweí. Lyû had seen vastly more potential profit in politics than trade and a golden opportunity now right before his eyes. So he passed his concubine on to the hostage from Qín, who with his help was returned to Qín. There he would reign from 249 as King Zhuangxiang (281-246), with Lyû as prime minister, but died after two and a half years, leaving the throne to his thirteen year old son.[9]

Canny entrepreneur, Lyû Bùweí then became the boy king's step-father (*zhòngfù*), regent, tutor and prime minister. In 239, Lyû published a monumental encyclopaedia of philosophy, *Lyû Clan's Springs and Autumns*, in which he revealed his ambitions. In a postscript to this ecumenical work, which could be described as a practical exposition of *Lâozî*, Lyû dared imply he, with his royal stepson, was thus following the legendary example of the Yellow Emperor instructing his heir Zhuanxù.[10]

Its words of wisdom, geared to a year's progression through the months, encapsulate intellectual unification in the shape of an almanac (plus fourteen 'reviews' and eight 'theses'). Much as in the Roman Empire, unification was both religious and geo-political, the emperor himself acting as the centre piece of a belief-system, a form of state-based Daoism. Despite obvious fascination with the Yellow Emperor, and Lâo Zî (Lâo Dan) whom he ranks above Confucius for breadth of vision, Lyû Bùweí betrays no sign that he knew *Héguanzî*, then barely or just completed, either the (Mâwángdui) 'Yellow Emperor scrolls'. Yet their theme of imperial unification was only too familiar to him.

Lâo Zî had been the first to expound the doctrine of unity in both spiritual and political realms. *Héguanzî* and 'Yellow Emperor scrolls' freely quote his writings. *Lâozî* lived early in the era of Warring States (ca. 483-221). This was when barons usurped the title of 'king' (*wáng* 王), formerly exclusive property of Zhou, and became known as 'baron-kings' (*hóuwáng*), a title retained after unification by imperial Qín for regional grandees and used by *Lâozî*.

---

[9] Simâ Qian: *Shîjì* (Bênjì, VI) dì-39c; (LXXXV, Lièzhuàn 15, Lyû Bùweí) dì-418-419a.

[10] *Lyûshì Chunqiu* (I Mèngchun) 4 Guì Gong 8b-9a; (XII Jìdong) Xùyì 9b, Qín 8th year, 239 BC.

Thus, First Emperor's given name Zhèng, 'governor', chimed with such a line from *Lâozî*. Its second half is repeated there, in the work ascribed to legalist Shang Yang, and in two 'Yellow Emperor' scrolls:[11']

Baron-kings get unity **to become Under-Heaven's governor.**

It is absent from *Héguanzî* but used three times by Lyû Bùweí on rulership, and elaborated by him under 'Respect the Teacher', thus subtly paying himself the supreme compliment for grooming an emperor to be:[12]

He who has the Great Dynamic
may 'become Under-Heaven's governor'!

(*Yôu Dàshì kê'yî weí Tianxià zhèng'-yî!* 有大勢可'以爲天下正'矣!)

In a more sinister, but immediately apposite sense, as we saw, this word 'governor' could also mean 'campaign' or punitive attack. Thus, the Yellow Emperor was advised to purify himself with austerities before going on to pacify the Chinese world.[13] Then, having overcome his foe Chiyóu, the Yellow Emperor dismembered him, used Chiyóu's skin on his shield, hair for his banner, entrails in a bag for target practice and pickled the bones and flesh for soup to feed the troops before the High God (Shàngdì) intervened to prohibit it.[14]

---

[11] *Lâozî* (XXXIX): *Hóuwáng déyi* **yî weí Tianxià zhèng** 侯王得一以為天下貞[=正], absent from Guodiàn. (XLV): Pure and still may **become Under-Heaven governor**, *Qing jìng* **weí Tianxià zhèng** 清靜為天下正. *Shangjun Shu* (XXVI, Dìngfen): He who knows law edicts' meaning *is the Under-Heaven's governor. Pú zú-yî zhi fâlìng-zhi weí-zhê* **yîweí Tianxià zhèng** 樸足以知法令之謂者以為天下正. *MWD Jingfâ* Sì-Dù 51, 44a: Kings and duke hold ***[unity?] **to be the Under-Heaven's governors**... *Jingfâ* Dàofâ 44, 8b. *Shîjì* (VI, 219 BC, dì-43a) Qín Shîhuáng's Lángyé stele with names of his subject 'baron kings'.

[12] *Lyûshì Chunqiu* (IV Mèngxià) 3 Zunshi 6b; (XVII, Shênfèn Lân) 2 Junshôu 4a: still and tranquil **may become Under-Heaven governor**; 8 Zhíyi 16b: The King grasps unity **to become myriad things' governor**. See concordances in *Appendix I*.

---

[13] *MWD* Shíliù-Jing (Wû-Zheng; Zhengluàn). *Jingfâ* (Junzheng).

[14] *MWD* Shíliù-Jing (Zhengluàn) 103-106. *Hánfeizî* (LI, Zhongxiào) 358 accuses Confucian paragons Tang, founder of Shang (1766 BC) and 'Martial King' Wûwáng, founder of Zhou (1122 BC), of like desecration of their defeated predecessors' corpses.

Once King Zhèng had achieved unification, by annexation of his rival six kingdoms, he broke precedent by canonising himself. Yet *Lâozî* (XXIX; *Hánfeizî* VIII Yángquán 30) states: "the Sage man rejects extremes, rejects extravagence, **rejects the grand** (*qu Taì*)."

So King Zhèng, quoting 'reject the grand' from *Lâozî*, modestly proclaimed himself 'First Augustan Emperor', literally 'First Augustan God', Shî Huáng Dì.[15] Showing filial piety, Zhèng then canonised his deceased father King Zhuangxiang (r. 249-246) with the title 'Grand Superior Augustan', combining both *Héguanzî* titles, Taìhuáng and Shànghuáng. 'Grand Superior' was the term *Lâozî* (XVII) for the ideal ruler of the pristine age, used in *Héguanzî* (ix-a), while it is to 'Grand Augustan' that the god Grand Unity, Taìyi, expounds his scheme for unification in *Héguanzî* (x-a, xi-a). Then, to pre-empt posterity, he abolished all future posthumous titles on the pretext that they infringed protocol by being necessarily awarded by juniors to deceased seniors.

'Augustan' (Huáng), in this messianic title, is a pun on 'Yellow' with fiery shamanic overtones, as in 'Yellow Emperor'.[16] *Héguanzî* anticipated the First Emperor's title, linking 'Augustan' to 'God' (Dì) as in *Héguanzî*'s epithet 'innate Augustan, inner God' and *Guânzî*'s line: 'He who is enlightened to Unity is Augustan, he who discerns the Way is God.'[17]

First the messianic figure, 'Augustan/Yellow God', Huáng Dì (皇/黄帝), must correct and purify his person. Pankenier (2004: 234-235) links the etymology of 'Dì' for God-Emperor to 'join' or 'unite'. The God-Emperor's body was deemed a microcosm and paragon of measure and standards. (ix-c) He unites Heaven's timing, Earth's resources and human accord to transform the mysterious Way into transparent Law.

The *Yellow Emperor*, *Way's Law* and *Lâozî* scrolls, entombed at Mâwángdui less than forty years from the fall of Qín, contain many distinctive phrases, lines or passages matching those in *Héguanzî*. (*Appendix I*) Like *Héguanzî*, these scrolls are filled with aspirations for unification, amenable to justify Qín's imperialist policies. Yet, once unification had been achieved, and Qín replaced, there would be no need for them. Accordingly, they were then conveniently buried, to be forgotten for over two millennia.

---

[15] *Shîjì* (VI, Bênjî, year 26) dì-41c: on his self-canonisation and abolition of posthumous titles *shì* 諡.

[16] Lewis 1990:195-196, 315: endnote 116. Pines 2014: 258-279 'The Messianic Emperor'.

[17] *Héguanzî* (ix-g): *sù Huáng, neì Dì* 素皇內帝. *Guânzî* (XVII, Bingfâ) 94: *Míng yi-zhê Huáng, chá Dào-zhê Dì*, 明一者皇 察道者帝.

Qín's final triumph over its rival six kingdoms in 221 BC, and their annexation, was not just a politico-military conquest and annexation. Lyû Bùweí coined the phrase 'Under Heaven Grand Peace' (Taìpíng), destined to resonate in future millenarian uprisings. It looked to Qín's achievement of unification under the aegis of Grand Unity. The First Emperor was to twice celebrate this epoch-making expression on his great mountain steles, copied by calligraphers as models of 'small seal script'.[18]

Unification involved the standardisation of weights, measures and scripts in a dictionary named after Yellow Emperor's minister Cangjié, hailed repeatedly, by Héguan Zî himself, as inventor of writing and hence of calendar and law. (vii-c 3x, ix-g) Numbering was to be based on the number six. (*Shîjî* VI, year 26, 42a)

The remarkable preservation of earlier literature and histories in the newly standardised script, including *Héguanzî* itself, as if trophies from all six kingdoms to the time of their annexation, indicates there was more to Qín than the infamous 'burning of the books'.[19] Indeed it was Hàn that more effectively suppressed knowledge of Qín and Yellow Emperor 'Way's Law' philosophy until their modern rediscovery.

In 219 BC the First Qín Emperor, emulating the Yellow Emperor, enfiefed the holy Grand Mountain, Taìshan (Shandong). Simâ Qian reports that he worshipped eight gods: 1. Heaven, 2. Earth, 3. Arms as Chiyóu, 4. Yin, 5. Yáng, 6. Moon, 7. Sun, and 8. the Four Seasons with famous mountains and rivers, sacrificing to the four directions, coloured green for east, red south, white west and yellow centre. Black north and Grand Unity were conspicuously absent.[20]

Liú Bang, Hàn dynasty founder, having captured the Qín capital of Xiányáng (next to Xi'an) in 206 BC, enquired why there was no fifth temple to black, god of the north.[21] Evidently the First Emperor had assumed for himself the embodiment of that direction, symbol of Grand Unity, the polar axis which Confucius had revered as the archetype of virtuous rule by 'non-contrivance' (wúweí).[22]

---

[18] *Lyûshî Chunqiu* Zhòngxià 3b V-2 *Tianxià Taìpíng* 天下太平. *Shîjî* (VI, Bênjî) dì-44a, 215BC Mt Jieshí; 45b, 210 BC Mt Kuaìji: 'Taìpíng' 泰/太平. Dông Zhòngshu: *Chunqiu Fánlù* (XVII-78) 95b: 'non-contrivance induces Grand Peace' *wúweí zhì Taìpíng* 無爲致太平.

[19] Pines 2014: 228. Jiâ Yì: *Xinshu* (I, Guò Qín-shàng) 7 accused the First Emperor of burning books of the 'hundred philosophers' to make people ignorant.

[20] Poo Mu-chou 2014: 192. *Shîjî* (XXVIII Fengshàn Shu) dì-223b, c; 3rd year after unification dì-222c, eight gods.

[21] *Shîjî* (XXVIII) dì-225a: White, Yellow, Green, Red: but without Black, North Emperor God, Beîdì 北帝.

[22] *Lúnyû* (II-1) 15. *Lúnyû* (ii Weízhèng) 1 on the Pole Star and virtue's rule; (xv Weì Líng) 8 on Shùn's non-contrivance.

Hàn's Martial Emperor (Wûdì r. 140- 87) set out in 113-110 to imitate the Yellow Emperor, and so outdo Qín's First Emperor, by sacrificing on Grand Mountain. Clairvoyant Gongsun Qing revealed to him that: "Exalted eras are equal in virtue to the Nine Augustans but still take scholastic skills to adorn them."[23] (*Gaoshì bîdé yú Jiû-huáng ér pocaî Rúshù yî wén-zhi*. 高世比德於九皇而頗采儒術以文之) Qing went on to adduce a precedent for sectarian persecution: "The Yellow Emperor both warred and studied the way of the immortals. Concerned that the hundred clans might condemn his way, he decided to behead those who denied the demons and gods."[24]

Martial Emperor worshipped Grand Unity at Ganquán (Shânxi) with the five directional gods below.[25] Yet despite his own spiritualist obsessions, he established Confucianism as sole governing ideology, ending study of the Way's Law and Huáng-Lâo, as scholiast Dông Zhòngshu (ca. 179-104) had urged.

Water, likened by Lâo Zî to the highest good,[26] symbolic of black and north, had been adopted by the First Emperor, renaming the Yellow River 'Virtue Water', as emblem of his dynasty to extinguish the red 'fire' of Zhou, in accord with cyclical five agent theory. Qín, occupying a source of the Wèi and great Yellow River at Tianshuî 'Heavenly Water' (Gansù), doubtless saw further significance in this equation'. Hàn, despite having overthrown Qín, retained 'water virtue' as their own icon for a century until 104, when Martial Emperor finally changed black to yellow for 'soil' to absorb or overcome, as it were, the 'water' of Qín.[27]

Qín's First Emperor believed himself to have attained Daoist invulnerability and, in 212 BC, 'True Man' became his self-designation.[28] *Héguanzî* uses the term simply as 'true men', paired with 'gentlemen' (xii-a). 'True Man' in this transcendental sense was seen in *Zhuangzî* and in the Owl Rhapsody (174 BC) of Confucian scholiast Jiâ Yì who mocked futurism and perhaps *Héguanzî*. (*Postscript I*).

---

[23] *Shîjì* (XII, Bênjì, Xiàowû Dì) dì-83a; (XXVIII) dì-228b: ref. no. 1395.

[24] Ess 2014: 253, SMQ 1393. *Shîjì* (Bênjì, XII) dì-82b; (XXVIII) dì-227c: *naî duàn zhân fei guîshén-zhê* 乃斷斬非鬼神者.

[25] *Shîjì* (XXVIII) dì-227c.

[26] *Dàodé Jing* (VIII).

[27] Ess 2014: 244-248. *Shîjì* (VI) dì-42a, 221 BC, Qín Shîhuáng; (XII) dì-84c *Taìchu Yuánnián*, 104 BC; (XXVIII) dì-225b, 167 BC, the abortive change under Wéndì 'Civil Emperor'.

[28] *Shîjì* (VI, Bênjì, Qín Shîhuáng, year 35) dì-44c. cf. *Zhuangzî* (I Xiaoyáoyóu).

A 'Daoist' encyclopaedia in early Hàn, edi`ted by ill-fated Prince Liú An (179-122) of Huaínán (Anhui), after the example of Lyû Bùweí in Qín, informs us that 'God-Emperors embody Grand Unity', adding: the 'True Man' is never parted from Grand Unity.[29]

Rationaliser Dông Zhòngshu explained the Nine Augustans as titles in the set of five emperors and three founder kings of Xià, Shang and Zhou dynasties, ritually conferred in reverse succession to dead kings until they reached that of Ninth Augustan, but without astral connections.[30] (see *Table 3*)

Nearing the end of the former Hàn dynasty, Daoist revelation turned to a new messianic saviour in the Western Queen Mother, Xiwángmû of the 'Grand Peace Way' Taìpíng Dào which promised a more egalitarian society. Fifteen years later, Wáng Mâng, acting with the infant emperor's maternal clan, seized power with a program of reform to found a New Dynasty (9-23 AD).

Wáng re-established the primacy of the old Zhou dynasty sacrifice to Heaven but merged it with Grand Unity as August Heaven's Supreme Emperor of Grand Unity. Despite attempts to conjure celestial powers of the Dipper to its side, the New Dynasty collapsed within a decade.

Hàn rule was restored and lasted two more centuries. Buddhism and Daoism began to emerge as rival hierarchies, aspiring to independence from the state. Emperor Huán in AD 165 reconciled Confucius with Lâo Zî as a god on a par with Grand Unity and Buddha newly arrived from India. Two sectarian rebellions then broke out. The Yellow Turbans in the northeast, raised the aegis of Huáng-Lâo as god of Yellow Central Grand Unity in the movement of 'Grand Peace'.[31]

---

[29] *Huaínánzî* (III, Tianwén) 5a; (IX Zhûzhú) 1b; (VII, Jingshén); (VIII, Bênjing) 7ab: *Dì-zhê tî Taìyi* 帝者體太一; (XIV, Quányán) 1a. *Shĭjì* (XXVII, Tianguan Shu) dì-209c. Werner 1922: 85. Puett 2002: 160ff.

[30] (Hàn) Dông Zhòngshu: *Chunqiu Fánlù* (VII-23 San-daì gaîzhì zhíwén) 43a. *MWD* (Jiû- Zhù) lists 'Nine Rulers', one 'lawful' (fǎ) and eight bad. 29 and 33 refer to a diagram. Cf. *Kôngzî Jiayû* (III, Guan Zhou) 1b-2a speaks of temple portraits of good and evil past rulers.

[31] Lagerwey and Kalinowski 2009: 23-25; 'A Religious State': 28. *Taìpíng Jing* (160.450 Tian Taìyi). *San-guó Zhì* (I) 10 commentary: Zhonghuáng Taìyî. Hendrischke 2006: 22-23. Gé Hóng (283-343): *Bàopú Zî* (xvii: 301) on Taìyi dùnjiâ astrology and Dipper constellation pacing. *Jinsuô Liúzhu Yín* scripture foot diagram paces Five Dippers in paired steps. Andersen 2008: 238-239. Steavu-Balint 2010: 261ff.

In the south-west, Five-Pecks- of-Rice rebels rose under Zhang Dàolíng (d. 184), inspired by a deified Lâo Zî. They failed to gain power but morphed into personal religions independent of the state. Zhang's cult eventually became 'Orthodox Unity' (Zhèngyi) Daoism, with its base on Lónghû 'Dragon-Tiger Mountain in Jiangxi. Its 'Grand Unity' was internalized as the 'true self' (zhenwú 真吾).[31] (see *Appendix II*)

3. Nine Augustans re-incarnated

Daoism was now facing strong spiritual competition from Buddhism, the 'foreign' religion. Yet Daoism also had international appeal and could relate to ths shamanism of tribal invaders from the north in the Three Kingdoms and Six Dynasties period of disunion that followed the fall of Hàn in 220.

The Táng dynasty, who ruled a united China for nearly three hundred years (618-906), were of Turkic ancestry but claimed descent from Lâo Zî through their surname Lî. Emperor Sùzong (756-762), on advice of ritualist Wáng Yú, erected a temple south of his capital Cháng'an to Grand Unity the Great Lord (Tàiyi Dàjun).[32]

After the fall of Táng, and half a century of disunity, the Sòng reunited the country but failed to regain territories on its northern frontiers. In response its emperors sought to reaffirm Hàn ethnicity and Daoism as the national religion. Emperor Zhenzong of Sòng in 1012 after a dream revelation declared himself heir to the Yellow Emperor and one of the human Nine Augustans. Portraits of these holy figures were commissioned for the gigantic Zhaoying Gong state temple in Dàliáng (Kaifeng), refounded in Hángzhou by Southern Sòng.

In 1073 Shénzong ordered the god of Central Grand Unity (Zhong Tàiyi) enshrined.[33] Lù Diàn (1042-1102), who had served reforming emperor Zhézong (r. 1085-1100) as minister and ambassador to the Khitan Liáo, first edited *Héguanzî*. In this period esoteric texts of Dipper meditation and visualization practices connect Nine Augustans to nine human orifices and attainment of longevity or immortality.[34]

---

[32] Andersen 2005: 29-30; under 'Jiao' in Pregadio 2008: i 542-543. He cites *Suí History* on a Zhèngyi Daoist night ritual to Heavenly Augustan Grand Unity (Tianhuáng Tàiyi) with the Five Planet Emperors.

[33] Lî Tào 1183: *Xù Zizhì Tongjiàn, Chángbian* (LXXIX-6) 1797-1798 'Rén Huáng Jiûrén'. The Língbâo Temple was dedicated to 'Central Grand Unity', Zhong Tàiyi. ndersen 2005: 29-30; under 'Jiao' in Pregadio 2008: i 542-543. He cites *Suí History* on a Zhèngyi Daoist night ritual to Heavenly Augustan Grand Unity (Tianhuáng Tàiyi) with the Five Planet Emperors.

[34] Huang 2010: 57-90. *Beîdôu Yánshòu Jing* 81-83, inLi(1906): *Dàozàng Jíyaò* 道藏輯要.

Shénzong's son Huizong, the aesthete emperor and ardent Daoist, subsequently came to believe himself a Ninth Empyrean deity. Next. we learn of Grand Unity's diffusion into a set of ten. This may represent a merging of Grand Unity with the Nine Augustans.[35] Finally, following the dangerous King Lear-like precedent of 'yielding the throne' in emulation of ancient sages, Huizong abdicated to his son. In 1127 both were captured from their capital at Kaifeng by erstwhile Jurchen allies who then established their own 'Golden' Jin dynasty in North China.

The new emperor Gaozong (r. 1127-1162), Huizong's ninth son, invoking the aid of the Dipper Mother managed to hold out and establish a Southern Sòng dynasty based at Hángzhou. There, in 1148, he erected a Tàiyi Temple filled with images of the Three Augustans and Five Emperors of antiquity. Yet his piety was insufficient to restore the cracked vase of empire.[36]

4. Three-in-One religion

Meanwhile Jurchens, ancestors of the Manchus, founded their Jin Dynasty in the north. In 1148 they granted official recognition to a Grand Unity Religion from Hénán. Its scriptures survive from stele inscriptions collected by court scholar Wáng Yùn (1227-1304).[37] The Jurchens, being of non-Hàn ethnicity, favoured syncretism and patronised Complete Truth (Quánzhen) Daoism under Qiu Chûji (1148-1227) who integrated Confucianism and Buddhism into a unity of the 'three religions'.[38]

Mongols under Genghiz Khan and his successors, cleverly naming their dynasty 'Prime' Yuán, likewise saw value in Complete Truth Daoism. In 1247 they undertook a century-long construction of a monumental shrine to its saint Lyû Dòngbin at Yônglè 'Eternal Joy', his birthplace by the Yellow River in Shanxi.[39] Eternal Joy's Temple walls, inaugurated in 1280, depict two hundred and eighty-two gods paying court to Lâo Zî as the Prime, synonymous with the dynasty. A line of so- called 'Ten Grand Monads' are in fact the nine Dipper stars with thunder god, attending the Golden Empress of the West above. Two of the nine masters wear pheasant-feather caps. (Plate 11)

[35.]Chén Zhèngmíng 1997: 2. Shàngqing Língbâo Dàfâ, 1119-1125, includes Ten Grand Unities.

[36] Huang 2001: 13-14. Gesterkamp 2011: 50-54.

[37] Lagerwey 2010: 46. Grand Unity Religion (Tàiyi Jiào) was founded under Jurchen Jin by Xiao Bàozhen (d. 1166) of Jíxian (Hénán). Kirkland 2004: 108.

[38] Kirkland 2004: 164ff on Jurchen patronage of Daoism, especially Quánzhen. Unity of the three religions was championed at the time by Lî Chúnfú who later became a Buddhist.

[39] Liao Ping 1985: 52-53, 64. Lagerwey 2010: 45-48.

A Southern Sòng scroll, conserved in a Japanese shrine, paints these nine stars as priests. (*Plate 12*) Among other awesome martial deities, is a six-eyed Cangjié, minister of the Yellow Emperor, personally hailed by Héguan Zî as inventor of writing, calendar and law. (vii-c, ix-g) On the inner east wall Grand Unity, resonating with the solar Eastern Augustan Grand Unity of ancient Chû, is the 'Eastern Pole's Purifier of China, Grand Unity Saviour of the Distressed'.[40]

Grand Unity maintains this role in the Complete Truth sect White Cloud Monastery, Baíyún Guan at Beîjing. There he is incarnate as a lion-riding saviour with sword held aloft like Manjûsri, bodhisattva of wisdom. (*Plate 9*) In 1273, Kublai Khan, battling remnants of Southern Sòng ordered the fifth patriarch of the Grand Unity sect to place a seat for True Warrior in Beîjing's new Zhaoying Temple.[41] Yet the fall of Yuán spelt eclipse for the cult of Grand Unity.

In 1368, ethnic Hàn uprisings of Daoist and Manichaean inspiration drove the Mongols back to the northern steppes and established the 'Shining' Míng dynasty at Nánjing. Its third emperor, taking the reign name 'Eternal Joy' Yônglè (r. 1403-1424) after the Complete Truth Daoist shrine, overthrew his Confucian nephew the Jiànwén emperor and re-instated Beîjing as capital.[42] He commissioned a giant compendium of literature, inserting into *Héguanzî* (xi) a novel passage, alleging "Law's righteousness and degree's order were obliterated in the Central Palace," as if to justify his revolt and usurpation. (*Postscript II*).

Imperial interest resurfaced under Qing emperor Qiánlóng (r. 1736-1796) who cherished a Míng moveable-type edition (Yongxiang Lu ed. 2014: *History of Chinese Science and Technology*, Springer, 219). By the seventeenth century Míng's problems sparked renewed interest in *Héguanzî*, just prior to their conquest by the Manchu Qing 'Pure' dynasty. A new edition was printed with appreciative comments on the upper margin by leading intellectuals.[43] Grand Unity was reborn in popular imagination with Míng prose epic *Investiture of the Gods* and recently Japanese manga cartoon.

---

[40] Chén Zhèngmíng 1997: 3 on Nine Palace Grand Unities of Píngyángfû Daoist shrine west mural (Royal Ontario Museum, Toronto). They stand haloed between two martial deities and a haloed priest who dominates the Emperor and Empress gods. White 1940: 200 in Gesterkamp 2011: 259-276 'Daoist Priest as Central Deity'; pls. 13, 15; Drawing 2B, nos 3-10. Liao Ping 1985: 48-53.

[41] Dongjí Qing Huá Taìyi Jiùkû Tianzun 東極清華太乙救苦天尊. Liao Ping 1985: 56. Gesterkamp 2011: 178; 263 footnotes 42, 43; 326 table "II, East Pole Emperor."

[42] Chan 1976 *passim*. Wells 2013: 65-66.

[43] Wells 2013: 80. Huáng Huaíxìn 2004: 10 cites Chén Shen 陳深 1591: *Héguanzî Pínjié*; Zhu Yânghé 朱養和 1625: *Héguanzî Jípíng*.

It recounts Zhou's dynastic war to replace Shang in quasi sci-fi terms. King Tang, founder of Shang, alias Heavenly Unity, is named Grand Unity, thirteenth generation scion of the Yellow Emperor. Later a Daoist saint, named Grand Unity the True Man, announces the conception of a 'unicorn son' to his mother in a dream.

Grand Unity acts as 'god-father' and tutor to Nézhà (Nata), son of Táng generalissimo Lî Jìng. Father and son turn out to be Buddhist avatars of North Mountain King war god, 'Pagoda Bearer' Vaishrâvana, and Nalakubera.[44] Like the Indian Nachiketa who delivers himself to Death, learning the secrets of fire ritual and immortality of the soul, Nézhà frees himself by suicide of his earthly body and with his fiery chakra wheel is worshipped as 'Third Prince' (San Taìzî) in spirit- possession cults. After seizing the throne in 1403, real-life Emperor Yônglè who also had a conflicted relationship with his father, rebuilt Beîjing, site of the Mongol capital, popularly known as Nézhà city after its spiritual guardian and symbolic embodiment.[45] (*Plate 20*; *cf. Postscript II*)

An alchemic meditation text was published under the name of Grand Unity, ascribed to Complete Truth sect patriarch Lyû Dòngbin. It credits Grand Unity with the mystic source of true energy and light in quasi-Manichaean terms. Translated by Richard Wilhelm as *The Secret of the Golden Flower*, it visualises generation of mystic light within the 'womb' of the meditator's abdomen as a miniature Buddha.[46] Grand Unity's politico-social dimension had been virtually forgotten.

5. Chinese Messianism

Religion and soteriology is a subject long neglected in readings of pre-Hàn history. Yet messianic movements have been prominent throughout. Dynastic founders from earliest times invariably claimed divine sanction. Messianism was already inherent in the Confucian Gongyáng commentary on 'capture of the unicorn' in 481 BC. (Gentz 2005: 227-254) Under Hàn, Lî Hóng reputedly proclaimed himself Lâo Zî re-incarnate, followed in 142 AD by 'Heavenly Master' Zhang Dàolíng, forerunner of Zhèngyi 'Correct Unity' Daoism. (Seidel 1969, 1983 , 1984) Buddhist messiahs identified with Maitreya (Mílèfó). More widely recognized are

---

[44] *Fengshén Yânyì* (I) 1 on Shang dynasty founder Chéng Tang as Taìyi; (XIII-XIV) Taìyi Zhenrén and Nézhà. *Xún Zî* (XXV, Chéngxiàng) 515 identifies Chéng Tang with 'Heavenly Unity' Tianyî.[45] Werner 1922: 305ff birth of Nézhà 哪吒; 229. Dudbridge 1970: 146 on Nata legend. Jordan 1972: 123 'San-Taìzî' 三 太 子 . Phillips 2016: *passim*. Nachiketa in *Natha Upanishad*.[46] *Grand Unity's Golden Flower Lineage Meaning, Taìyi Jinhua Zongzhî* 太乙金華宗旨. Wilhelm 1931: 5; 21.

the periodic rebellions, from the Hàn up to the 'Grand Peace Heavenly Kingdom' (Taìpíng Tianguó) of 1850-1864. This last, led by 'God's Son' Hóng Xiùquán, at his capital Nánjing, showed Christian inspiration.

Héguanzî, predating such politico-religious movements, has been overlooked in this field. Nearing the climax of the Warring States just prior to Qín conquest, it reflects yearning for unification as by Mencius (Ia-6), or Machiavelli's *Il Principe* in Renaissance Italy. *Héguanzî* preaches an ideal future: "If you wish to know the future, examine the past" (vii-b) and "divine governance is in the future" (viii-d and xviii-a). It points to nine stars in the Dipper (iv-a) who came to represent nine gods under their Dipper Mother (Dôumû) in a cult that gained imperial patronage in the Sòng dynasty (ca. 1100).

From *Héguanzî* (iv-a, ix, x), it is clear the Ninth Augustan (Jiû- Huáng), and Complete Ninth (Chéngjiû 成鳩=成), were not merely of antiquarian significance but harbingers of a new age, a utopia due in the near future. There is a parallel Virgil's vision (*Eclogues* iv) of the dawning of a Golden Age as foretold by the Sybil for Augustan Rome.

Here, a detailed program for political unification with religious sanction is revealed by the god 'Grand Unity' (Taìyi), the Great Monad or Great One, a philosophic concept and an oracle that speaks. (x) Grand Unity is traditionally linked to the north polar axis, equated in Sòng dynasty cosmology with Taìjí, the Grand Polarity, union of opposites *yin* and *yang*, encapsulated in the spiral black and white disc, and embodied by the Emperor 'Heaven's Son' (*Tianzî*).[47]

Grand Polarity was first defined in an appendix to the *Book of Change* (*Yìjing*, Xící-shàng XI). There, it divides into dark and light (*yinyáng*), the cardinal directions, eight trigrams (*ba-guà*) to represent basic phenomena and ultimately sixty-four hexagrams, by a process of binary sub-division (1>2>4>8>16>32>64). (*Table I*) *Héguanzî* makes what just one metaphorical reference to these (xv-b).

Héguanzî locates Grand Unity, inspirer of the Nine Augustans' (Jiû-Huáng), at the centre. He is equated with the note *do* (*gong*) and the one to whom the hundred gods look up (x-a). The Nine Augustans' sacred transmission includes a Grand Augustan and Complete Ninth to inaugurate a new age of unity. (ix-d, x-a, xi-a) This prophecy was soon to be realized, not quite in the manner envisaged, but by Qín conquest.

---

[47] Luó Bì (of Southern Sòng, prefaced 1170): *Lù Shî* (Qiánjì I) 1: Now Grand Polarity (Taìjí) is Grand Unity (Taìyi). *Fu Taìjí-zhê Taìyi-yê.* 夫太極者太一也. Defoort 1997: 15.

Parallels, between Qín authoritarianism and the Ninth Augustan's program (ix-c,d), could be explained by collaboration with schemer Lyû Bùweí and First Emperor's father, hostage in Zhào. After release of the latter from Zhào in 249 to inherit the Qín throne as King Zhuangxiang, he would likely have been hoped amenable to Zhào, as the expected Ninth Augustan incarnate. An escape-clause to *Héguanzî's* interdiction of hereditary monarchy, 'if he could accept the teaching', could have been inserted to accommodate such an eventuality. (xi-b, end)

Alas, it was not to be.

Instead, as we saw, the First Emperor's father, having reigned just over two years, canonized 'Grand Superior Augustan', only after he was safely long dead and buried. Disappointment and rejection of Qín's ominous regime, installed by this tragic king's successor, may be reflected in the denunciation of tyranny in Manifest Hope (ii).

6. Authorship, Message and Mode

Héguan Zî, 'Pheasant Cap Master', was by tradition said to be a hermit of Chû, the great kingdom of south China. (*Plate 23* map) In 299 BC, its King Huaí had been detained by Qín, escaped to Zhào but was deported back to Qín where he died in 296. A prince of Chû, the poet statesman Qu Yuán, allegedly drowned himself to protest at this king's appeasement of Qín. It is plain from its contents that *Héguanzî* is focused on the northern state of Zhào, but shows signs of Chû influence, including the figure of Grand Unity, shamanic celestial flights akin to those paeaned by Qu Yuán and even passionate anti-Qín resistance.

Héguanzî is written in verse, mostly in quatrains and couplets of four-character lines. Reproduction of its rhymes would require the reconstruction of a dialect from over two thousand years ago. The work was written over a period of years. Its basic themes are of political unification, meritocracy, equality, multi-racialism (ix-g, xi-b) and spiritual transcendence. This mix of varied voices reflect the cauldron of ideas fermenting in the lead-up to Qín's imposed unity. It represents, from pluralistic angles, a discourse on topics of unification that was about to be indefinitely adjourned.

Héguan Zî, his nom-de-plume meaning 'Pheasant Cap Master', maintained a low profile. The work betrays no explicit information on its author. It receives no mention, presumably supressed or secreted in the imperial library, until Liú Xin presented his *Seven Summaries* to the emperor in 6 BC. This was the period of turmoil leading up to Wáng Mâng's radical revolution, and proclamation in AD 8 of the short-lived 'New' Xin dynasty, whose radical ideals echo those of *Heguanzî*.

The reason for Héguan Zǐ's use of pseudonym may be surmised from the radical nature of his ideas, glorification of hostage-taker Cáo Mò and denunciation of reigning monarch (vii-b). The Mâwángdui 'Yellow Emperor' scrolls' overlaps with *Héguanzî*, and no other, are so numerous as to imply co-authorship I count sixty-six instances. (*Appendix I*)

Héguan Zî in person appears here only in five chapters (vii-ix, xiv-xv), all in dialogues with Páng Zî, 'Master Páng'. This work, like most of the period, must be a compilation edited by disciples. Among these, the chief must be general Páng Xuan, presumably Páng Zî, who is interviewed by King Diàoxiang (r. 244-236, xvi) of Zhào. The text's high number of internal cross-concurrences argue for its integrity, though not uniformity.

Graham (1989a: 527-529) isolates "three utopias" in the opus as having 'Daoist' or 'primitivist' (iii, v, xiii), 'Legalist' (ix) and 'Confucian' (xv) tendencies respectively. The 'Legalist' (ix) chapter gives the blueprint for Qín's First Emperor's centralisation into thirty-six 'commanderies and counties' (*jùnxiàn*, ix-c), building on that of early reformer in Qí (Shandong), Guân Zî. It harnesses time to a program of reporting by the cyclical sixty-day solar calendar (viii-c, ix-d, g).

Yet, Héguan Zî makes an outspoken critique of harsh legalism. (viii-a,b) In the 'Confucian' chapter (xv), he preaches submission by the Sage to the teacher in moral education and study. Themes of unity, wide meritocratic recruitment, adherence to contracts, divine law, and military preparedness in resistance but not aggression, are paramount.

Héguan Zî in person delivers a lesson from history, reconciling five systems of governance matched to five luminaries. Their citation without explanation by a 'Yellow Emperor' scroll, implies the primacy to *Héguanzî* which provides detailed exegeses for them.[48] (viii-c, d; cf. iv.) His first governance is from the mythological age of Augustans, which he calls 'divinely reformative' (*shénhuà*). Second is divinely illuminated 'bureaucrative' (*guan*) governance, on mathematical models, which will lay the foundation for unification.

Third, 'educative' (*jiào*), is that of the great founder kings, who led by moral example and were idolised by Confucius. Fourth is 'adaptative' (*yin*) governance, by baron-kings of the Warring States period. Its 'mind technique' combines the psychology of Lâo Zî and theory of adaptation developed by Shèn Dào (ca. 350-275) of Zhào. Fifth is 'operative' (*shì*) governance practised by Five Hegemons, notably King Huán of Qí guided by premier Guân Zhòng (ca. 720-645).

---

[48] Levi 2009: 138, footnote on 'Five Regulations and Five Clarities'. Huáng 2004: 153; 2014: 147.

Héguanzî frequently quotes *Lâozî*, without attribution as then usual, except for Confucian citations of the ancient classics. I count thirty-nine cases. (*Appendix I*) He interprets *Lâozî*'s quatrain, absent from Guodiàn *Lâozî* (ca. 300 BC), on a mysterious presence as the 'Night Walker' (iii-b, Yèxíng), implying a covert operator. *Héguanzî* (viii-b, xix-a) also quotes pioneer strategist Sun Zî in like vein. The primacy given to 'Man' (vii-a), in the trilogy Heaven-Earth-Man (i-a, iv-a, xiv-a), and 'mandate' recalls Confucius' *Analects* (*Lúnyû* XV, XX end) and Mencius (*Mèngzî* IIb-1). Yet his pre-occupation with 'human employments' is unparalleled.

The penultimate chapter (xviii-a) gives us a lyrical play on *dé*, as 'virtue', with 'getting', and the 'Way' *Dào*, which echoes those, with contrasting foci, painted by *Zhuangzî's* 'Great Lineage Master' (VI, Dàzongshi) and *Hánfeizî's* 'Explaining *Lâozî*' (XX, *Jiê Lâo*). Clearly these three shared a common milieu.

7. Unity of opposites: the Question of Gender

Lâozî (LI) had linked Way to Virtue, and material form to dynamics. *Héguanzî* delights in exposing the unity of opposites, complementary or antagonistic (v-d, xii-d). (*see lists, below*) All this was to argue for political unification. Dialogues, ascribed to Pheasant Cap and Grand Unity, respect the 'individual' ego (*wô/jî*) as the integer of society. Positive emphasis is placed on on integrity of the 'self's' continuing existence within the multitude. (*jî, zì*, xi-a,-c, xvi-a, xviii-b)

This multi-pointed vision of unity supports preservation of individual integrity and diversity within a dynamic, not static, whole (v-d, ix-f, x-c). It touches on the paradox of the one and the many, unity and multiplicity as in the debate of Parmenides and Aristotle. (Jowett 1892: 110) In the field of causation, this involves 'dynamics' (*shì* 勢), opposing spatio-temporal forces, to which one must adapt, or must divide. (See: introductory to iv.)

Héguanzî explains this idea of 'dynamics', expounded by Sun Zî in a military setting, and politically by Shèn Dào and *Hánfeizî* (XL), by mechanics (xiv-a) and internalises it to self (xviii-b).[49] Above this is *Héguanzî*'s concept of a great dynamic in the rotation of the cosmic axis, most plainly manifested by the Dipper constellation, and the physical cycle of five 'elements', of water, wood, fire, earth and metal, better translated as 'agents' since they are in constant state of change. (v *passim*).

---

[49] Giles tr. 1910: *Sun Tzu* (*Sunzî* V) 15-16 gives 'energy', 'momentum'; Ames 1983, 65: 'positional advantage'; Sawyer 1993: 429-433 'strategic configuration of power'; Jullien 1995, 178- 182: *ropensité*, *'efficacité'*; Wells 2001: 'dynamics' with a bridge to Aristotle's *dynamis*. Amongst other candidates for *Shì* are 'potential' and 'power'. Kohn 2014: 65, 217-218. Thompson 1979: 5, Fung Yu-lan 1934 tr. 'circumstances'; 169-170 Shen Tzu fragment **13**; 236.

Building on the paradoxes of *Lâozî*, here imbued with a pro-active mission to reform society, *Héguanzî* analyses phenomena by complementaries and oppositions, their mutual dependence and transformation. The nature of classical Chinese does not intrinsically distinguish male or female, singular or plural, personal or impersonal, abstract or concrete nouns, cosmic theory or practical aims (iv-a>e, v-a), past, present or future verbs. All must be adduced from context. Is it 'Ninth' Augustan' or 'Nine Augustans'; Night 'Walker' or 'Walking'? Grand Unity may be masculine, feminine or neuter, but *Lâozî* speaks of 'Myriad Things' Mother'.

Daoist tradition reveres a Way or Dipper Mother, linked to the Pole Star who gives birth to the Nine Augustans' constellation. One may perhaps detect feminine touches in the mysterious authorship of the present work, with its unusual interest in music, flavours and colours, 'love' (*aì/hào* 愛/好), 'hero', mother's loom (iv-c), and positive citation of shamans (v- d). Like *Zhuangzî*, it stresses feelings as 'emotive reality' or truth (*qíng* 情) or 'humane realism' (*rénqíng*) in place of the Confucian 'humane' (rén 仁). Kohn 2014: 59-60). *Héguanzî* thus reconciles objective with subjective perceptions but does not renounce the world.

8 . Divine Luminaries

The nature of *shénmíng* here includes both internal 'divine illumination' and astral 'spirit luminaries', presumably that of the Nine Dipper Augustan stars. The bureaucrative form of governance is 'embodied' by Divine Luminaries (*tî/shi shénmíng* viii-d; ix-bx2; ix-g; xi-a). 'Grand Unity' (Taìyi), him or herself, and 'Grand Augustan' (Taìhuáng) in dialogue (x-a) are clearly divine and semi-divine personages.

They are akin, in form and language, to the mythic interlocutors in 'Yellow Emperor' scrolls excavated from the early Hàn tomb at Mâwángdui. Both have a marked resemblance in form to spirit writing by spirit medium cults as still practiced. (Seaman 1987: 12ff. Dean 1997: 254-256)

Traditional Daoist cosmogony equates the Nine Augustans with seven stars, whose right-side two point to the Pole star, plus one on each side to make up nine. From *Héguanzî*'s description (iv-a), these last two must be first- magnitude stars Arcturus and Capella, spanning the sky (*Plates 1-3* This differs from the received version in which they are two nearly invisible stars by its western tail, as shown in the Táng star map from Dunhuáng. (*Appendix II*)

This constellation, known as the Northern Bushel (Beî Dôu 北斗) and in the West as the Plough or Dipper of the Great She-Bear (Ursa Major), has been revered since antiquity. Excavations in 2020 of a Neolithic capital at Shuanghuaíshù near Zhèngzhou (Hénán), ca. 3,000 BC, have revealed the Dipper's nine stars outlined by the pattern of nine buried pots. (*Plate 3*) *Héguanzî* does not explicitly equate the Nine Augustans with the Dipper stars but a connection may be inferred from the importance given them (iv-a, v-b, xvii-d) and the 'embodiment of divine luminaries' in ideal governance (viii-d; ix-b x2; ix-g; xi-a).

The Nine Augustans continue to be celebrated by Chinese in Southeast Asia. In the Hokkien community's 'Vegetarian Festival', witnessed on the Thai island of Phuket, the Nine Augustans are greeted with their palanquins at the shore on the first day of the ninth lunar month and given a tumultuous send-off on the ninth. Unusually, no visual depictions or images of the Nine Augustans are displayed there. (*Plates 16-22*) The only site where, in 2015, I found their statues, life-size, was far away to the northwest, at Tianshuî 'Heavenly Water' in Gansù, cradle of Chinese civilisation in the ancient kingdom of Qín. (*Plates 13-15, 19*)

During the Phuket festival, devotee mediums perform acts of auto-sacrifice and spirit-possession in their honour, practices characteristic of major temple rituals. It is alleged that in 1825, the 'Nine Emperor Gods' were invited to Phuket from a Dipper Mother temple in 'Kansai', Jiangxi, home of orthodox Zhèngyi Daoism, to end a plague.[50] (*Plates 20-21*)

𝟫. Grand Unity generates Water

Lâo Zî's *Way and Virtue Classic* (XLII) places 'unity' second only to the Way in the line of evolution:[51]

The Way > **Unity** > Duality > Trinity > Myriad Things

---

[50] Cohen 2001: 21ff, 24, 51, 91 on Nine Augustan Grand God 'Kiu Ong Tai Tae' festival in Phuket, their incense urns, empty sedan chairs and lack of their images. Tourism Authority of Thailand, Phuket Office 2015: 7, 9. Cheu Hock Tong 1993: 28-38. Ingo Wandlet 1993: 309-310. Elliott 1955: 34, 78. Werner 1932: 247. On mainland China, Jiangxi has major Dipper Mother temples: in Changjiang, Jîngdézhèn, and Chéngxù Temple, Zhouzhuang.

[51] *Lâozî* (X) 116; (XIV) 117; (XXII) 120; (XXXIX) 101; (XLII) 102 on Unity and genesis. *Zhuangzî* (XXIII) 785; (XXXII) 1047: Grand Unity's form is vacuity, *Taìyi xíngxu* 太一形虛 ; (XXXIII) 1093: Lâo Zî and the Pass Keeper...founded it on constantly not-having, ruled it by Great Unity, *Lâo Zî, Guan Yín...jiàn-zhi yî cháng wúyôu, zhû-zhi yî Dàyi* 老子關尹···建之 以常無有主之以大一. Allan 2003: 275-276. Puett 2002: 160ff; 174; 183.

Allied to this abstract unity, is the element of water which *Lâozî* likens to the Way: "highest goodness is like water." (*Lâozî* VIII) Other early writings exalt water and credit it with five virtues (*Guânzî* XXXIX 'Water and the Earth') or take it as a metaphor for fluid troop maneuvers (*Sunzî Bingfâ* VI).

A bamboo-strip book, from a tomb (ca. 300 BC) at Guodiàn (Húbeî), found with the earliest known drafts of *Lâozî*, is named from its first line (*Guodiàn Chûmù Zhújiân* 1998: *Taìyi shengshuî* 太一生水), which places water first after Grand Unity, even before Heaven, in its genesis:

Grand Unity begot Water.
Water returned to nourish Grand Unity and
by this means begot **Heaven**...

It makes Grand Unity 'the Myriad Beings' Mother', a phrase from *Lâozî* paralleling 'Under-Heaven's Mother' as kenning for the vacuous Way (*Lâozî* I, XXV, LII). These titles impute to primal unity a female aspect like Dipper Mother of Nine Augustans in traditional Daoism.

The importance of water's generation by Heaven, according to the conventional sequence, in the form of rain, and its denial to practitioners of 'savage law' is clear from *Héguanzî* (viii-a). Unusually, its produced from by a dialectic of opposites: Heaven though dry generates Water, Earth though wet generates Fire.

Water is one of the elemental Five Agents (*wû-xíng*). *Hàn History's* Five Agents Record explains the *Documents Classic's* Vast Plan sequence by the interaction of opposites: **odd** (+) Heavenly and **even** (-) Earthly forces, *yáng* and *yin*: 1. Water + > 2. Fire - > 3. Wood + >, 4. Metal - > 5. Soil +.

Cosmologist Zou Yàn (ca. BC 300) is credited with the Five Agent production theory of Wood > Fire > Soil > Metal > Water, correlated to the seasons. (*Table I*) This sequence is found in *Héguanzî* (x-c). A conquest order of Metal # Wood; [# Soil #] Water # Fire, with Soil moved from centre to end also occurs (xiv-a), and an inverted conquest sequence (xvii-d). (cf. Bodde 1974: 31-32)

The *Change Classic* (*Yìjing*) does not mention the Five Agents but an appendix gives a trigram (*ba-guà*) sequence by compass points from Thunder trigram as Wood at East to Water trigram at North, after Heaven. Southerly trigrams (SE to W) are conversely 'shady' (*yin*), and northerly trigrams (NW to E) 'sunny' (*yáng*). Trigrams of broken (0) and unbroken (1) lines are shown here in binary Leibnizian form by zeroes and ones.[52]

---

[52] Wilhem/Baynes 1967: 268-269, Shuoguà 5, 'Later Heaven' Hòu Tian, sequence: *Dì chu-hu Zhèn...*帝出乎震*... Taìyi sheng shuî* 太一生水 Lî Xuéqín ed 1998. Shaughnessy 2005.

Table I. Five Agents and Eight Trigrams in Correlative Cosmology

EAST *left* **Spring** *Humanity*	SE	SOUTH *front* **Summer** *Loyalty*	SW Centre	WEST *right* **Autumn** *Righteous-ness*	NW	NORTH *rear* **Winter** *Sagacity*	NE
1.WOOD *mù* 木		*2.FIRE* *huô* 火	*3. SOIL* *tû* 土	*4. METAL* *jin* 金		*5.WATER* *shuî* 水	
Green Dragon Sol (*zhǐ*)		Red Bird La (*yû*)	Yellow Emperor Do (*Gong*)	White Tiger Re (*shang*)		Black Warrior Mi (*jué*)	
100 Yáng +	011 Yin -	101 Yin -	000 Yin -	110 Yin -	111 Yáng +	010 Yáng +	001 Yáng +
1. Zhèn 震 arousing	2. Xùn 巽 gentle	3. Lí 离 bright	4. Kun 坤 nourishing	5. Duì 兑 joy	6. Qián 乾 war	7. Kân 坎 trouble	8. Gen 艮 stillness
Thunder	*Wind*	*Fire*	*Earth*	*Lake*	*Heaven*	*Water*	*Mountain*
4.Hare Mâo 卯	*5.Dragon* *6.Snake* Chén, Sì 辰, 巳	*7.Horse* Wû 午	*8. Sheep* *9. Monkey* Weì, Shen 未, 申	*10.Cock* Yôu 酉	*11.Dog* *12.Boar* Xu, Haì 戌, 亥	*1.Rat* Zî 子	1. *OX* 2. *Tiger* Chôu, Yîn 丑, 寅

In order to reconcile the twelve-unit cycle used for zodiac, months and double-hours, at bottom, with the eight-unit cycle of the trigrams, an extra four of the latter each join one of the former (as above). The Dipper constellation, as it appears to revolve across the firmament over the solar year, was seen as a celestial clock pointing out the time for each month's 'station' (*jiàn* 建) in the sky.

The twelve-unit cycle starts from winter and North, while that of the trigrams starts from springtime and East. In the same way, Grand Unity normally identified with the north polar region was celebrated in the southern state of Chû as Eastern Grand Unity (*Chûcí: Dong Taìyi*). In the *Yìjing* genesis, "God goes forth in Thunder (of the East)," while a 1993 excavated text from Guodiàn (Húbeî) dated ca. 300 BC begins: "Grand Unity generates Water…"

Héguanzi viii-c gives Unicorn and Dark Hollow as variants for the north quadrant mascot of war and water. The word for 'dark', which can also be translated as 'black' or 'mysterious' (*xuán* 玄), written as 'prime' (*yuán* 元), in taboo name avoidance. 'Primal energy' aroused interest as a putative proto-scientific Chinese identification of primordial matter. (xi-a; Defoort 2015: 285-286) Indeed, *Héguanzî* might be called a bible of qì 'energy' and *shì* 'dynamic', for its bountiful usages of such terms in unprecedentedly physical contexts.

1 0. Ritual Propriety and Music

Confucius (541-478) paired Music with 'Ritual/ Propriety', homonym for rational principle (*lî* 禮 / 理), in the Six Arts of his curriculum. Confucian polyglot and poet Xún Zî (ca. 313-238) of Zhào, who criticized Lâo Zî' for passivity,[53] was reputedly teacher of both Hán Fei Zî and Qín premier Lî Si. He took 'Propriety', not water, as prime mover after Grand Unity:[54]

Grand Unity > **Propriety** >
Heaven and Earth > Sun and Moon > Four Seasons >
Planets and Stars > River Systems > Myriad Things

The genesis in classic *Ritual Record* is similar, but with a final theistic twist:[55]

Grand Unity > **Propriety** > Heaven and Earth > Shady and
Sunny (*yin-yáng*) > Four Seasons > Demons and Gods.

On a more cheerful note, entreprenr and 'king-maker' Lyû Bùweí replaced Propriety with Music, a synonym for joy (*yuè*), in first place but no gods, just natural dialectics:[56]

Grand Unity > the Way's degree and measure, embodied
in **Music** > Two Shapes [Shady-Sunny, *yin-yáng*]...

For Héguan Zî, musical notes and modulations, geared to heaven's clockwork, are a perfect mathematical model for moral and social order. Thus they, more than arms, are the key to battle and warfare, and serve as a metaphorical rebuke for war mongers to heed 'Heaven's Balance' (vii-b, xii-d, xvii-f; xix-b). It was his way of saying the way to unite the Under-Heaven is by benevolence and `not to delight in killing men', as Mencius once chastened a baron king.[57]

---

[53] *Xúnzî* (XVII, Tianlùn) 343: Lâo Zî had insight into contraction but no insight into expansion.

[54] *Xúnzî* (XIX, Lîlùn 'Propriety Theory') 379-380: All Propriety starts from Grand Unity. Heaven and Earth by it are joined. *Fán Lî shî Dàyi [Taìyi]. Tiandì –yî hé.* 凡醴始大一天地以合.

[55] *Lîjì* (IX, Lîyùn) 382: Propriety must be rooted in Great [Grand] Unity which divides into Heaven and Earth... *Lî bì bên –yú Dà-yi, fen –ér weí Tiandì* 醴必本於大一分而爲天地. *Kông Zî Jiayû* (VII Lîyùn) 9a.

[56] *Lyûshì Chunqiu* BC 239: (Jì V-2, Dàyuè 'Great Music') 3a-b.

[57] *Mèngzî* (Ia-6). *Lâozî* (XXXI).

Its cosmology is that of the Five Agents (*wû-xíng*) or 'elements'. It relates them to notes of the five-note scale, the cardinal compass points and seasons. Notes of scale (*sheng*) are termed 'precedent' (*gù*), keynotes and pitchpipes (*yin*, lyù) are for 'mode' (*diào*). Modulation is a recurring concept in *Héguanzî*. (iii-a, v-c, ix-c, x-a, c) It prescribes the musical intervals of the major chord: the third and fifth (xvii-f). The relation of modulation to the five flavours, colours and musical notes, suggests a code or euphemism for redistribution of foods, clothes and ranks respectively according to the five social grades (i-a; viii- a, c; x-c).

Five 72-day and six 60-day gradated periods of reporting to the centre are fixed in a 360-day solar calendar, consistent with the First Emperor's predeliction for the number six. There were to be no longer any hereditary dukedoms and baronages. This conforms to *Héguanzî*'s pervasive message urging 'promotion of worthies' and 'wide selection', in direct opposition to both the conservative Confucius' *Lúnyû* and *Lâozî* (III). Instead, 'commanderies and counties' (*jùnxiàn*) were to be instituted under appointed officials subject to draconian penalties. (ix) These were soon to be adopted in practice by the unified Qín empire and essentially continued ever since in place of semi-autonomous hereditary fiefs.[58]

While *Héguanzî* preaches centralised unity under the Way's Law, it warns against 'savage law' (viii-a) and 'usurped love' (x-c). Emotive reality/real feeling' (*qíng*), is its hallmark. I count thirty-four uses of this word, allied to the 'human reality' of feelings (*rénqíng*) and humanism. Yet it warns against hedonism in 'trusting to it to cultivate life' (iv-d). The humane and righteous rejoice in 'formless internal governance' (x-c).

Héguanzî makes just a single use of the word 'human-nature' (*xìng*, xiv), absent from *Lâozî*, a hot topic for good or evil in Confucian debate between Mencius and Xún Zî, neutral in newly unearthed Guodián text, which here simply means 'physique'. To Lyû Bùweí, in relation to sensory pleasures, it has an equally corporeal scope. Instead, *Héguanzî* and Mâwángdui scrolls propound a novel concept, which I translate as 'commonality' or 'constitution' (*fàn* 范) to link humanity (ix-g, x-c, xi-a).[59]

---

[58] Hsing I-tien 2014: 186 in Pines *et al.* 2014. Bodde 1974: 26-34 on twenty-four 'solar nodes'.

[59] Guodián: *Xìng-zî mìng chu* 性自命出 start. Nakajima 2007: 436. *Lyûshì Chunqiu* (I) 4b: 'complete physicality Way', *quánxìng-zhi Dào* 全性之道. *MWD* 'Nine Rulers' Jiù- Zhû 29, 360-362: 'Heavenly constitution/ commonality', Tian fá = fàn, 天乏/範. 'Enlightened Lords' Míngjun 35, 408.

Prior to Qín unification, the cosmology of the *Book of Change* appendices was yet unknown. Xún Zî did not count *Change* among the classics. Rather, as Graham argued, it was imperial Qín strictures on the Confucian classics, exempting works on divination, that first induced scholars to invest the *Change* appendices with philosophical content.[60] *Héguanzî*, in common with other pre-Qín writings, shows no inkling of eight trigram theory.

1 1 . Grand Unity, Dipper Mother and Pacing the Dipper

Grand Unity is located at the celestial North Pole, known as the 'Purple Aura' (*zîwei*), and directs the turning of the Dipper.[60] Confucius had likened rule by 'non-contrivance' (*wúweî*), practiced by filial sovereign Shùn of prehistory, to the unmoving Pole Star.[61] From there, emperors were said to rule by 'south-facing' (*nánmiàn*) and non-contrivance, as *Héguanzî* remarks (vii-b, x, xi).

Laôzî promoted laissez-faire 'non-contrivance' as the ultimate, but also as a tactical tool, meaning timely action appears like inaction, because the problem has been arrested before it was generally apparent: "contrive it before it is there, govern it before it is disordered."[62] Timely action achieves great results with little effort and so has the appearance of 'non-contrivance'. *Héguanzî*'s doctor-of-medicine provides instances of this ilk (xvi). *Héguanzî* (vi-a, xiii-a), like *Laôzî*, blames 'mutually having-contrivance', with 'intelligence and cunning', for causing the conflicts that wrecked primeval 'Eden'. Contrivance in this sense implies actions taken with ulterior motives of a selfish and covert nature.

The North Pole was also identified with the Dark Warrior (xvii-d), in the shape of a tortoise entwined by snake. Thus, Grand Unity too can assume a martial role. A repainted and tattered, miniature banner in the Mâwángdui mound (BC 168), is headed by a wild staring figure, labelled 'Grand Unity About to March (Taìyi Jiangxíng)' to serve as a protective charm. Grand Unity is flanked by gods of thunder and rain, a baby green dragon with yellow head between his legs, over four demonic warriors. Below them prance big green and yellow dragons.[63] (*Plate 8*)

---

[60] Graham 1989: 134, 327, 330, 359, cites '*Doctrine of the Mean*' *Zhong yong* (XXVIII-3) 411 which refers to standardisation of axel widths and writing postdating Qín unification.

[61] *Huaínánzî* (III) 5a: Grand Subtlety is Grand Unity's hall, Purple Palace is Grand Unity's seat...Purple Palace grasps the Dipper to revolve anti-clockwise (left about). *Taìwei-zhê Taìyi-zhi tíng-yê. Zígong-zhê Taìyi-zhi ju-yê...Zígong zhí Dôu-ér zuô xuán.* 太微者太一之庭也紫宫者太一之居也 紫宫執斗而左旋. *Lúnyû* (II, Weízhèng) 1; (XV, Weì Líng) 8.

[62] *Lâozî* (LXIII-LXIV): *weí zhi-yú weìyôu, zhì zhi-yú weì luàn.* 為之於未有 治之於未亂.

[63] Lewis 2007: 186-187. Lî Líng 1995, 2: 1-39. *Zhongguó Huìhuà Dàquán* I, 2010: 'Taìyi jiangxíng tú' gives a high-resolution reproduction of this silk painting in colour. (Lai Guolong 2014).

These nine spirit companions conform in number and shape (3-4-2) to the nine Dipper stars. Given its credited efficacy in battle, one can dare in a flight of fancy to imagine this banner as a relic from an old campaign, green and yellow dragons in the 'vertical coalition' of Chû and Zhào, making a last stand against Qín, under the aegis of Grand Unity.

Ritual Record proclaims: the army marches with "Red Bird in front (south), Dark Warrior behind (north), Green Dragon on the left (east), White Tiger on the right (west) and Beckoner above."[64] Beckoner (Zhaoyáo i.e. Tianpéng) is the star at the point of the Dipper constellation. The military classic *Six Satchels*, ascribed to legendary Yi Yîn, strategic mastermind to King Tang in his campaign to overthrow corrupt Xià, advises a similar astral array with sun, moon, stars, planets and Big Dipper.[65] (see *Appendix II*)

Dipper Mother, Dôumû, of indubitable femininity, is unattested in classic texts, except, arguably, as the virginal Woman Qí who "without coupling begot nine sons" at the opening of 'Heavenly Questions' in *Chû Lyrics'* traditionally ascribed to dissident Qu Yuán. At the head of 'Nine Songs' addressed to nine deities, from the same work, is a hymn to a sword-wearing 'Eastern Augustan, Grand Unity', Donghuáng Taìyi, whose name implies solar rather than polar provenance.[66]

Dipper Mother, also known as the 'Way's Mother' (Dàomû) is said, to have by tradition, gave birth to Nine Augustans who ruled the world as Human Augustans, before becoming 'star lords' (*xingjun*) in the Dipper, where they exercise awesome power as enforcers of heavenly law. Due to Buddhist influenced Daoism, Dipper Mother has subsequently been portrayed as the multi-armed Indian goddess Mârîcî in her chariot drawn by seven pigs as in *Dipper Mother Primal Dignity's Nine Augustan Classic*, from a compilation ascribed to Zhang Sanfeng. (*Plates 13-15*)

---

[64] *Ritual Record, Lǐjì* (I Qulî-shàng) 43-44 describes chariot banners with: Red Bird in front (south), Dark Warrior behind (north), Green Dragon on the left (east), White Tiger on the right (west), Beckoner above.

[65] *Liù-Tao* 32; Sawyer 1993: 80. Lewis 1990: 204 "follow the Dipper to attack."

[66] *Chûcí* 楚辭, Hawkes (tr. 1959) 48: Tianwèn 天問 19-20; 36: Jiû-ge 九歌 1-15.

This mysterious Complete Truth Daoist recluse was enshrined in the huge True Warrior temple at Wûdang Mountain (Húbeî) by Míng emperor Yônglè to bolster his dubious claim to the throne,.[67] As we saw, his great compendium of literature included an edition of *Héguanzî* with a unique interpolation appearing to bestow on him divine sanction as the awaited messiah, and thus justify his ensuing usurpation. (*Postscript II*)

Nine stars figure in the Daoist ritual of 'Pacing the Dipper' (*Bùgang*) or 'Yû steps', named after Great Yû, founder of the Xià dynasty who   in taming primaeval floods became lame, a theme recalling the Grail's Fisher King and royal auto-sacrifice in world folklore.[68] The word for king *wáng* 王/亡 is a homonym for 'lost' or 'doomed' (i-b, vii-b, etc) and etymologically close to 'lame victim' wâng 尪 . Auto-flagellation. a form of sacrifice, is still practised at festivals outside the mainland. (Plates 21-22)

At Mt Wûdang in Húbeî, a Daoist monk ang enacts a shamanic dance of limping steps, as if in a sacrifice for rain (v-d), on Dipper stars' 'Nine Palace Steps' embodying cosmic flight. (xviia, Plate 11). In Beîjing opera, on the ninth of the ninth lunar month, actors paid homage to the Nine Augustans star-gods with papier-maché statues. In Taíwan, a Beîguân actor, as witnessed in 1984, danced a ritual exorcism in the guise of demon-queller Zhongkuí tracing the outline of the Dipper stars.[69]

Héguanzî describes Grand Unity's extra-terrestial travel and rotating heavenly motion (xi-a, xvii-a). In a magic square, symbolising the cosmos, known as the Luò River Map of Yû, numbers one to nine in any straight line of three numbers (horizontal, vertical or diagonal), with five in the centre, always total fifteen. Marked in zig-zag or '**double-helix**' patterns of ordinal sequences, it is also used in Daoist 'Pacing the Dipper' as well as in martial arts such as *baguàzhâng* and *taìjíquán*:[70] (*Diagrams 1-3. Cf. Appendix II*)

---

[67] *Dôumû Yuánzun: Jiû-Huáng Jing*, in *Sanfeng Quánjî*: 405ff.

[68] Campbell 1968: 416ff 'The Maimed Fisher King'. Frazer 1922: 109ff 'Magicians as Kings', 115 'shaman', 375ff 'King Hop'. Lewis 1990: 194-195. Wells 2013: 12-14.

[69] Wilhelm/Baynes 1967: 310, Figure 5.Li Hongchun 1982: 404. 408-409. Chu Kunliang 1991:102, 152, 156-157

[70] *Dà Dai Lǐ* (Míngtáng), in Needham 1959: 57. Andersen 1989: 29-35. Kalinowski 1998- 99, *Early China* 23/24: 125. *Taìyi Shù Tôngzong Dàquán* 1780 (III, 1-4 Jiû-Gong Guìshén Tôngxíng Biànxiàng Shù) lists Nine Palaces in Luò River sequence. Guo Pú 郭璞 (276- 324): *Língyào Jing* (II-zé 4) 17b lists prayer, troop deployment and sacrificial offerings for each. Mak 2015: Method of Flying Stars, 242ff: Nine Palace chart, Figs 18. Mroz 2011: 145: "Nine Palace Trajectory used in Daoist ritual and martial art of baguazhang"; 146: Fig 27 *Jiugong* Nine Palace trajectory; 163: Figs a-p '*Wudang Taiyi Wuxing quan*'. Huang Shih-shan 2010: 81-83. Boretz 1995: 93-109 on 'martial violence' in Chinese popular religion. Sun Fúquán (Lùtáng) 1924: IV-14 Guo Yúnshen's *xíngyì* boxing footwork on Luò River diagram. Chén Xin (pref 1919): *Taiji Quán Túshuo*, 62 'chánsijing/jìng'. Wells 2005: 66.

In 1977, the 165 BC tomb of Marquis Rûyin (Anhui) was found to contain a 'Grand Unity Walking the Nine Palaces Divination Board' in Luó River Map sequence. Following these squares or 'palaces' (*gong*) in numerical sequence produces a trajectory of zig-zags turns just as in Pacing the Dipper'.[71] *Diagrams* 2 and 3 show the Luò River Map sequence co-ordinated with Eight Trigrams, as compass-points plus centre, for pacing the Nine Dipper stars by Daoists in Southeast Asia. A contrast could be drawn with celestial gyrations, but only anti-clockwise practised by Mevlevi Sufi 'whirling dervishes' (*sema*) in Konya, Turkey.

Diagram 1. Luò River Map trajectories clockwise and anti-clockwise

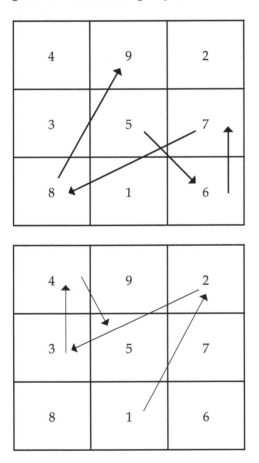

---

[71]   Harper 1978, *Early China* 4: 1-10. Csikszentmihalyi 2008: 868, DZ 1294 'flying Nine Palace steps'

Diagram 2. Pacing the Nine Dipper Stars as Eight Trigrams plus Centre, according to the Luò River Diagram[72]

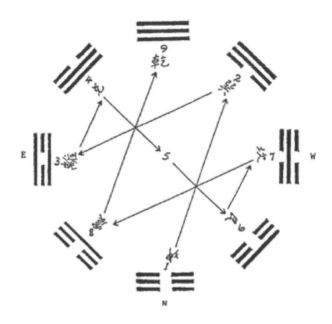

Diagram 3. Dipper Nine Star names with Eight Trigrams
(Kun is paired with both Earth at Centre and North at bottom).[73]

Star	Direction	Numeral	Element	Trigram
Tianying	South	9	Fire	Qian
Tianren	Northeast	8	Earth	Zhen
Tianzhu	West	7	Metal	Kan
Tianxin	Northwest	6	Metal	Gen
Tianqin	Centre	5	Earth	Kun
Tianfu	Southeast	4	Wood	Dui
Tianchong	East	3	Wood	Li
Tianrui	Southwest	2	Earth	Xun
Tianpeng	North	1	Water	Kun

[72] Cheu Hock Tong 1993: 42-43.

[73] Cheu Hock Tong 1993: 42-43.

28

12. Translation, Notes and Charts

Classical written Chinese is wonderfully flexible. Verbal functions, whether as noun, adjective or verb, are largely determined by dynamic position and context. In the case of *Héguanzî*, comprehension is facilitated by the number of shared items with better known texts of the period. On the other hand, *Héguanzî*'s unique socio- political outlook, coupled with textual corruptions and lack of an early commentary, present serious problems of interpretation, which none have so far attempted comprehensively to undertake in English until now. (cf. Wells 2013; Defoort 1997; 2015: 286-287)

To retain the maximum of the original's poetic style and sense, I follow its word order as closely as possible. To flag its important terms, I try where possible to render each occurrence with the same English word, adding clarifications where necessary, so the reader can follow the scope of their usages.

Chinese words are spelled here according to the official Chinese *pinyin* system, modified slightly to accord with standard keyboards. The umlaut on '*lu*' or '*nu*' has been rendered here by '*lyu*' and '*nyu*'. Unlike in other English language books on China, speech-tones in current pronunciation are marked. This should help differentiate words with otherwise identical spelling but different meaning:
1. High level tone: unmarked e.g. 'high' *gao* 高.
2. Rising tone: marked by acute accent e.g. 'humane' *rén* 仁.
3. Falling-rising tone: marked by circumflex e.g. 'Law' *fâ* 法.
4. Falling tone: marked by grave accent e.g. 'Way' *dào* 道.

Cross-references to chapter numbers in the work are shown by bracketed Roman numerals. The italicized acronym *HGZ* denotes the present work; *MWD* is for Mâwángdui scrolls. Authors are spelled in this form: e.g. 'Lâo Zî' or 'Héguan Zî' ('Zî' being the honourific appellation for 'Master'), while the works themselves are italicized and consolidated: '*Lâozî*' or '*Héguanzî*'. The original's chapter titles are in two Chinese word-syllables, except for the last (xix) which has three. Punctuation, paragraphing and sub-titles within each chapter have been supplied by the translator to assist the reader. The text has been transmitted with only one commentary, that by Lù Diàn (1042-1102), whose preface notes problems with corruptions in the text and admits limitations in his understanding, coloured by orthodox Daoism.

My interpretation, while recognising disparate strands, is based on a holistic reading of its totality within the geo-political context of the Warring States just prior to Qín unification. Within the limitations of a literal rendering, an attempt has been made to strive for coherent sense with the aid of some degree of lateral thinking.

There are indications in the text of substitution at certain points of alternative words due to taboo avoidance of the First Emperor's personal name Zhèng (正) 'Governor/ Correct'. There are cases of archaic characters, such as that for 'dynamics' (*shì* 執 = 勢 , easily confused with 執, or even 'who' *shú* 孰). Another case is that of the word I render 'reality', or 'emotive reality' (*qíng* 情), which seems to have been mistransmitted in some as 'invite' (*qîng* 請) or 'posthumous title' (*shì* 謚).

Complementaries
Design (wén) <> Reason (lî)
Flavour (weì) <> Colour (sè)
Flavour/foods (weì) <> Energy (qì)
Form (xíng) <> Dynamic (shì)
Heaven (Tian) <> Earth (Dì)
Human (Rén) <> Reality, Feelings (Qíng)
Individual (wô) <> Multitude (zhòng)
Leaves (yè) <> Flowers (hua)
Modes (sheng) <> Keynotes (yin)
One (yi) <> Myriad (wàn)
Principle (lî) <> Dynamic (shì)
Reality (qíng) <> Principle (lî)
Shady (yin) <> Sunny (yáng),
Things (wù) <>Species (leì)
Way (Dào) <> Virtue (dé)
Yin (negative) <> Yáng (positive), shady/sunny Energy (qì)

Oppositions
Dynamics (shì) >< Investigation (chá); Form (xíng)
Fire (huô) >< Water (shuî)
Form (xíng) >< Spirit (shén); Dynamics (shì)
Flavours/foods (weì) >< Poison (dú)
Medicine (yào) <> Poison (dú)
Name (míng) >< Substance (shí)
Penalties/Form (xíng) >< Virtue/Favour (dé)
Precedent (gù) >< Modulation (tiáo, diào)
Way (Dào) >< Law/penalties (fâ/xíng)
Wet (shi) >< Dry (zào)

Correlative Numerology
One: Unity, prime, energy (qì).
Two: shade-sunshine, negative- positive (*yin- yáng*).
Three: Heaven-Earth-Man, Kings, Pole-Dipper-Galaxies, 'triangulation'.
Four: aims, directions, seasons, social programs (iv-a>e).

Five: agents/conquests, colours, commonalities (fàn 范/範, x-c), flavours, God-Emperors; Governances (iii-a, viii-c, d; cf. iv-a, b, c, d, e), keynotes, (xii-d, xvii-f), luminaries, offices, modes.

Six: attainments/laws/hexagrams (xv-b), offices (x-d), co-ordinates (up-down, east-west, north- south), pitchpipes in two whole-tone sets. Qín's First Emperor made six the basis of his numbering.

Eight: directions, extremities, winds.

Nine: Heavens, Augustans (iv-a, x-a, xi-a), barbarians, design, Dipper stars (iv-a), expanses, orifices, regions, Ways (viii-c, xv-a).

Ten: unlabelled list of sorites: 'unity > things' (v-a).

Eleven: unlabelled list of meritocratic assessments (vi-c).

Thirteen: unlabelled list of 'proofs' (yàn, iii-a).f

Thirty-six 'to contrive the year's format' (viii-c).

Twenty-five 'to organize the Under-Heaven' (viii-c).

Sixty: sexagenary calendar of overlapping 10 and 12 unit cycles (ix-d).

Seventy-two: day reporting periods, a fifth of the 360-day year (ix-d).

Hundred: battles, operations (shì), enterprises (yè), fathers, gods, laws (vii-c), lineages, men, reforms (huà), selves, tribes (zú).

Myriad: chariots, commoners, enterprises, explanations, generations, lives, mouths, nations, men, metamorphoses, people, souls, species, turns, things/beings, undertakings, years.

Three-hundred-and-sixty day year (ix-g)

Eighteen Thousand [2x 9000?]: years of Complete Ninth (ix-g).

Core Vocabulary

ace, hero, top grade: jùn 俊, 雋

actuality, truth, emotive reality: qíng 情

adaptation, adaptive, yin 因 (viii-d, xix-a)

agents, five agents/elements, here 'five conquests' wû-xíng/shèng 五行/勝

aims: qi 期 (iv-a>e, v-a)

analysis, by three and five, triangle and square: canwû 三五/參伍

arms: bing 兵

Augustan, Emperor: Huáng 皇

Augustan of Heaven and Earth, Huáng Tiandì 皇天地

balance, power, expedience: quán 權

Beckoner, leading star in the Dipper handle: *Zhaoyáo* 招搖

baron-king: hóuwáng, 侯/后王 (viii-d)

bureaucracy, bureaucrative, official: guan 官 (viii-d)

campaigns: zheng 征/正. Cf. correct; governance

change, revolution, transform: biàn 變

civil, culture, pattern, design: wén 文

colours (five), black, white, red, green, yellow; clothes: sè 色

commonality, constitution: fàn 范/範/乏 (ix-g, x-c, xi-a; *MWD Jiû-Zhû* 29, 360-362; *Míngjun* 35, 408.)

commandery (province), county: jùn, xiàn 郡, 縣 (ix-c)

conquest: shèng 勝 cf. agents

Complete Ninth: Chéngjiû 成鳩/九 (ix-a, b, f, g)

contracts, pledges, covenants: yue 約 (v>vii, ix)

control, system: zhì 制

correct (govern/punish-attack): zhèng 正(政/征), in Zhào Zhèng, name of Qín's First Emperor

courage: yông 勇

culture, civilization, design: wén 文, related to Propriety and Principle.

customs, morals, vulgar: sú 俗

Daoism: Dàojiào 道教

decide, decision (cut): duàn 斷

Dipper (Northern), Bushel, Plough, Ursa Major: Dôu 斗 (iv-a)

Divine Sage: shénshèng 神聖 (x-b,-c; xi-a,-b)

Divine Luminaries/ illumination, astral bodies: shénmíng 神 明 (viii-d; ix-bx2,-g; x-a; xi-a,-c)

dynamics, potential, power: shì/yì/shè 勢, 埶,設 (iv-c x2, v-d, vii-b, viii-a,-b, x-b, xii-d x2, xiv-a x2, -b, xvii-e, xviii-a, -b x2: = 16x) often confused with 'skill' yì 藝/蓺, 'grasp' zhí 執, 'who?' shú 孰

Earth, cosmic nature, paired with Heaven, the sky: Dì 地 Cf. soil

education, educative: jiào 教 (iv-d, viii-d)

ego, I, we: wô, wú 我, 吾 cf. self

embody/'encorpse' divine illumination: tî/shi shénmíng 體/尸神明 (viii-d; ix-bx2; ix-g; xi-a)

emotive reality, feelings with human, things: qíng 情

Emperor, God, Thearch: Dì 帝. See: Augustan, huáng: 皇

energy, weather: qì 氣 (42x)

expected man: xirén 人 (ii-a)

face to face: zhèngmiàn 鉦=正面 (ix-g, xii-d) see: correct

factual, result: guô 果

fathom, determine: cè 測

fence-in, rule by division: yòu 宥

flavours (five), sweet, sour, salt, bitter, pungent; foods: weì 味

Form, penalties, physical body: xíng 刑, 形情

generation, world: shì 世

get, win: dé 得(81x), attain unity in the Way, pun on Virtue Dé 德 (v-d, ix-g, x-a, xii-c,-d, xviii-a,-b)

God, Emperor: dì 帝

god, spirit, divine: shén 神

governance, government: zhèng 政/正 (iv-c, viii-d)

Grand Unity, god and Pole: Taìyi 太/泰一, 泰壹, Taìyî 太乙, Dàyi 大一 (7x)

Great Dynamic: Dàshì 大勢/埶(v-d, 1x)

having contrivance, activist: yôuweí 有為 (xiii-a)

Heaven, sky, God, God-given nature: Tian 天

Heaven's Son, King, Emperor: Tianzî 天子

Heavenly Melody, bi-monthly reporting by six pitchpipes: liù-lyù 六律, Tianqû 天曲 (Cf. Solar Numbering, ix-b.-d; divine melody, xvii-f)

Heavenly Hero: Tianying 天英 (xvii-f)

Heavenly Warrior: Tianwû 天武 (xix-a)

hegemon, paramount ruler after Zhou lost power: Bà/bó 霸/伯

hero, third grade: ying 英 (see: ace, valiant)

household, family, school (of philosophy): jia 家

humane: rén 仁 (ii-c, vi-b,-c)

human reality/feelings: rénqíng 人情 (iv-a,-d, ix-b,-g, xii-a, xiii-a, xv-a)

ideas: yì 意

individual, self: jî 己, wô 我 cf. self

intelligence, knowledge, cunning, wise: zhi, zhì, huì 知/智,慧

keynote, in pentatonic scale: yin 音

king, divine sovereign of first three dynasties Xià 夏, Shang 商, and Zhou 周 ; title usurped by barons; linking heaven, earth and man: wáng 王, pun on 'doomed' 亡 (vii-b)

Law, model, constitution: fâ 法, 灋 (78x)

man, human; humane: rén 人; 仁

mandate, mission, divine destiny, command: mìng 命 (47x)

martial, military, warrior: wû 武

meaning, call: weî 謂

Messiah, primal/Divine Sage, expected/ultimate/true man, Augustan: yuán/shén Shèng 原/神聖, xi/zhì/zhenrén 希/至/真人, Huáng 皇

mode, sound: sheng 聲

model, pattern: zé 則

modulate, tune: tiáo 調

motive, cause, fixed: gù 故

myriad things/beings, phenomena: wàn-wù 萬物

names, titles, terms, words, reputation: míng 名

nation, state: guó 國

primal Sage: yuan Shèng 原聖 (viii-c, xviii-a)

Night Walker: yèxíng 夜行 (iii, xix-a)

nine, Ninth/dove: Jiû: 九/鳩, number of Dipper stars, Augustan (ix-a)

non-contrivance, inaction, laissez-faire: wúweí 無 爲 (vii-b)

numbering, technique, art: shù 數/術

One Man: Yi-rén 一人. (iv-e; vi-c)

operation, employment: shì 事 (iv-e, viii-d)

Pacing the Dipper: Bùgang 步罡; limping Steps of Yû: 禹步 Cf. shaman

Phoenix, Fire Bird constellations (viii-c): Fènghuáng, Chúnhuô 鳳凰, 鶉火

pitch, tuning: jun 均

pitchpipes, six whole-tones: lyù 律

Pole Star, Cf. Grand Unity

precedent, cause: gù 故

principle, rationality: lî 理, closely related to propriety

propriety, ritual, morality: lî 禮 Cf. principle

punitive attack：zheng 征

reality, sensory and emotional reality, feelings: qíng 情 (yì 諡 x2; qîng 請 x3; 34x) cf. human reality reason, rationality, see: principle

reformation, reformative: huà 化 (iv-b, viii-d)

revolution, alteration, transformation: biàn 變

return, revert: fù, fân 復; 反 Cf. rotator

rhetoric, deceptive, superfluous language: yíncí 淫辭

rhythm, timing, regulate: jié 節

rotator, turn：huán 還 (xvii-a), see: return

Royal Axe: Wángfû/fu 王斧/夫 (i-a,-b, ix-f)

Sage King: Shèngwáng 聖王 (iv-a,-e; vii-a; viii-c; xi-b) Cf. Messiah

Sage Man: Shèngrén 聖人 Cf. Messiah

save, regulate: dùo, dù 度

scale of five notes (do, re, mi, sol, la): sheng 聲

seasons, times: shí, jié 時節

self, jî, zì, 己, 自, cf. ego, individual

self-so, natural, spontaneous: 自然

shady and sunny, opposites: yin-yáng 陰陽

Shady Warp, covert operations: Yinjing 陰經 (xix-a) cf. Night Walker

shaman, witch: wuxì 巫覡,'teacher' shi 師 (v-d) cf. Pacing the Dipper

sign, evidence, portent, opportunity: yàn 驗; ji 稽, 幾, 機

soil, the physical substance, one of the five agents: tû 土 cf. Earth

Solar Numbering: Rìshù 日術 Cf. Heavenly Melody (ix-b,-d)

soul, efficacious, magic: ling 靈

space-time: yûzhòu 宇宙

spirit, divine, gods: shén 神

spirit medium, spirit possession, victim: wang 伬, 尪, cf. shaman, embody

substance, facts: shí 實

suchness, nature: rán 然, cf. self-so

suicide, cutting throat: wênjìng, zìjîng 刎脛, 自到

tally-stick, broken into halves to verify the identities: fújié 符節

teacher, shaman: shi 師 cf. shaman: wu 巫

technique, numbering, mathematics: 術/數

things, beings: wù 物

times: shí 時; see: seasons jié 節

true man/men: zhenrén 真人 (xii-a, Owl Rhapsody, *Postscript I*)

ultimate man: zhìrén 至人 (xii-d; xviii-c, Owl Rhapsody, *Postscript I*)

Under-Heaven, the world, empire: Tianxià 天下

Unicorn, Dark Hollow (Black Hole?) constellation of north: Qílín,
    Xuánxiao 騏麟, 玄枵 (viii-c)

Unity, unification, one, oneness: yi 一/乙/壹 (38x)

valiant, second grade: háo 豪 (see: Ace, Hero)

valiant knights: lièshì 烈士

Virtue, blessings, power, to do good to: Dé 德 (55x) Cf. pun on 'get'

warehouser, district official: sèfu 嗇夫 (ix-b,c)

Water, produced by Heaven: shuî 水 (viii-a)

Way: Dào 道 (152x)

Way's Law: Dàofâ (v-b) worthy: xián 賢

Dramatis Personae, Antiquity's Hall of Fame
n.b. dates are B.C., unless otherwise indicated.

Bâilî Xi 百里奚, premier to Hegemon Duke Mù 穆 (r. 659-621) of Qín.

Biânquè 扁鵲, doctor of legendary skill. Baron Wén (r. 636-628) of Jìn, elsewhere Baron Huán (r. 714-695) of Caì, refused his treatment until the disease was beyond control. (xvi)

Bîgan 比干, loyal adviser, martyed by tyrant Zhôu of Shang. (xiii-b)

Bóyí 伯夷, son of ruler of Guzhú (Korea?), brother of Shúqí. Each abdicated to the other, then went west where they met Wû of Zhou, carrying a wooden idol of his father in a carriage, on campaign to overthrow Shang. To protest violence, they starved to death on Mt Shôuyáng (Shanxi), their principles ridiculed here as futile (xiii-a).

Cangjié 蒼頡, legendary inventor of writing, calendar, bureaucracy and law, allegedly under the Yellow Emperor. (vii-c, ix-g)

Cáo Mò (Jù) 曹沫, patriotic general of Lû 魯 who at a conference in 681 held Duke Huán 桓 of Qí 齊 hostage, forcing him to restore territory to Lû. (xii-b)

Chéngjiû 成鳩, see Complete Ninth.

Chiyóu 蚩尤, demon, primaeval rebel killed by Yellow Emperor in Mâwángdui scroll 'Crushing Rebellion' (Zhengluàn). (xii-a)

Chóu Mù 裘牧, loyal minister of Sòng, struck dead by minister Nángong Wàn who assassinated Duke Mín in 682. (xiii-a)

Complete Ninth, Chéngjiû 成鳩 = 成九. 'Nine' (*jiû*) is written with the bird radical which I take as honourific as, literally, 'Complete Dove'. (ix-a,-b,-f,-g). In ancient south Chinese 'bird script', bird images (鳥) were added to names. (cf. Goujiàn)

Diàoxiang, King, 卓襄王 (r. 244-236) of Zhào, defeated by Qín. (xvi)

Fàn Lî 范蠡, counsellor to King Goujiàn of Yuè and instrumental in the recovery of his kingdom in 473. (xvi)

Feì Zhòng 費仲 sycophant who served tyrant Zhôu of Shang.

First Augustan Emperor, Qín Shî Huángdì 秦始皇帝 (r. 221-210), named Zhào Zhèng 趙正, because born in Zhào.

Five Emperors, Wû-Dì 五帝, pre-dynastic god-kings of legend (xii-a).

Fuchai 夫差, Hegemon King of Wú 吳 (r. 495-473).

Goujiàn 勾践/鳩淺, Hegemon King of Yuè 越 (r. 496-465), confined in 494 by Fuchai of Wú. In 473, using Fàn Lî's counsel, he regained his kingdom. A sword was found inscribed with his name written 'Jiuqian' 鳩淺, *'jiu'* 'nine plus bird' as in 'Complete Ninth'. (ix-a)

Goumáng 勾萌, 'Hooked Spike', crop-sprout god of Spring. (vii-a)

Grand Augustan, Taìhuáng 泰皇, chief of the Nine Augustans and acolyte of Grand Unity. Worshipped in Chû as Eastern Augustan of Grand Unity, Donghuáng Taìyi 東皇太一. (x-a)

Grand Superior, Taìshàng 泰上, used to qualify the Ultimate Way of the Complete Ninth and its golden age. *Lâozî* VII: "Under the Grand Superior, subordinates do not know he is there." (ix-a, xix-a) Qín's First Emperor canonized his father, Zhuangxiang (r. 249-246), 'Grand Superior Augustan'.

Grand Unity, Taìyî 泰一, monad, star, god and principle. Also written Taìyî, and associated with Heavenly Unity, Tianyi, Tianyî. (x-a, xi-a)

Guân Zhòng (d. 645), Guân Zî 管仲 premier to first great Hegemon, Duke Huán 桓 of Qí. (xii-d, xiii-b, xvi)

Hán Xuan Zî 韓宣子,with Weì 魏 and Zhào 趙 defeated tyrannical usurper Zhì Bó at Jìnyáng in 453 and divided his state of 晉 among themselves. (xix-a)

Huán 桓, Duke (r. 685-643) of Qí, first Hegemon who with Guân Zhòng (qv), in place of the Zhou king, nine times convened the barons.

Huáng Dì, see Yellow Emperor.

Ji Zî 姬子, Grand Teacher to tyrant Zhôu of Shang who imprisoned him. He escaped death by feigning madness. On the fall of Shang, he reputedly led his followers to Korea where he founded a state.

Jiân Shú 蹇叔, advised Duke Mù of Qín against attacking Zhèng. His advice was ignored and Qín suffered defeat in 627. (xiii-b)

Jiang Zîyá, see Taìgong Wàng.

Jié 桀, tyrannical last king of Xià (trad. d. 1766).

Jù Xin (d. 242) 劇辛, general of Yàn 燕, originally of Zhào, who cut his throat after his abortive invasion of Zhào. (xii-c)

Lî Si (c. 278-208) 李斯, ex-pupil of Xún Zî (313-238) and premier to Qín's First Emperor. Cited in Jiâ Yì's *Owl Rhapsody*.

Líng, King of Chû 楚靈王 (r. 540-529), in 533-531 employed his younger brother Qìjí to annex the small border states of Chén and Caì, but was overthrown by Qìjí and committed suicide.

Lyû Bùweí 呂不韋 (291-235), merchant in Zhào, editor of 'Daoist' encyclopaedia, 'step-father' (zhòngfù), and premier to Zhào Zhèng, future First Emperor of Qín.

Lù Diàn 陸佃 (1042-1102), ed. *Héguanzî* under Daoist emperor Huizong.

Nine Augustans Jiû-Huáng 九皇, series of divine monarchs.

Páng Huàn 龐煥 (c. 300), adviser to King Wûlíng of Zhào 趙. (xix)

Páng Xuan 龐暖 general of Zhào, leader of last failed combined assault on Qín in 241. Possible descendant of strategists Páng Huàn and/or Páng Juan (d. 341) whose lost work on alliance-brokering is listed in *Hàn History*. (vii, xvi)

Qu Yuán 屈原 (ca. 300 BC), reputed author of *Chû Lyrics*. (cf. *Postscript I*)

Shang Róng 商容, musician and ritualist, imprisoned after admonishing tyrant Zhôu of Shang, re-instated by King Wû of Zhou after revolution.

Shen, Biao, Baoxu 申鳳, 包胥, of Chû, ex-friend of Wû Zîxu (q.v.) who fled to Wú in 522 and in 506 returned with an army to capture Chû capital Yíng. Shen fled to Qín and in 505 BC with its help restored King Zhao of Chû but declined office. (xiii-b, xvi)

Shen Túdí 申徒狄, a protest suicide in the Yellow River. *Mòzî* fragments record he had urged regent Duke Dàn of Zhou (d. 1032 BC) to employ worthies. (xiii-a)

Shùn 舜 (trad. 2225-2206) legendary predynastic Emperor chosen on merit by Emperor Yáo to succeed him. Shùn in turn appointed Yû.

Shúqí 叔齊 see: Bóyí.

Taìgong Wàng, 'Grand Duke', Jiang Zîyá, Lyûshàng 太公望, 姜子牙, 呂尚 strategist of Zhou victory over Shang in 1046 BC, ex-butcher, famously discovered fishing on the banks of the Wei, and premier to founders Wén and Wû of Zhou.

Taìhuáng 太/泰皇, see Grand Augustan.

Taìyi 太/泰一/壹, see Grand Unity.

Tang, Chéng 湯, 成 'the Victorious', (r. 1766-1754?), founder of the Shang商 dynasty, alias Tianyî 天乙, or in late fiction Taìyî 太乙.

Three Kings, San-Wáng 三王 founders of Xià, Shang and Zhou dynasties.

Wén, Hegemon Duke of Weì/Jìn 魏/晉文侯 (r. 636-628).

Wén, King 文王 'Civil King' (1099-1050) of Zhou 周, father of Wû, q.v.

Wû, King 武王 'Martial King' (r. 1049?-1043), Zhou founder, overthrower of Shang.

Wûlíng, King 武靈 王 (r. 325-299 d. 295) of Zhào, military reformer who asked advice from Páng Huàn. He unwisely abdicated. Wùlaí 惡來 villainous strongman of Qín under Shang tyrant Zhôu. (xix)

Wû Zîxu 伍 子 胥 After King Píng of Chû killed his father, in 522, he fled to Wú where in revenge he counselled its victory over Chû in 506. Later, he was slandered and executed by Wú, his body thrown into the river Huaí. He is still commemorated, along with Qu Yuán, by dragon boat races. (xiii-b). cf. his friend Shen Biao, Baoxu.

Yáo 堯 legendary predynastic Emperor who abdicated to the Sage Shùn. Yellow Emperor, Huáng Dì 黃帝 legendary unifier in pre-dynastic era. (xii-a)

Yi Yîn 伊尹 ex-publican, Daoist sage, promoted by King Tang, founder of Shang to be his chief military adviser and premier. (xiii-b, xvi)

Yû 禹 the Great ('r. 2205-2197') founder of Xià dynasty, famed for flood control and channeling rivers, defeated Yôumiáo. (xii-a, xiii-b) His eventual lameness gave his name to the shamanic hopping step, Yûbù 禹步. (v-d)

Yuán Jì 原季 minister to hegemon Duke Wén 文 (r. 636-628) of Jìn晉. (xvi)

Yúfù 俞跗 doctor of legendary skill, like Qíbó 岐伯, under the Yellow Emperor. (xvi)

Zhao 昭, King of Chû (r. 515-489). (xvi)

Zhào She 趙奢, leading general of Zhào. His widow warned king against appointment of their unqualified son, Zhào Kuò, whose army suffered annihilation by Qín at Chángpíng in 260. (*Plates 23-25*; vii)

Zhào Zhèng 趙正/政 (259-210), King of Qín who became First Emperor and unifier of China, annexing the Six Kingdoms.

Zhì Bó 智伯, usurper in Jìn, was killed and his head lacquered after the battle of Jìnyáng in 453. Jìn then split into the three states of Zhào, Weì (Liáng) and Hán (Shanxi, Hénán and Hébeî). (xix-a)

Zhôu Xin 紂辛, last king of Yin-Shang 殷商, tyrant killed by Martial King Wû of Zhou in 1046 BC.

Table II. Classic Philosophies in outline

Time Line	Individu-alist	internal <	< centrist >	> external	Politico- Militarist
B.C.	**Way**, Dào 道		**Scholiast**, Rú 儒		**Law**, Fâ 法
700					Guân Zî Zhòng 管子仲 ca. 720-645
500			Confucius, Kông Zî, Zhòngní 孔子仲尼 541-478		
450				Mò Zî, Dí 墨子翟	Sun Zî Wû 孫子武Wú Zî, Qî 吳子起
350		Lâo Zî, Dan 老子耽			Shang Yang 商鞅 390-338 Shen Bùhaì 申不害
300	Zhuang Zî Zhou 莊子周	Shèn Dào 慎到 (ca. 350-270)	Mencius, Mèng Zî Ke 孟子軻 372-289	Xún Zî Qing 荀子卿 313-238	Sun Bin 孫臏 Páng Huàn 龐煥(xix)
250		Lyû Bùweí 呂不韋 d. 235	'Pheasant Cap' Héguan Zî 鶡冠子	Way's Law; Huáng-Lâo 道法; 黃老	Hán Fei Zî 韓非子 d. 233
150		Jiâ Yì 賈誼 201-169 Huáinán Zî 淮南子179-122	Dông Zhòngshu 董仲舒c.179-104		

Table III. Geo-Politics in Early China

Prehistory B.C. 3000+ **'Reformative'** Huà 化	Legendary Five Emperors Wû-Dì 五帝	Yellow Emperor, Huángdì 黄帝 vanquished Chiyóu蚩尤, 'inventor of weapons' (xii-a)	Cangjié 倉傑, 'invented writing, calendar and law' (vii-c, ix-g)
		Yáo 堯 abdicated	Shùn 舜 elected emperor
		Shùn 舜 abdicated	Yû 禹 elected emperor
'Educative' Jiào 教	Xià dynasty 夏代	Yû the Great 夏禹	Tamed flood waters
1500	Shang dynasty 商代	King Tang, Chéng the Victorious, 成湯 1766	Yi Yîn 伊尹 wise adviser (xiii-b), *MWD* 'Nine Rulers' scroll'
1000	Zhou dynasty 周代	Civil King Wénwáng 文王 Martial King Wûwáng 武王 overthrew Shang in 1046	Taìgong Wàng 太公望 strategist
700 **'Operative'** Shì 事	Chunqiu 春秋, Wû-Bà 五霸	'Spring and Autumn: Five Hegemons Period'	
	Qí 齊	Duke Huán of Qí 齊桓公 (r. 685-643)	Guân Zhòng 管仲 (d. 645) (xii-d, xvi) Cáo Mò 曹沫 of Lû 魯 (xii-b)
	Qín 秦	Duke Mù of Qín 秦穆公 (r. 659-621)	Baîlî Xi 百里奚, Jiân Shú 蹇叔 (xiii-b)
	Jìn 晉	Duke Wén of Jìn 晉文公 (r. 636-628)	Yuán Jì 原季 (xvi)
	Chû 楚	King Zhao 楚昭 of Chû (r. 515-489)	Wû Zîxu 伍子胥. Shen Biao Baoxu. 申應包胥 (xiii-b)
	Yuè 越	King Goujiàn 越勾踐 of Yuè (r. 496-465)	Fàn Lî 范蠡 helped recover kingdom. (xvi)
500 **'Adaptative'** Yin 因	Warring States 戰國	King Xiàochéng 趙孝成 of Zhào (r. 265-245) lost battle of Chángpíng (260)	Lìn Xiangrú 藺相如 with general Zhào She 趙奢's widow petitioned king. (vii)
250 **'Bureaucrative'** Guan 官	Qín dominance 秦國	Zhuangxiang (r. 249-246). Zhào Zhèng 趙正 (b. 259, r. 246-210), King of Qín, future 'First Emperor'	Lyû Bùweí 呂不韋 (d. 235) Merchant, premier, edited first encyclopaedia.
221-206	Imperial Qín dynasty. 秦朝	First Emperor, Shî Huángdì 始皇帝 (d. 210) annexed six kingdoms unified China	Lî Si 李斯 (ca. 278-208), premier, centralised law and imperial bureaucracy, 'burned books'.
206 BC – 201 AD	Hàn dynasty.漢朝	Liú Bang 劉邦, Emperor Gaozû 高祖 (r. 203-180); 'Martial Emperor' Wûdì 武帝 (r. 140-80)	Jiâ Yì 賈誼 (201-169). Maintained centralization. Established state Confucianism.

Table IV. Succession of 'Nine Augustans' (Jiû-Huáng 九皇)

Jiâ Yì (201-169 BC)'s *New Book* (*Xinshu* ix, 68-72) lists ten foundational monarchs, adding two names: Zhou King Wû's father the uncrowned 'cultured' Wén, and Wû's son the 'completer' Chéng, to the conventional eight shown below. Dông Zhòngshu (ca. 174-109)'s *Springs and Autumns Luxuriant Dew* (*Chunqiu Fánlù* VII-23, 43a) explains the succession of ritual titles for revered ancestral rulers as Nine Augustans. Cf. *Héguanzî* xii-a 'Dynastic Revolutions'.

'Prehistoric' **Legendary:** *Five God Emperors, Wû-Dì* 五帝:
Yellow Emperor, Huángdì Xuanyuán = Grand Augustan 泰皇?
Zhuanxù Gaoyáng 顓頊高陽
Kù Gaoxin 帝譽高辛
Yáo 堯, paradigm of filial virtue
Shùn 舜, paradigm of filial virtue
Dynastic Founders: **Three Kings, San-Wáng** 三王:
Yû the Great 大禹, founder of the Xià dynasty 'r. BC 2205-2197'
Chéng Tang 成湯, founder of the Shang dynasty r. 1766-1754?
Wû 武王 'martial' founder of the Zhou dynasty r. 1049?-1043
Awaited Messianic Ruler ? **Ninth Augustan, Jiû-Huáng**

TOP SCROLL

i. WIDE SELECTION (Bóxuân 博選第一)

The messianic ruler will grasp the sacred weapon, the royal halberd or pole-axe of power and military command wielded by Yellow Emperor, Chéng Tang (r. 1766-1754?) of Shang, and Martial King of Zhou.[74] It is also the symbol of the messianic Complete Ninth (ix-f).

To inaugurate the new era, he will recruit men superior to himself in ability and honour them as Sage teachers. Under such protocol, Mencius stood on his dignity as teacher, refusing to be treated like a servant by the king (*Mèngzî* IVb; Lílóu: 149). When recruitment of the good depended on their treatment with respect, even a king should 'face north' as subject, rather than 'face south' as otherwise befitted a ruler.

Yet China's unification would soon elevate the emperor's person to the status of both king and Sage, like the 'philosopher king' in Plato's Republic. Meritocratic theory could justify this only by a pious fiction that the monarch was Heaven's choice as the one worthy to rule and not merely hereditary scion. Like *Mòzî*, *Héguanzî* opposes hereditary principles which Confucius held dear. It here urges 'wide selection'. Thus it endorses Mò Zî's call to 'promote the worthy' (xi-b, xiii-b) which Xún Zî accepted, but conservatives Lâo Zî and Mencius opposed for encouraging strife and threatening the social order.

Individual evaluations are listed in five grades by multiples of ten. By inverse proportions a social pyramid of employment emerges: 1 king > 10 ministers > 100 knights > 1,000 servants > 10,000 slaves. In virtue, the top grades are Ace > Valiant > Hero. This numbering theme is resumed in the penultimate chapter (xviii-c). *Huaínánzî* (XX, 10b-11a), presented to the Hàn court in 139 BC, assesses by the same yardstick but in quotas of intelligence (zhì). Detailed criteria for character assessment are presented in vi-c and for accomplishments in xv-a.

Here we have here the idea, in foetus form, of competitive examination for office. This was first implemented in 165 BC by Hàn Emperor Wén under the ascendency of Way's Law (Dàofâ) philosophy in the dynasty's early years. (Creel 1970: 87) This evolved into a national institution for civil service recruitment, based instead on the Confucian classics.

---

[74] 'Axe' fu 鈇 means 'halberd/pole-axe' fûyuè 斧鉞. *MWD* Shíliù-Jing: Wû-Zheng 65, 94b; Zhengluàn 67, 104a write it qiang yuè 鏘鉞. Cf. Lewis 1998: 19, 23, 126 royal axe; 206-207 Yellow Emperor's axe; 301n.54 thunder god's axe; 175, 202-204, 316n.133 axe tallies, spells. Jade axe heads were found at Shímâochéng ca. 2000 BC.

To implement such reforms, hope is placed in the appearance of a great leader. Royal Axe is a symbol of power and decisive action. Three 'Yellow Emperor' texts give variants of a rhyme used by Fàn Lî in advice to King Goujiàn (r. 496-465) of Yuè (Zhèjiang) on timing his campaign against Wú (Jiangsu) to recover his throne:[75]

> You must at Heaven's timing decide (`cut', duàn).
> If what must be cut is uncut, you will get disorder (luàn).

The word 'cut' (duàn), meaning 'decide', rhymes with 'disorder' (luàn), as of tangled strands. The Six Satchels, ascribed to Taìgong Wàng, Grand Duke of Zhou strategist of Zhou's victory over Shang in 1046 BC, warns: "If you grasp a knife you must cut. If you hold an axe you must attack." The timing is that for the final battle. This opening chapter starts and ends with 'Royal Axe', emblematic of the Nine Augustans' transmission (ix-f), in an appeal for resolute action: "No death, no birth. No decision ('cutting'), no completion" (i-b). The remaining question is who to do it? The time is at hand.[76]

a) Meritocracy

The Royal Axe is not one generation's weapon.[77]
王鈇非一世之器者.
It is thick in virtue, lofty in heroism.
厚德隆俊也.
The Way altogether has four signs:
道凡四稽:
> First is Heaven,
> 一曰天,
> Second is Earth;
> 二曰地,
> Third is man;
> 三曰人,
> Fourth is mandate.
> 四曰命

---

[75] *Guóyû* (XXI Yuèyû-xià: 3b) Fàn Lî to Goujiàn: "If you get the time and do not complete, you will on the contrary receive its disasters." Liù-Tao 1.7; Sawyer 1993:46.

[76] *MWD* Shíliù-Jing (Guan): 63, 90a: At Heaven's timings always cut. When you must cut, but do not, you will receive its disorder. Dang Tianshí, yû-zhi jie duàn. Dangduàn bùduàn, jiang shòu -qí luàn. 當天時與之皆斷當斷不斷將受其亂; Bingróng: 71, 118b; Cheng 81, 149b: Heaven has revolving penalties. You on the contrary will receive its disasters. Tian yôu huánxíng, fàn shòu qí yang. 天有環刑反受其殃). Shuîhûdì tomb almanac (Rìshu) 197: Do not on a sì (巳, 6th of 12 cyclical days, pun on 'death' sî) day conduct prayers, or on the contrary you will receive its disasters.

[77] cf. i-b; ix-f. Jiâ Yì: *Xinshu* (II, Zhì–bùdìng): Expedient dynamics and law's controls   are the master of men's weighty axe. Only when dynamics are settled, and expedients sufficient, then you may employ humane justice and merciful generosity...

Assessment of men has five grades:
權人有五至:
    First is as an hundred individual-selves;
    一曰伯己;
    Second is as ten individual-selves;
    二曰什己;

    Third is as an individual-self equal;
    三曰若己;
    Fourth is as a servant;
    四曰廝役;
    Fifth is as a slave.
    五曰徒隸.

'Heaven' means things' principles in emotive reality (*truth*).
所謂天者物理情者也.
'Earth' means constancy in not departing from it.
所謂地者常弗去者也.
'Man' means hatred of death and joy in living.
所謂人者惡死樂生者也.
'Mandate' means nothing but the duty of rulership.
所謂命者靡不在君者也.

The ruler governs[78] by the Divine Luminaries.
君也者端=政神明者也.
Divine Luminaries in men make their basis.
神明者以人爲本者也.
Men in worthy Sages makes their basis.
人者以賢聖爲本者也.
Worthy Sages in wide selection make their basis.
賢聖者以博選爲本者也.
Wide selection from five grades makes its basis:
博選者以五至爲本者也.

b) Recruitment
So, if you face north (as a subject) to serve them,
  故北面而事之,
then those like a hundred selves will be induced.
則伯己者至.

---

[78] Here is the first use of duan 端 'upright/principle' as taboo avoidance for 'correct/govern' (zhèng 正/政), personal name of Qín Shǐ Huángdì.

If you prioritise exertion before rest,
先趨而後息,
and questioning before silence,
先問而後默,
then those like ten selves will be induced.
什己者至.
If others exert themselves before you exert yourself,
人趨己趨,
then your self-equals will be induced.
則若己者至.
If you lean on your desk and rest on your staff,
憑几據杖,
waving a flywhisk to command,
指麾而使,
Then servants will be induced.
則廝役者至.
If when pleased you grunt, and annoyed shout,
樂嗟, 苦咄,
then slaves will be induced!
則徒隸之人至矣!
Thus, Emperors with teachers associate.
故帝者與師處.
Kings with friends associate.
王者與友處.
Doomed lords with slaves associate.[79]
亡主與徒處.

So, he who does virtue (*good*) to a myriad men is called an 'Ace.'
故德萬人者謂之儁.
He who does virtue to a thousand men is called 'Valiant.'
德千人者謂之豪.
He who does virtue to a hundred men is called 'Hero.'
德百人者謂之英.[80]

---

[79] *MWD* Shíliù-Jing (Cheng): 81, 145b-46a: An emperor's ministers are called ministers, they are actually teachers. A king's ministers are called ministers, they are actually friends. A hegemon's ministers are called ministers, they are actually guests. An endangered ruler's ministers are called ministers, they are actually servants. A doomed ruler's ministers are called ministers, they are actually slaves.

[80] *Zhànguó Cè* (XXIX Yàn Cè) 11, Guo Weî counseling King Zhao (r. 311-279) on the restoration of Yàn: Hegemons with ministers abide and places doomed nation rulers with servants. *Wénzĭ* (VII Weimíng) 58; (XII Shàng Lĭ) 97 define four classes of merit equal to 10,000 men = 'hero' ying 英; 1000 men = 'ace' jùn 儁; 100 men = 'champion' jié 傑;

10 men = 'valiant' háo 豪. *Huaínánzĭ* (XX) 10b-11a's order is ying, jùn, háo, jié. Vankeerberghen 2001: 118. *Hànshu* (Rénwù Zhì) cites Má Gong: Shi Zhuàn that a person above a myriad men is called 'hero.' Cf. xv-a, 7; xviii-c, fn 363.

Virtue's notes mean their sound (*reputation*).
德音者所謂聲也,
You never hear notes issue forth
未聞音出

whose echo surpasses their sound.
而響過其聲者也.

The noble have knowledge,
貴者有知,
the rich have wealth,
富者有財,
the poor have their bodies.
貧者有身.

If good faith's tally-sticks do not match,[81]
信符不合,
employment undertaken will not succeed.
事舉不成.
If some do not die, others will not live:
不死, 不生.

If you do not take decisions, there will be no achievements.[82]
不斷, 不成.
Assess achievement before rewarding,
計功而償,
Weigh virtues before speaking.
權德而言.

The Royal Axe resides in these things.
王鈇在此. ,
Who is able to put it to work?
孰能使營?

---

[81] Tally-sticks were broken, each party to a contract retaining half, like invoice and receipt. Verification was made by re-fitting the broken halves together. They symbolised rule of objective law.
[82] *MWD* Shíliù-Jing (Zhèngluàn) 67, 106b.

ii. MANIFEST HOPE (Zhùxi 著希第二)

A messiah, the 'Expected Man,' is to fulfill Heaven's mandate and restore morality in a corrupt world. He will be a 'gentleman', upholding the Way and Virtues of humanity, ritual propriety and justice. Its criticism of contemporary morality attacks hypocrisy which masks real feelings. Graham suggested it is an attack on 'false prophet' Qín Shî Huángdì. If so, it must post-date 221 when he became First Emperor. More likely, its target is the future First Emperor, when still just Zhào Zhèng, King of Qín.

Here we see the pairing of the Way and Virtue (dàodé), as in Lâo Zî's *Dàodéjing* (alias *Lâozî*), terms pregnant with early religious import, tied to the God Grand Unity. (Jia Jinhua 2009, passim). In traditional usage, the compound 'Way-virtue' became a synonym for morality in general.

The Way may derive from 'Heaven's Way', manifest in the sky, and is a basic to all ancient Chinese schools of thought. 'Virtue' has the same sound as 'getting' (dé 得) and covers the dual senses of benefit spiritually and empowerment physically. Unlike Mò Zî who equated 'profit' (lì 利) as 'benefit' with righteousness, but more like Mencius who rejected 'profit' as its contrary, Héguan Zî declines to equate 'profit' with human emotive reality. He has altruistic aspirations and refuses to equate a corrupt world with 'fixed reality' (dìngqíng 定情).

a) The Way's Virtue

The Way has signs,
道有稽,
virtue has proofs.
德有據.

If men's ruler does not hear its essentials,
人主不聞要,
he constantly with destiny revolves
故尚[=常]與運堯[繞] and lacks means to see.
而無以見也.

If his Way with virtue lodge,[83]

道與德館,

but he lacks the means to mandate,

而無以命也,

it is because his righteousness does not match its standard

義不當格

and he lacks the means to alter it.

而無以更也.

If he were thus installed,

若是置之,

though settled, he would not be fixed.

雖安, 非定也.

b) The Conduct of the Expected Man

Regular and irregular have their places,

端倚有位,

Names and titles do not deviate from them.[84]

名號弗去.

So the Expected Man

故希人者

will not disobey real feelings.

無悖其情.

The Expected Generation

希世者

will not falsify its substance.[85]

無繆其賓.[=實?]

---

[83] *Guânzǐ* (XXXVI Xinshù-shàng) 220-221 defines 'Virtue' homophonically: **Virtue** (**dé** 德) is the Way's lodge, that which things **get** (**dé** 得) to be born. It generates wisdom to **get** employment of the Way's essence. So **Virtue** is **getting**. **Getting** means what you **get** to be so. **Dé**-zhê Dào-zhi shê. Wù **dé**-yî sheng. Sheng zhì **dé**-yî zhí Dào-zhi jing. Gù **dé**-zhê **dé**-yê. Qíweì suô**dé**-yî rán-yê. 德者道之舍 物得以生 生知得以職道之精 故德者得也其謂所得以然也. Cf. x-a, xviii-a.

[84] 'Regular' here is written duan 端 for zhèng 正, as if in taboo avoidance of the First Emperor's name. *MWD Jingfǎ*'s Dàofǎ 43, line 7b: When the regular and irregular have their positions, names and titles do not depart from them.

[85] I read 'falsify' (miù 謬) for 'entwine' (miú 繆) and 'substance' (shí 實) here for look-alike 'guest' (bin 賓) to complement 'real feelings' (qíng 情).

Civilized propriety's[86] desolation,
文禮之野,
with birds and beasts becomes the same in form.
與禽獸同則.
Words and speech's violence,
言語之暴,
with barbarism is the same in meaning.
與蠻夷同謂.

Now, the gentleman is easy to relate to,
夫君子者易親,
yet hard to corrupt.
而難狎.
He is wary of disaster yet hard to repulse.
畏禍而難卻.
He is fond of profit, yet does not contrive it by doing wrong.
嗜利而不爲非.
In timeliness he moves yet does not opportunistically act.
時動而不苟作.

Though his body is at ease in something,
體雖安之,
he does not dare abide there:
而弗敢處:
and so ritual propriety is born.
然後禮生.
Though his heart desires something,
心雖欲之,
he does not dare give rein to it:
而弗敢信:
and so righteousness is born.
然後義生.

Now, righteousness regulates desires in order to govern.
夫義節欲而治.
Propriety returns to real feelings in order to discriminate.[87]
禮反情而辨者也.

---

[86] *Xúnzǐ* (XIX Lǐlùn) 379-381 equates ritual propriety (lǐ 禮) with rational principle (lǐ 理), identical to it in sound, in the new expression 'civilised rationality' (wénlǐ 文理) whose genesis he traces back to 'Great Unity,' a variant of 'Grand Unity.'
[87] *Lǐjì* (XIX Yuèjì 'Music Record'): 614: to join real feelings (qíng) and decorate appearances are music and ritual's task.

So, the gentleman does not disregard real feelings when taking action,
故君子弗徑情而行也,
does not consider endangerment as the Way,
以中險爲道,
does not consider profit as reality.
以利爲情.

c) Lament for a Degenerate Age
Now, a disordered generation
夫亂世者,
considers crude knowledge as creative ideas.
以麤智爲造意.
Considers endangerment as the Way,
以中險為道,
considers profit as reality.
以利為情.
To those who do not share their hatreds,
若不相與同惡,
they cannot relate;
則不能相親;
For those who share their hatreds,
相 與 同 惡 ,
they have dislike.
則有相憎.

Speech of benevolent humanity,
說者言仁,
they consider lying.
則以爲誣.
Motivation by righteousness,
發於義,
they consider boasting.
則以爲誇.
A fair mind's honest report,
平心而直告之,
they do not believe.
則有弗信.

So, worthies in a disordered generation
故賢者之於亂世也
are cut off from prospects and have no means to succeed.
絕豫而無由通.
They are of a different species
異類
and so have no means to tell of their suffering! Alas!
而無以告苦乎!哉!

d) Life under Tyranny

Worthy men hide in a disordered generation.
賢人之潛亂世也.
Above, they have to follow their lord,
上有隨君,
below, there is no straight speaking.
下無直辭.
When the lord is arrogant in behavior,
君有驕行,
the people have many taboo words.[88]
民多諱言.

So, men distort their honest sincerity.
故人乖其誠.
Capable knights conceal their substantial reality (*true feelings*).
能士隱其實情.
In mind, though unhappy,
心雖不說 (=悅?),
they dare not but praise.
弗敢不譽.

In working at enterprises, though disapproving,
事業雖弗善,
they dare not but labour.
不敢不力.
In support or rejection, though in disagreement,
趨舍雖不合,
they dare not but follow.
不敢弗從.

So, observe worthy men
故觀賢人
in a disordered generation,
之於亂世也,
they take care not to take it as fixed reality.
其愼勿以爲定情也.

---

[88] *Lâozî* (LVII): When the Under-Heaven has many taboos, people become ever poorer.

iii. THE NIGHT WALKER (Yèxíng 夜行第三)

The chapter sets out from a teleological world in which everything has a purpose, in its legalist model of thirteen signs. *Lâozî* calls 'thirteen' the number of life and death.[89] Here it is the enumeration of the totality of physical phenomena. Music here may be an analogy for society with the five grades outlined above (i-a), corresponding to the five-note scale, and the goal of social mobility with promotion by merit, represented by modulation.

Then, in contrast to these palpable phenomena, verses from *Lâozî* are used to introduce an invisible, transcendent presence at work behind the scenes, divine or political. This recalls the 'Harun al-Rashid' theme where an ideal ruler goes out at night among his people in disguise to ascertain their true conditions. Night Walker fits the role of immanent deity and hidden messiah, the second coming "like a thief in the night' of Christianity or the occultation of the Twelfth Imâm in Islâmic tradition. *Guânzî* (II) associates it with rule by 'non-contivance' (wúweí). Identification of Dipper or Pole Star with the supreme deity is explicitly stated in the next chapter (iv-a). Significantly, the 'night walker's Way' is resumed in *Héguanzî*'s final chapter (xix-a), with 'shady warp's law', in a sense of tactical emergency.

a) Thirteen Signs

Heaven is for design
天文也,
Earth for principle (*rationality*).
地理也.
Moon is for forms (*punishments*),
月刑也,
Sun for virtues (*rewards*).[90]
日德也.
Four seasons are for inspections,
四時檢也,
Degree and number are for regulation.
度數節也.

---

[89] *Lâozî* (L): 'Thirteen' (shîyôusan 十有三) literally 'ten having three' is archaic 'thirteen'. *Hánfeizî* (XX Jiê Lâo): nine orifices plus four limbs. As the imperial numerology of nine gained dominance, Wáng Bì's interpretation in later Hàn as 'three out of ten' was accepted. Yet thirteen never lost its mystique in folk culture and music, mostly as five agents plus eight trigrams (sixth, seventh and eighth in the fibonacci series), not seven plus six as here. *Shangjun Shu* IV lists a total of 'thirteen factors' (shísan shù 十三數) essential for the state.

[90] Moon and Sun represent penal and civil law, respectively. Cf. HGZ ix-a, x-a.

Shade and sunshine (*yin and yáng*) are for energies (*qì*),
陰陽氣也,
Five agents (*metal, wood, water, fire, soil*) are for enterprises.
五行業也.
Five Governances are for the Way. (*cf. iv, viii c, d*)
五政道也.
Five keynotes for tuning, (*adjustments*)
五音調也,
Five modes are for precedents. (*customs*)
五聲故也.
Five flavours (*foods, salaries*) are for employments,
五味事也,
Five penal fines are for contracts.[91]
五罰約也.

These all have proofs by which they are so.
此皆有驗有所以然者.

b) Song of an Invisible Presence

Pursue him and you will not see his back,
隨而不見其後,
Meet him and you will not see his head.
迎而不見其首.
'He achieves success and finishes the job.'[92]
成功遂事.
No one knows his appearance.
莫知其狀.

Pictures cannot convey him,
圖弗能載,
Names cannot raise him.
名弗能舉.
If forced, I will try to describe him, saying:
強爲之說曰:

Vacuity! Nothingness!
芴乎芒乎!
In its midst is an image!
中有象乎.

---

[91] I add 'five' and delete 'rewards' to match the preceding format. According to the first legal text 'Lyǔ's Penalties', Lyǔxíng (in Documents Classic, *Shàngshu*), the 'five fines' were for lesser offences than the 'five penalties' (wǔ-xíng).

[92] *Lâozî* (XVII): He achieves success and finishes the job. Cf. xi-a, xi-b, xvi.

Nothingness! Vacuity!
芒乎芴乎!
In its midst is a being!
中有物乎!

Mystery! Darkness!
窅乎冥乎!
In its midst is an essence!
中有精乎!
Utmost faithfulness, ultimate reality,[93]
致信究情,
reverts back to facelessness.
復反無貌.
If ghosts were visible,
鬼見,
they would be unable to do men's enterprises.
不能爲人業.
So, the Sage Man values Night Walking.[94]
故聖人貴夜行.

---

[93] *Lâozî* XIV (absent from Guodiàn *Lâozî*): No appearance's appearance (zhuàng), Nothing's image (xiàng 象). This means a misty mirage (máng). Follow it and you don't see its back (hòu), Meet it and you don't see its head (shôu). Received texts reverse the lines: placing 'head' before 'back' etc. (XV): If forced to contrive its appearance... (XXI also absent from Guodiàn): The Way, as a thing (wù 物), Is just mirage, just misty (wù 霧). Misty oh! Mirage (máng 茫) oh! In its midst is an image (xiàng 象). Mirage oh! Misty (wù) oh! In its midst is a thing (wù). Mysterious oh! Dark (míng 冥) oh! In its midst is essence (jing 精). Its essence is utmost truth (zhen 眞) in its midst is goodfaith (xìn 信). *Lyûshì Chunqiu* (Jì V-2 'Great music' Dà Yuè) 4a: No appearance's appearance approximates to knowing it! The Way is utmost essence. It may not be formed, may not be named. If forced to contrive it, I call it 'Grand Unity.'

[94] *Guânzî* (II Xíngshì) 4: To summon the distant, employ non-contrivance in it. To befriend the near, speech has no business in it. Just night walking alone has it; (LXIV Xíngshì Jiê) 327: Night walking is mental operation. If you can mentally operate virtue then in the Under-Heaven none can with you contend; (XVII Bingfâ) 95 on 'night operations', signalled by a lunar standard, the second of nine battle standards. *Huaínánzî* (VI Lânmíng) 3a. *Wénzî* (II Jingchéng) 9. *Chunqiu Fánlù* (III-5 Jinghuá) 23: uses this couplet without 'night walking'.

iv. HEAVEN'S MODEL (Tianzé天則第四)

Heaven here serves as a model comparable to the Ideals of Plato. It centres on the Dipper (Plough)'s seven stars in the Great Bear (Ursa Major) constellation, plus, it seems, the 'Bear Guardian' Arcturus and Capella, to make up nine stars to mirror the Nine Augustans. (Plates 1-3, Appendix II) The traditional Horn star is a perfect match for Arcturus, whereas the Chinese name for Capella in Auriga the 'Charioteer' is now 'Pentagon Chariot 2' (Wû-Che 2), a coincidence which may reflect Greek cultural influence on Qín through importation of war horses from central Asia. 'Sage' and 'king' are one and the same. The 'constitutional' monarch has become absolutist. He will become 'Ninth Augustan' to establish world unity through his person.

The Ninth Augustan's new political program has five objectives, of which economy is first: a) the Sage: social welfare; b) reformation: spontaneous co-operation; c) governance: self-motivation; d) education: critique of sense perception; e) operations: practical realism. The last three, governance, education and operations/employment, elaborate on aims of the seven outlined in Guânzî's Establishing Government, though in different order.[95] Three headings (b, d, e) match those in chapter viii's 'Five Governances', leaving a) and c) to compare with its bureaucrative and adaptative categories. (viii-c, d; MWD Shíliù-Jing (Wû-Zheng) 65, 91b cf. iii-c; iv-a>e passim)

People are paramount. Law derives from the particular, the 'this' and the 'here' (cî 此. See also iv, viii). Operations here do not rely just on penal law (xíng) to 'herd' (mù) the people, but on adaptation and 'fencing' (yòu 宥). (iv-e) Rulers cannot be divorced from the subjective 'human realities' of their subordinates. Their suppression will produce deception but trusting to them will lead to failure. Recruitment and promotion will be from the eight compass points, offices will not be transmitted father to son. Re-use of the line: 'his application does not slacken' (iv-a) in Rhapsody of the Hero (xii-d) implies close linkage.

'Reliance on dynamics' (rènshì 任勢,iv-c) was the theory propounded by Shèn Dào (ca. 350-270) whose work survives only in fragments. There are four evidentiary links between Héguan Zî and Shèn Dào to whom Zhuangzî (XXXIII) ascribes the relativist concept of 'equalising the myriad things' (qí wàn- wù).

First, association with the state of Zhào. Second, reverence for Cangjié whom Héguan Zî in person credits with the invention of writing, whence calendar and law, and Shèn Dào places before primal culture hero Fúxi. Excavated Shang dynasty oracle bones (BC 1200) confirm the importance of calendric signs (jiâzî 甲子) in early writing. Third, theories of dynamic

---

[95] Guânzî (IV Lìzhèng, Qi-guan) 12-13. The seven are: education, instruction, customs, goodfaith, Way, employment, governance.

adaptation and law. Fourth, repeated recourse to the distinctive trope in argument: 'From this we observe...'[96] (Yóu-shì guan-zhi...由是觀之)

Héguanzî's three uses of this expression precede discussions of dynamics, relative (1) to the unity of individuals as separate entities and en masse (ix-g); (2) to shifts of appointed mandates over time (xiii-b); and (3) to effects of size and scope in the dimension of space (xvii-b), as in Zhuangzî XVII's Autumn Waters.

a) Sage's Program of Social Welfare

The Sage King listens to the subtle
聖王者有聽微
so as to resolve doubts in the Way.
決疑之道.
He has the ability to dismiss slanders to assess facts.
能屏讒權實.
He opposes superfluous language,
逆淫辭,
cuts short rumours and discards the useless.
絕流語, 去無用.
He blocks factionalism.
杜絕朋黨之門.

Thus envious and malicious men
嫉妒之人
do not get publicity.
不得著明.
None but gentlemen, skilled and numerate knights
非君子術數之士.
Will get advancement.
莫得當前.
So evil cannot subvert him,
故邪弗能奸,
Disasters cannot strike him.
禍不能中.

He in Heaven and Earth's infinity
彼天地之以無極者,
guards degree and measurement,
以守度量,
so that there is no excess.
而不可濫.

---

[96] Thompson 1979: 128: **8, 13, 49;** 233, 236, 260. *Shîjî* LXXIV Shèn Dào. *Hánfeizî*: XL Nán Shì. Wells 2001: tr. 185ff. cf. Mòzî (III) 24/ *Zhuangzî* (XVII) 580: Zì-/Yóu-cî guan- zhi 自/由此觀之.

As the sun does not transgress in its dawnings,
日不踰辰，
And the moon lodges in its stations:
月宿其列：
According to names, he manages employment.
當名服事．
As the stars hold their positions without deserting them,
星守弗去，
Crescent and full moons waxing and waning,
弦望晦朔，
He finishes and starts in orderly succession.
終始相巡．
Over passing years and accumulated harvests,
踰年累歲，
His application does not slacken.[97]
用不縵縵．

This is what his Heaven holds for handle as it looks down:
此天之所柄以臨：
The Dipper constellation's
斗者也
central three complete positions,
中參成位，
its four energies contrive governance.
四氣爲政．
In front its light extends, behind is the Ultimate (*Pole*).
前張後極，
At left is the Horn (*Arcturus*), at right the Halberd (*Capella*):
左角右鉞：
Its ninefold design conforms to principle.[98] (Plates 1-3)
九文循理．
It monitors official multitudes (*of stars*),[99]
以省官眾，

Small and great are all included.[100]
小大畢舉．

---

[97] The line yòng bù-mànmàn 用不縵縵 recurs in xii-d. Rhapsody of the Hero; and ix-g, with variation.

[98] The three end-stars make the 'Beckoner' (Zhaoyáo). Cf. xvii-d. The two extra stars, at left and right, fit the traditional nomenclature of 'auxiliaries' (fǔ 輔, bì 弼). Super bright stars Arcturus (Dà Jué 大角) and Capella (traditionally Wǔ-che Èr 五車二) align with the Dipper almost equidistantly from its centre. (see Appendix II)

[99] I read 'official' (guan 官) for the similar ideograph 'palace' (gong 宮).

[100] Defoort 1997: 190-91, 275n.60-63 citing Williams' interpretation (1987: 231n.103) concludes "the positions given here are less than perfect... Pheasant Cap Master was more a philosopher than an astronomer."

In future will be neither grudges nor hostile disasters;
先無怨讎之患,
In the past, neither ruined reputations nor disgraced conduct to blame.
後無毀名敗行之咎.
So, his awesome power will above extend and below interact.
故其威上際下交,
his bounty to the four directions will spread inseparably.
其澤四被而不鬲.

Heaven does not deviate,
天之不違,
because it does not depart from Unity.
以不離一,
If Heaven abandoned Unity,
天若離一,
it would revert to being a thing.[101]
反還爲物.
He does not initiate nor create.
不創不作,
With Heaven and Earth he shares virtue.
與天地合德.

Tallies and seals are mutually faithful,
節璽相信,
just as moon responds to sun.
如月應日.
This is how the Sage Man suits his generation.
此聖人之所以宜世也.

Knowledge sufficient only to corrupt government,
知足以滑正,
policies sufficient only to temporize disaster:
略足以恬禍:
this is why endangered nations may not be secured,
此危國之不可安,
why doomed nations may not be preserved.
亡國之不可存也.

---

[101] *MWD* ('Nine Rulers' Jiǔ-Zhǔ) 3-52: If a ruler is unlawful, he will revert to being a thing.

So, Heaven's Way first values shelter,
故天道先貴覆者,
Earth's Way first values support.
地道先貴載者.
Men's Way first values employment,
人道先貴事者,
mutual protection first values food.
相[酒]保先貴食者.
These depend on things.
待物也.

The leader of energies is the seasons;
領氣時也;
to generate (*in spring*) and kill (*in autumn*) are its laws.
生殺法也.
Compliance with degree in decisions
循度以斷
is Heaven's rhythm.
天之節也.

It lays out the Earth and protects it,
列地而守之,
divides the people and deputises them.
分民而部之.
The cold will get clothing,
寒者得衣,
the starving will get food.
饑者得食.
The wronged will get reason (*justice*),
冤者得理,
the laboured will get rest.
勞者得息.
This is what the Sage aims for.
聖人之所期也.

To tailor clothing,
夫裁衣,
you must know how to select the tailor.
而知擇其工.
To tailor the kingdom, you must know how to seek men.
裁國, 而知索其人.
This is certainly in this generation's public interest!
此固世之所公哉!

It is just in conformity that we see Heaven;[102]
同而後可以見天；
just in difference that we see the human;
異而後可以見人；
Just in transformation that we see seasons;
變而後可以見時；
just in reformation that we see the Way.
化而後可以見道。

It is just when faced with profit, that we see goodfaith;
臨利而後可以見信；
just when faced with wealth, that we see the humane;
臨財而後可以見仁；
just when faced with hardships, that we see courage;
臨難而後，可以見勇；
just when faced with employment, that we see skilled and numerate knights.
臨事而後，可以見術數之士。

In the Ninth Augustan's system,
九皇之制，
the ruler is not in vain King.
主不虛王。
Ministers are not in vain noble.
臣不虛貴階級。

Honourable and base names and titles
尊卑名號
Are for the ruler to employ people.
自君吏民。
Apart from this there is no kingdom.
次者無國。

Successive generational favours, successive emoluments
歷寵歷錄
should match the purpose of appointment.
副所以付授。
If they are with Heaven and men uncorrelated,
與天人(不?)參相結連，
a system of cross-checks not being prepared is the cause.
鉤攷之具不備故也。

---

[102] See *Mòzǐ* (xii Shàngtóng-shàng) 46: If the Under-Heaven's hundred clans all above conform to Heaven's Son, but do not all conform (tóng 同) to Heaven, then disasters will not depart. (iv Fǎyì) 12: Heaven's motion is broad and unselfish.

When subordinates are suppressed,
下之所逜,
superiors may be deceived.[103]
上之可蔽.
This is because they are divorced from human realities (*feelings*)
斯其離人情
and lose Heaven's rhythm.
而失天節者也.

When relaxed to be lazy,
緩則怠,
Under pressure to be in difficulty,
急則困,
to see an opening and use the irregular to exploit it[104]
見閒則以奇相御
are humanrealities.
人之情也.

To promote (*people*) from the eight directions, (*everywhere*)
舉以八極,
to be faithful to them but not trust to them,
信焉而弗信,
is Heaven's model.[105]
天之則也.

When there are discrepancies and falsehoods,
差繆之閒,
words do not match,
言不可合,
temperament is off-key.
平不中律.

---

[103] Cf. vii-c, ix-e: "wûshàng bìshàng" 逜下蔽上. *MWD* (Jiû-Zhû 'Nine Rulers') 29, 31; n5.

[104] I translate 'odd' (qí 奇) as 'irregular.' *Sunzî Bingfâ* (V Shì, 'Dynamics') 'unorthodox tactics.' *MWD* Jingfâ (Dàofâ) 43-7b: 'by asymmetries mutually control' yî qí xiang yù 以奇相御.

105 Promotion to office should be by universal selection but offices are not to be permanently held. See: Education's aim, below.

The moon full, at dawn
月望而晨
Will be annihilated in the sky.
月[=將?]毀於天.
The pearl fills the oyster
珠蛤贏[=贏/盈?]蚌
vainly in the deep sea.[106]
虛于深渚. [=海?]
(i.e. *The great perish while the worthy languish in obscurity.*)

b) Reformation's Aim

Superiors and inferiors are equal yet separate.
上下同離也.
Before being ordered, they know how to act.
未令而知其爲.
Before being despatched, they know where to go.
未使而知其往.
Though superiors do not increase their tasks,
上不加務,
people spontaneously do their utmost:
而民自盡:
this is what reformation aims at.
此化之期也.

When those despatched do not go,
使而不往,
when what is forbidden is not stopped,
禁而不止,
when superiors and inferiors are rent apart by falsehood:
上下乖謬者:
the Way is not mutually got.
其道不相得也.

When superiors preside but subordinates meddle,
上統下撫者,
distant multitudes hide from them.
遠眾之慝也.
If shade and sunshine (positive and negative) do not connect,
陰陽不接者,
principles have no means to reach each other.
其理無從相及也.

---

[106] I read 'sea' haì 海 for 'islet' zhǔ 渚. In Chinese tradition, oysters generate pearls from moonlight. *Lyǔshì Chunqiu* (Qiujî IX) Jingtong 9a: When the moon is full, the oyster is impregnated… Yuè wàng ér bangge shí… 月望而蚌蛤實…

If calculations do not match,
算不相當者,
men will not respond to superiors.
人不應上也.
If tally-sticks are lost here,
符節亡此,
how can they ever be joined?
曷曾可合也.

c) Governance's Aim

To contrive but not harm,
爲而無害,
to win and be undefeated;
成而不敗;
For one one man to sing and a myriad men reply in chorus
一人唱而萬人和
as limbs follow the mind:
如體之從心:
This is government's aim.[107]
此政之期也.

Altogether, it is like mother's cotton loom in concerted motion.
蓋毋[=如?]錦杠悉動者.
Its essential is in unity.
其要在一也.

I have never seen anyone who, without getting a prognosis,[108]
未見不得其診[?]
could eradicate a disease.
而能除其疾也.

If the civil and military, alternately applied,
文武交用,
do not get operations' substance,
而不得事實者,

---

[107] Guânzî (IV Lìzhèng, Qi-guan) 13: As the hundred organs follow the heart-mind. Rú bai-tî zhi cóng xin. 如百體之從心.
[108] I take the obscure graph (言+爾) = (言+尔) as 'prognosis' (zhên 診).

It means law's edicts are promulgated
法令放
without the means to execute them.
而無以梟[=效?]之謂也.
By discarding the 'this' to rely on the 'that',[109]
舍此而按之彼者,
how could they ever be gotten?
曷曾可得也?

To understand words is easy,[110]
冥言易,
to comply with words is hard.
而如言難.
Thus, a father cannot obtain it in his son,
故父不能得之於子,
and the ruler cannot obtain it in a minister.
而君弗能得之於臣.

I have seen how Heaven has more goodfaith than things.
已見天之所以信於物矣.
I have not seen how humans have more goodfaith than things.
未見人之所信於物也.

To sacrifice things and rely on dynamics is Heavenly.
捐物任勢者, 天也.
It sacrifices things and rely on dynamics, (*cf. ix-d*)
捐物任勢,
so, none may command except by Heaven.
故莫能宰而不天.
Now, things if crooked may be altered,
夫物故曲可改,
men may be employed.
人可使.

---

109 The 'that/this' (there/here, bî/cî 彼此) dichotomy implies subjective versus objective factors. *Lâozî* (XII, XXXVIII, LXXII): He takes this and rejects that. Qu bî, qû cî 去彼取此. *Hánfeizî* (XX Jiê Lâo) 99: What is meant by 'discarding that and taking this' is to discard appearance directly and take

the path of rational principle. It is to love reality's substance. Suôwei qùbî qûcîzhê, qùmào jìng jué, ér qû yuánlî, hào qíngshí-yê. 所謂去彼取此者去貌徑絕而取原理好情實也. *Guânzî* (XXXVI *Xinshu*-shàng) 220: The means of knowing that is the means of knowing this.

110 I read 'understand' (míng 明) for 'dark' (míng 冥) here.

Law manifests[111] things and is not self-permissive.
法章物而不自許者.
It is Heaven's Way to promote education.
天之道也以爲奉教.
Ostensible loyalty in subjects is insufficient to rely on.
陳忠之臣, 未足恃也.
So, law is the crooked's controller.
故法者曲制.

Offices are prepared for the ruler's use.
官備主用也.
Elevation of good cannot be done in secrecy,
舉善不以宵宵,
correction of errors cannot be done in the dark.
拾過不以冥冥.
To decide 'here':[112] is what law values.
決此:法之所貴也.
If millstones are not given something to grind,
若礱磨不用賜物,
No matter how exerted they will be ineffective!
雖詘, 有不效者矣.
If between superiors and subjects there is a gap,
上下有閒,
Then erected barriers and informational cover-ups together arise.
於是設防知蔽並起.
So, when government is usurped by a private house
故政在私家
and they cannot restore it,
而弗能取,
When important men lose authority
重人掉權
and they cannot prevent it,
而弗能止,
When rewards are presented to those with no achievements
賞加無功
and cannot be taken back.
而弗能奪.

---

[111] Defoort 1997: 200, end-note 9: Joseph Needham, editor of epoch-making encyclopaedic series Science and Civilization in China, proposed 'mould' for 'manifest' (zhang 章) here.

[112] A 'comma' punctuation jù 句 in the original serves as a colon after the 'here' (cǐ 此) to highlight it. 'Here' is the same word translated as 'this' elsewhere. It has the sense of here and now, to judge each case by its merits on the spot, as per the axiom "justice delayed is justice denied," extrapolated from *Magna Carta* (1215), clause 40.

When law is abandoned and disrespected
法廢不奉
and cannot be established,
而弗能立,
punishments are executed on the wrong men
罰行於非其人
and cannot be rescinded.
而弗能絕者.
No communication with the people is the reason.
不與其民之故也.

d) Education's Aim

Now, to cause the hundred clans to disregard self
夫使百姓釋己
and with their superior to be of the same mind,
而以上爲心者,
is what education aims at.
教之所期也.

If eight directional undertakings
八極之舉
cannot in time interchange,[113]
不能時贊 [=替?],
they may become obstructions.
故可壅塞也.
Formerly, those who had the Way
昔者有道
took up government not by ears and eyes.[114]
之取政非於耳目也.

---

[113] I read 'interchange' (tì 替) for 'commend' (zàn 贊). Sòng dynasty editor Lù Diàn 陸佃 (ca. 1100) takes 'eight directions' in a metaphysical sense and cites King Tang's question about the size of the universe, as in Lièzî (V Tangwèn).

[114] Cf. Isaiah 11.3-4: He shall not judge by what he sees; nor decide by what he hears. He shall judge the poor with justice... i.e. he judges not by appearance nor hearsay.

Now, the ear is master of listening,
夫耳之主聽,
the eye is master of illumination.
目之主明.

If one leaf covers the eyes,
一葉蔽目,
they will not see Grand Mountain.[115]
不見太山.
If two beans obstruct the ears,
兩豆塞耳,
they do not hear thunder peals.
不聞雷霆.

For the Way's opening to be blocked
道開而否
is unheard of.
未之聞也.

To see something dropped and not pick it up
見遺不掇
is opposed to human reality.[116]
非人情也
Yet if you trust in emotive reality to cultivate life,
信情脩生,
even though not by Heaven punished,
非其天誅,
you will encounter human slaughter[117]
逆夫人僇
and not discharge your responsibilities.
不勝任也.

---

[115] This example, with the following, serve to illustrate the limits of sense perception, subject to physical obstrucions, contrasted with the absolute values of the Way's truth. Grand Mountain, the holy Tàishan in Shandong near Confucius' home, is proverbial for great
size and importance. Cf. xviii-b.

[116] Under the law of Zhèng of reformer Zǐ Chân (d. 522), people: on the roads did not (dare to) pick up dropped objects. Dào bù-shí yí 道不拾遺. *Hánfeizǐ* (Wài zuóshàng 5- shuo).

[117] Cf. *MWD Jingfà* (Lùnyuè) 57, 68a: If there is no Heavenly punishment, there will necessarily be human slaughter.

e) Employments' Aim

To contrive completion and seek to get it
爲成求得者
is what employment aims at.
事之所期也.
To contrive for the people
爲之以民
is the Way's essential.
道之要也.

When people know the limits,
唯民知極,
do not replace them.
弗之代也.
This how the Sage King in bestowing enterprises
此聖王授業
keeps control.
所以守制也.

If his teaching is bitter,
彼教苦,
people's behavior will be insincere.
故民行薄.
If lost at the root,
失之本,
it will be disputed at the periphery.
故爭於末.

Men have divisions in their dwellings,
人有分於處,
dwellings have divisions by Earth.
處有分於地.

Earth has divisions by Heaven,
地有分於天,
Heaven has divisions by times.
天有分於時.
Time has divisions by numbers,
時有分於數,
numbers have divisions by degrees,
數有分於度,
degrees have divisions by units.
度有分於一.
Heaven sits high, yet its ear is low.
天居高而耳卑者.
This is its meaning.
此之謂也.

So, the Sage King
故聖王.
Heavens it, Earths it, Mans it.[118]
天時[=之]人之地之.
Without herding he can adapt
雅[=雖]無牧能因
and so his achievements are many.[119]
無[=其]功多.

To elevate rulers and humble ministers,
尊君卑臣,
he does not go by kinship.
非計親也.
To appoint the worthy and employ the able,
任賢使能,
he does not favour his hometown.
非與處也.[120]
Water and fire do not mutually encroach.
水火不相入.
This is Heaven's control.
天之制也.

What luminaries cannot illumine,
明不能照者,
the Way cannot get.
道弗能得也.
What compasses cannot encompass,
規不能包者,
force cannot lift.
力弗能挈也.
When intelligence and cunning appear,
自知慧出,
they cause jade to be reformed into rings and crescents,
使玉化爲環玦者,
governance conversely becomes deceitful.[121]
是政反爲滑也.

---

[118] x-a, fn 246; xiv-a, fn 313: Heaven them, Earth them, Man them; xvii-f, fn 341. *MWD Jingfâ* Liù-fen 49, 28b. Shíliù-Jing (Bingróng) 71, 116b. *Mèngzî* (II) 1. *Guóyû* (XXI) 1-2.

[119] Cf. *Guânzî* (I Mùmín) on 'Herding the People'.

[120] *Guânzî* (I-5 Liù-qin, Wû-fâ) warns against favouritism by kinship or hometown.

[121] This metaphor of jade carving seems to allude to the Daoist ideal of the uncarved block (pú 樸), symbol of natural integrity cf. HGZ x-b. *Lâozî* (XVIII): When knowledge and intelligence appear you have great hypocrisy, Zhìhuì chu yôu dàwei 智慧出有大偽; (XXVIII): Return to the uncarved block. The uncarved block dispersed is turned into utensils. Cf. HGZ xiii-a on abuse of intelligence to cheat.

If fields are not adapted to Earth,
田不因地,
they cannot succeed in producing grain.
不能成穀.
If you contrive to reform but do not adapt to the people,
爲化不因民,
you cannot succeed in inducing morality.
不能成俗.

Severity and haste are excesses,
嚴疾過也,
joy and anger are enemies.
喜怒適[=敵?]也.
These four wound the self.
四者已仞.
They are not a teacher's techniques.
非師術也.

When forms (penalties) accumulate yet disorder increases,
形[=刑?]嗇而亂益者,
dynamics are not mutually regulatory.[122]
勢不相牧也.
Virtue that is with the person preserved or doomed
德與身存亡者
may not be taken as law.
未可以取法也.
Formerly those who 'fenced in' a generation
昔宥世者,
never separated Heaven and men
未有離天人
and so were able excellently to share the kingdom.[123]
而能善與國者也.

---

[122] I translate 'penalties warehouse' (xíngsè 刑嗇) as 'penalties accumulate' and 'mutually herd' (xiangmù 相牧) as 'mutually regulatory'. 'Form's dynamic' (xíngshì 形/刑勢) is also used for the power of fortified positions or terrain. Cf. *Guǎnzǐ* (VI Qi-Fa) 28; (XIII Ba-Guan) 73; *Hánfeizǐ* (XL Wǔ-Dú) 57. *Xúnzǐ* (XVI Qiángguó) 312; XVIII Zhènglùn) 354 on the power of material conditions.

[123] 'Fenced-in' (yòu 宥), to rule by dividing. See chapter introduction, above. Some versions omit 'Heaven' before 'men'. 'Fencing in', 'enclosing in pens' (yòu 宥 / 囿). *Zhuangzǐ* (XI Zàiyòu) 364: 'fencing in the Under-Heaven'; (XXXIII Tianxià) 1082. Graham (1989: 95-106)'s 'discard prejudice' (biéyòu 別宥) of Sòng Xíng, or 'separately fence.' *Lyǔshì Chūnqiu* (XVI.7 Quyòu 去宥) 15b-16b: 'reject prejudice'; (XIII.3 Quyóu 去尤) 5b-7a.

The First Kings of illustrious name
先王之盛名,
never negated what knights had established.[124]
未有非士之所立者也.

When errors are generated by superiors,
過生於上,
'criminals' die among subordinates.[125]
罪死於下.
Polluted generations take this as the norm.
濁世之所以爲俗也.
The One Man oh! The One Man oh!
一人乎!一人乎!
He is the Mandate's zenith.
命之所極也.

---

[124] I read 'kings' (wáng 王) for 'born' (sheng 生).

[125] This couplet on unjust incrimination of subordinates recurs in vii-b and viii-b.

v. CIRCULAR FLOW (Huánliú 環流第五)

This chapter opens with two ninefold geneses from unity via 'energy' (qì). Energy is the unifying plainstuff of phenomena, preceding 'ideas' (yì).[126] Marxist Hóu Waìlú found here primitive material dialectics and interpenetration of opposites.[127] This is evidenced by rhyming couplets as: "Flavours mutually oppose, yet as foods are equal" and "Energies both mutually benefit and mutually harm. Species both complement and mutually defeat." Poison can be made into medicine, limping may develop into a shaman's hopping dance. *Héguanzî* explains differing mandates and timings but adds a touch of inscrutability. The mandate like a father will choose his own. The worthy will not necessarily win or the unworthy lose. This sounds like an answer to the theological question of why the righteous suffer.

The Way of Virtue's Law is a cosmic force, the Great Dynamic manifest in the cosmic rotation of the Dipper's signalling seasons. Its role is co-ordinator in a world of different peoples and species. The reference to the shaman's lame hopping step (v-d) is interesting. This ritual is linked to the traditional Daoist practice 'Pacing the Dipper' (bùgang) symbolizing walking on its nine stars representing the Nine Augustans. (Figure 2). It is also known as Steps of Yû (Yûbù) after the lamed emperor who drained flood waters to found the Neolithic Xià dynasty. The priest is believed to embody both Yû and Grand Unity. (Appendix II)

a) Unified Energies
Having unity, there is energy.
有一, 而有氣.
Having energy, there are ideas.
有氣, 而有意.
Having ideas, there are schemes.
有意, 而有圖.

Having schemes, there are names.
有圖, 而有名.
Having names, there are forms.
有名, 而有形.

---

[126] *Zhuangzí* (XIII Tiandào) 471 on nine transformations (jiû-biàn): understanding Heaven, Way's virtue, humanity and right, divisions, form-names, adaptative appointments, inspections, right and wrong, reward and punishment. Makeham 1991: 362n. 90; Defoort 1997: 181-83.

[127] Needham 1956 (10. The 'Tao Chia' and Taoism) 75: "This is what Hou Wai-Lu calls the doctrine of cyclically recurring differences [xunhuan yibian lun 循環異變論]."

Having forms, there is employment.
有形, 而有事,
having employment, there are contracts.
有事, 而有約.
When contracts are decided, times are generated,
約決, 而時生,
when times are established, things are generated.
時立, 而物生.

So, energies mutually multiply to contrive times,
故, 氣相加而爲時,
contracts mutually multiply to contrive aims.
約相加而爲期.
Aims mutually multiply to contrive successes.
期相加而爲功.

Successes mutually multiply to contrive gains or losses.
功相加而爲得失.
Gains and losses multiply to contrive good or bad luck.
得失相加而爲吉凶.
Myriad things mutually multiply to contrive victory or defeat.
萬物相加而爲勝敗.

b) The Law of the Way
There is nothing that is not issued from energy,
莫不發於氣.
pervaded by the Way,
通於道, governed
by times. 正於時,
separated by names,
離於名,
completed by Law.
成於法者也.

Law being 'here' is termed near,
法之在此者謂之近,
Going out to reform 'there' is termed distant.
其出化彼謂之遠.
Near yet far-reaching is therefore termed divine.
近而至故謂之神.

Distant yet reverting is therefore termed luminary.[128]
遠而反故謂之明.
When luminaries are 'here', their light shines 'there'.
明者在此其光照彼,
If its operations are formed 'here',
其事形此,
its achievements will be completed 'there'.
其功成彼.
From 'here' to reform 'there' is Law.
從此化彼者法也.
The generator of Law is the self (ego),
生法者我也,
the completer of Law is 'the other' (there).
成法者彼也.
The generator of Law is daily present and untiring.
生法者, 日在而不厭者也.
Generation and completion in the self mean the Sage Man.
生成在己, 謂之聖人.
Only the Sage Man plumbs the Way's emotive reality.
惟聖人究道之情.
Only the Way's Law is impartial in governance and illumination.
唯道之法公政以明.[129]

When the Dipper handle points east,
斗柄東指,
the Under-Heaven is all springtime.
天下皆春.
When the Dipper handle points south,
斗柄南指,
the Under-Heaven is all summer.
天下皆夏.
When the Dipper handle points west,
斗柄西指,
the Under-Heaven is all autumn.
天下皆秋.
When the Dipper handle points north,
斗柄北指,
the Under-Heaven is all winter.[130]
天下皆冬.

---

[128] *Lâozî* (XXV): I do not know its name, I dub it the 'Way.' If forced to name it, I call it great, departing, distant, reverting.

[129] *MWD* Jing fâ (Dàofâ): 43: Way produces Law.

[130] Dàdai Lîjì (XLVII Xià Xiâozhèng) 61, 94 on the first month at dusk "the Dipper handle hangs down" and on the seventh month before dawn. *Huaínánzî* (IV Zéshì) gives the Dipper direction for each month.

As the Dipper revolves above,
斗柄運於上,
operations are established below.
事立於下.
The Dipper points one direction and
斗柄指一方,
the four sides are completed.[131]
四塞俱成.
This is the Way's application of Law.
此道之用法也.

So, sun and moon are insufficient to speak of illumination.
故日月不足以言明,
The four seasons are insufficient to speak of achievement.
四時不足以言功.

Unity makes them into Law
一爲之法
to complete its enterprise:
以成其業.
So none but will make it their Way.
故莫不道.

c) The Mandate's Law

When unified Law is established,
一之法立,
myriad beings will all come in allegiance.
而萬物皆來屬.

Law values being as good as its word.
法貴如言.
Speech is the myriad beings' lineage.
言者萬物之宗也.
Truth is that to which Law is kin,
是者法之所與親也,

---

[131] Lúnyû (VII Sù'ér): Confucius said: "If I raise one corner and you do not respond with three, I will not resume."

Untruth is that to which Law is alien.
非者法之所與離也.
Truth is with Law akin, so strong.
是與法親, 故強.
Untruth is to Law alien, so doomed.
非與法離, 故亡.
If Law is not as good as its word,
法不如言,
it will disorder its lineage.
故亂其宗.

So, what generates Law is mandate.
故生法者命也.
What is generated from Law is also mandate.
生於法者亦命也.
The mandate is self-such. (*natural*)
命者自然者也.
What mandate establishes,
命之所立,
the worthy will not necessarily get,
賢不必得,
the unworthy will not necessarily lose.
不肖不必失.
Mandate lifts up its own like a father.
命者挈己之文[=父?]者也.

Thus, there is one day's mandate,
故有一日之命,
there is one year's mandate.
有一年之命.
There is one season's mandate,
有一時之命,
there is life-long mandate and
終身之命
that never victorious.
無時成者也.
So, mandate has nowhere it is not present,
故命無所不在,
has nowhere it is not deployed,
無所不施,
has nowhere it does not reach.
無所不及.
In time someone afterwards will get the mandate.
時或後而得之命也.
Since there is time, there will be mandates.
既有時有命.

Extend your voice (*reputation*)
引其聲
To accord with your name.
合之名.
Get the right time for victory,
其得時者成,
your mandate will be called attuned.
命日[=曰?]調.
Extend your voice (*reputation*)
引其聲
To accord with your name.
合之名.
Miss the right time,
其失時者,
Essence and spirit both doomed,
精神俱亡,
Your mandate will be called awry.
命日[=曰?]乖.
Timely mandate only a Sage Man can decide.
時命者唯聖人而後能決之.
Now the First Kings' Way was fully prepared,
夫先王之道備然,
Yet generations have troubled rulers.
而世有困君.
They have lost its meaning.
其失之謂者也.

d) The Dynamic of Unity
So, what is meant by the Way is without self.[132]
故所謂道者無已者也.
What is meant by virtue is ability to get men.
所謂德者能得人者也.
From the Way of virtue's Law,
道德之法,
myriad beings take their enterprises.
萬物取業.

---

132 'Without self' (wújî 無己) could be read as 'unstoppable' (wúyî 無已) or 'necessity' (bùdéyî 不得已), like Latin 'un-ceasing' (ne+cessare) as Paul Thompson taught. Wells 2001: 67 in Mohist logic: Necessity is the unstoppable, Bì: bùyî-yê 必:不已也. Graham 1978: 38 B4. *MWD* Shíliù-Jing (Bênfâ) 75: The Way's action is from necessity (-bùdéyî), from necessity, so inexhaustible. Cf. Lúnyû (IX) 130: Confucius on a river said: "What is passing is like this, unceasing day or night." Jiâ Yì: *Xinshu* (IX Xiuzhèngyû- shàng): Yellow Emperor said: "The Way is like river water issuing unceasingly (wuyî), its running is unstoppable/-pping." *Hánfeizî* (XL): on dynamic necessity versus contradiction 'spear-shield' máodùn. Wells 2001: 67, Mohist logic: 'Necessity' of opposing dynamics, like younger and elder brother, one assenting, one dissenting, is necessity and un- necessity. This is not necessity." Graham 1978: 299- 300, A51.

Lacking form, but having divisions,

無形, 有分,

is called the Great Dynamic.[133] (*see Appendix I: Lâozî LI*)

名曰大埶. [=埶/勢?]

So, when east, west, south, and north

故東西南北

ways are correctly aligned,[134]

之道踹[=端]然,

their divisions are identical.[135]

其爲分等也.

Shady and sunny (*yin-yáng*) are not the same energy,

陰陽不同氣,

yet they in harmony share.

然其爲和同也.

Sour, salty, sweet, and bitter

酸鹹甘苦

flavours are mutually opposed,

之味相反,

yet as as foods are equal.

然其爲善[=膳]均也.

---

[133] I amend 'great who?' dàshú 大埶 to 'Great Dynamic' Dàshì 大埶=勢. *Lyûshì Chunqiu* (IV Mèngxià 3, Zunshi) 6b: He who has the Great Dynamic may become Under- Heaven's governor! Yôu Dàshì kêyî weí Tianxià zhèng-yî! 有大勢可以爲天下正矣. *Huaínánzî* (XIII Fànlùn) 10b: The ruler occupies a strong and great dynamic position, Jun chû qiángdà shìweì 君處强大勢位. *Liù-Tao* (II Wéntao: 15 Wénfá) 9: display with great dynamic, shì yî dàshì 示以大勢; cf. 12. (Míng) Romance of the Three Kingdoms starts: It is said: the Under-Heaven great dynamic when divided will always necessarily unite. Huàshuo: Tianxià Dàshì fen jiû bì hé 天下大勢分久必合. Form and dynamic are a pair: *Guânzî* (II 'Form and Dynamic' Xíngshì). *Lâozî* (LI): The Way generates them, Virtue nourishes them. Things form them, dynamics complete them. Dào sheng-zhi, dé xù- zhi. Wù xíng-zhi, shì chéng-zhi 道生之 德畜之 物形之 勢成之. Division of dynamics (fenshì) is a standard concept: *Hánfeizî* (XXXVIII-3, XLVIII); *Lyûshì Chunqiu* (XCVIII Shèn Shì) 14b; Mòzî (XXXII). Archaic shì 埶 and shú 埶 are often confused. Lù Diàn dutifully gives 'honest' (dun 敦) as alternative reading.

[134] 'Aligned' duan 端 may be another taboo avoidance for 'correct' zhèng 正.

[135] The magnetic 'south-pointing needle' (zhǐnán zhen) aligned to the North Pole may serve as metaphor for the dynamic of imperial rule. *Lúnyû* (II Weízhèng) 1. *Hánfeizî* (VI Yôudù) 25: The first kings established the monitor of south to determine dawn and dusk's [direction], xianwáng lì sinán –yî duan zhaoxì 先王立司南以端朝夕. *Guǐguzî* (X Móu 'Schemes') 71: the monitoring south chariot, sinán-zhi che 司南之車.

The five colours have not the same tint,
五色不同采,
yet in beauty are even.[136]
然其爲好齊也.
The five scale notes (*sounds*) are not the same pitch,
五聲不同均,
yet in enjoyment are one.
然其可喜一也.

So, things are nothing but species;
故, 物無非類者;
movement and stillness are nothing but energy.
動靜無非氣者.
For this reason, in having men,
是故, 有人,
to get one man's energy is auspicious.
將得一人氣吉.
In having households, to get one household's energy is auspicious.
有家, 將得一家氣吉.
In having nations, to get one nation's energy is auspicious.
有國, 將得一國氣吉.
The unlucky are contrary to this.
其將凶者反此.

So, sameness means unity.
故, 同之謂一.
Differentiation means the Way.
異之謂道.
Mutual conquests mean dynamics.[137]
相勝之謂埶 [=勢].

Auspicious or inauspicious means victory or defeat.
吉凶之謂成敗.
The worthy in a myriad undertakings have only one loss;
賢者萬舉而一失;
the unworthy in a myriad undertakings have only one win.[138]
不肖者萬舉而一得.

---

[136] *Guânzî* XI (Zhòuhé) 59: The five notes are not of the same sound yet can be tuned. The five tastes are not of the same substance yet can be harmonised. *Lâozî* II: Keynotes and modes mutually harmonise. Yin. Sheng xiang hé 音聲相和.

[137] I amend 'grasping' zhí 埶 to 'dynamics' shì 勢/埶. The archaic graphs are almost identical. Cf. 'great who?' (dàshú? 大孰?) above. Wells 2001: 61-71.

[138] Here is a rare appeal to statistical probability, rather than certainty, though the odds are heavily weighted at 10,000 to 1, as in *Hánfeizî* XL Nàn Shì 'Objections to Dynamics'.

Knowing unity may not unify,
知一之不可一也,
So, value the Way.
故貴道.
Sameness[139] means Unity,
空 [=同?] 之謂一,
nothing unprovided means the Way.
無不備之謂道.
To establish it means energy,
立之謂氣,
to communicate it means affinity of species.
通之謂類.

Energies (airs) which harm men are called unsuitable.
氣之害人者謂之不適.
Flavours (foods) that harm men are called poison.[140]
味之害人者謂之毒.
Now, at the land-altar without a blood-sacrifice, (*for rain*)[141]
夫社不夾, [=刲?]
you will not achieve even a mist.
則不成霧.

Energies therefore both mutually benefit and mutually harm.
氣故相利相害也.
Species therefore both complement and mutually defeat.
類故相成相敗也.

---

[139] Lù Diàn offers the alternative reading 'equality' (tóng 同), as in the previous stanza, to 'void' (kong 空). In viii-c it is used in the sense of 'aperture'. Defoort 1997: 126 interprets it: "Vacuousness is what we call the 'one'; nothing being incomplete is what we call 'way.'" (5: 24/8-9).

[140] 'Poison' (dú) rhymes with 'mist' (wù). This is another illustration for the unity of opposites.

[141] I read jiá (夾) as zhá (刲) here for cutting the throat in a blood sacrifice.

Accumulate limping to make lameness,

積往生跂,

with expertise you will become a shaman master.

工以爲師.

Accumulate poisons to make medicine,

積毒成藥,

with expertise you will become a doctor.[142]

工以爲醫.

Good and evil are mutually defining,

美惡相飾,

their mandate is called the return cycle.

命曰復周.

When things reach extremes they revert,

物極則反,

their mandate is called circular flow.

命曰環流.

---

[142] I follow Lù Diàn who cites Yáng Xióng: *Taixuán Jing* (53-18) 'hopping' qi (跂) but read 'lame', as in wâng (尪) for wâng (往) 'going.' Doctor and shaman (yi, shi) were related callings as in 'witch-doctor' (wu, yi 巫毉/醫). *Lúnyǔ* XIII (Zî Lù) 22: Confucius remarked: "Without constancy you cannot be (even) a witch or doctor... Don't prognosticate at all!" 'Constancy' (Heng 恒) is the name of hexagram no. 32 in the *Change Classic*.

vi. THE WAY'S GOVERNANCE
(Dàoduan 道端[=Dàozhèng正/政][143]第六)

This chapter has a detailed program of meritocratic recruitment and the right to remonstrate (jiàn 諫), freedom of speech to protest government policy. Despite the call for 'oneness' as unity, it warns against the monopoly of power and states the need for pluralism under the One Man. Personnel management is explained as recruitment of ministers with different qualities to serve separate functions in cabinet-style government. 'Four wefts' in Guânzî (I Mùmín: 2) meant propriety, justice, honesty and shame. Here they are humanity, righteousness, loyalty and sagacity, set to the cardinal points. Qín's First Emperor's stele of BC 219 has sagacity, wisdom, humanity and righteousness, replacing loyalty with wisdom.[144]

The lists of eleven virtues show signs of deletions and disorder. Parts of 'loyalty' and 'righteousness' are missing. Totally absent is the paramount Confucian virtue of filial piety, 'filialty' (xiào 孝) which, paired with righteousness, is to be inculcated in the Complete Ninth's Way (ix-c). The eleven are reducible to five pairs and one single: humanity and loyalty, propriety and righteousness, wisdom and courage, discernment and goodfaith, honesty and worth, concluding with sagacity. The ruler's person is subject to restraint by virtue and 'complete Law.' The homily ends with an exhortation to study, as urged by Xúnzî (I Quànxué), over the faith in innate goodness preached by Mencius (Mèngzî VIIa.15 Liángzhi Liángnéng).

a) Heaven and Earth's Governance
Heaven is how the myriad beings got established.
天者萬物所以得立也.
Earth is how the myriad beings got security.
地者萬物所以得安也.

Thus, Heaven settles them,
故天定之,
Earth places them.
地處之.

---

[143] 'Governance' (zhèng 政), written here as 'straight or aligned' (duan 端), appears to be a taboo avoidance of Qín First Emperor's personal name 'Governance' (Zhèng 正=政).

[144] Shîjî (VI), dì-43a Qín Shîhuáng, year 28, Lángyé Taí stele inscription. Guodiàn Chûmù Zhújiân: Six Virtues (Liù-Dé) 187.

Time develops them,
時發之,
Things receive them,
物受之,
the Sage Man models them.
聖人象之.

Now, cold and warmth's changes
夫寒溫之變
are not what one essence reforms.
非一精之所化也.
The Under-Heaven's employments
天下之事
are not what one man can alone know.
非一人之所能獨知也.
The sea waters' breadth and greatness
海水廣大
do not look to one stream's flow.[145]
非獨仰一川之流也.

Consequently, the illumined ruler
是以, 明主
to rule his generation urgently seeks men.
之治世也急於求人.
He does not alone attempt it.
弗獨爲也.
Together with Heaven and Earth,
與天與地,
he firmly establishes the four wefts
建立四維
(*Lù Diàn explains: 'Propriety, Righteousness, Modesty and Shame'.*)
to sustain the nation's governance.
以輔國政.

Hooks and strings are mutually extended,
鉤繩相布,
bits and halters mutually control.
銜橛相制.

---

[145] *Guânzî* (LXIV Xíngshì jiê) 329: Seas do not refuse water… *Mòzî* (II Xiushen) 3: Yangtse and Yellow River are not one spring's water… *Zhuangzî* (XXIV Xú Wúguî) 852. Shèn Dào (**53, 56**) A governed nation's rule is not one man's force... Jiâ Yì::*Xinshu* (IX Xiuzhèngyû-xià) 71: The Under-Heaven is not one family's possession. Dông Zhòngshu: *Chunqiu Fánlù* (VI 19, Lì Yuánshén) 38: Heaven's strength is not one essence's force; (VII 21, Kâo Gongmíng) 40: Sun and moon's brilliance is not one essence's light.

With threes and fives both prepared,[146]
參偶 (=參伍?) 具備,
established positions will then be firm.
立位乃固.

Warp energy has constants.
經氣有常.
Principles by Heaven and Earth move.
理以天地動.
To oppose Heaven's timing is inauspicious
逆天時不祥
and will ruin operations.[147]
有祟事.

b) Appointing the Worthy
If you do not appoint worthies
不仕賢,
you will have no success and inevitably fail.[148]
無功必敗.
Go forth to plumb its Way,
出究其道,
come in to exhaust its metamorphoses.
入窮其變.

When you extend the army to guard externally,
張軍衛外,
trouble conversely will be within.
禍反在內.
When what you protect is very distant,
所備甚遠,
traitors will be among those you love.
賊在所愛.

Consequently, the First Kings in appointing knights,
是以先王置士也,
promoted the worthy and employed the able.
舉賢用能.
They did not pander to their generation.
無阿於世.

---

[146] I read 'three and five' (canwù 參伍) for 'three and pair' (can'ǒu 參偶). 'Three and five' implies counter checking, vertical triangle (Heaven-Earth-Man) and horizontal square (4 directions and centre). See also xii-d. cf. Hánfeizî (VIII 32).

[147] Guóyǔ (XXI Yuèyǔ xià) 1-b.

[148] Lǎozǐ (III) opposes 'promotion worthies', one of Mòzǐ's ten theses.

Humane men sit on the left,
仁人居左,
loyal ministers sit in front,
忠臣居前,
righteous ministers sit on the right,
義臣居右,
the Sage sits in the rear. (*Facing south, a ruler has east on the left, west on the right.*)
聖人居後.

On his left is the law of humane benevolence,
左法仁,
thus springtime generates and reproduces.
則春生殖.
At his front is the law of loyalty,
前法忠,
thus summer's work is established.
則夏功立.
On his right is the law of righteousness,
右法義,
thus autumn completes ripening.
則秋成熟.
At his rear is the law of sagacity,
後法聖,
thus winter shuts down and stores.
則冬閉藏.
The First Kings by employing them
先王用之
became high but did not topple,
高而不墜,
secure and not doomed.
安而不亡.
They are the myriad beings' root and branch.
此萬物之本.

Heaven and Earth's gates and doors,
天地之門戶,
the Way and virtue's gains,
道德之益也,
these four are what the ruler takes from outside.
四大夫者君之所取於外也.

The ruler is Heaven.
君者天也.
If Heaven does not open gates and doors,
天不開門戶,
it causes subordinates to harm each other.
使下相害也.
If those who promote worthies are by their superior rewarded,
進賢受上賞,
then subordinates will not deceive him.
則下不相蔽.

Not waiting to be employed by men,
不待事人,
worthy knights will display unconcealable achievements.
賢士顯不蔽之功.
Then, entrusted with employment,
則, 任事之
there is nobody who will not exhaust loyalty.
人莫不盡忠.

Towns and villages will aspire to righteousness.
鄉曲慕義.
Reformed, they will sit and self-correct.[149]
化, 坐自端.
This is what his Way brings about,
此其道之所致,
what virtue completes.
德之所成也.

Their root issues from One Man,
本出一人,
so he is called 'Heaven.'
故謂之天.
None but accept his mandate.
莫不受命.

He may not be named,
不可爲名,
so is called 'divine.'
故謂之神.

---

[149] 'Erect' duan 端is used in the text here to avoid the taboo 'correct' zhèng 正.

He attains divinity's zenith,
至神之極,
manifesting it unerringly.[150]
見之不忒.

His breast he rides on the undoubted,[151]
匈[=胸]乖[=乘]不惑,
striving to govern a unified nation.
務正一國.
The unified nation's form
一國之刑
is concentrated in his body.
具在於身.

Through his person (*body*) he examines his generation,
以身老[=考]世,
to govern and establish the nation.[152]
正以錯國.
He submits to righteousness, practices humanity
服義, 行仁
in order to unite the royal enterprise.
以一王業.

Now humanity is the ruler's exercise,
夫仁者君之操也,
righteousness is the ruler's conduct,
義者君之行也,
loyalty is the ruler's governance,
忠者君之政也,
goodfaith is the ruler's teaching.
信者君之教也.
The Sage Man is the ruler's teacher.
聖人者君之師傅也.

---

[150] *MWD* (*Jingfǎ*:Lùn) 53, strip 52a-b: reaching divinity's extremity, he manifests it unambiguously.
[151] I read 匈 xiong 'inauspicious' as 胸 xiong 'breast,' and 乖 guai 'warped' as 乘 chéng 'ride.'
[152] *MWD* Shíliù-jing (Wǔ-Zheng) 65, 91a Anrán tells the Yellow Emperor: It begins in the body…
Seek the internal form…

c) Meritocratic Assessment

The ruler's Way is knowing men
君道知人.
The minister's technique is knowing employment.
臣術知事.

1) So, to oversee goods and divide wealth, employ the humane.[153]
   故, 臨貨分財, 使仁.
2) [To admonish the ruler, employ the loyal.
   矯拂王過, 使忠.]
3) To entertain and receive, employ the proper.
   賓奏贊見, 使禮.
4) [To save the weak and punish the violent, employ the righteous.
   救弱誅暴, 使義.]
5) To organize people so they abide peacefully, employ the honest.
   理民處平, 使謙.
6) To use the people and win multitudes, employ the worthy.
   用民獲眾, 使賢.
7) To cogitate on employment and settle plans, employ the wise.
   慮事定計, 使智.
8) To confront disasters and respond to trouble, employ the courageous.
   犯患應難, 使勇.
9) To deliver speeches and contract wordings, employ the eloquent.
   受言結辭, 使辯.
10) To exit fiefs, cross borders, and visit remote nations, employ the
    faithful.
    出封, 越境, 適絕國, 使信,
11) To control Heaven and Earth, and manage the barons, employ the
    Sage.
    制天地, 御諸侯, 使聖.

> 1a.) Now the humane [*minister's*] achievements are
> 夫仁[臣]之功
> in being good at giving and not quarrelling,[154]
> 善與不爭,
> so subordinates do not resent superiors.
> 下不怨上.

---

[153] The lists of a) nine and b) ten qualities exhibit signs of disorder and omissions which I have restored on the model of the third list c) of eleven qualities which appears complete and consistent. The received sequences of each list were as follows: list a) 1, (-), 6, (-), 5, 7 4, 2, 3, 8, 9; list b) 1, 4, 8, 5, 7, 9, 3, (-), 2, 6, 10. Restorations are italicized in square brackets.

[154] *MWD* (Cheng) 83, 166b: good giving and not quarrelling, shànyú bùzheng 善與不爭.

2a.) Loyal ministers' achievements are
忠臣之功
in correct speech and straight conduct,
正言直行,
to amend and reprove the king's excesses.
矯拂王過.

3a.) Proper ministers' achievements are
禮臣之功
in honouring the ruler and humbling ministers.
尊君卑臣.

4a.) Righteous ministers' achievements are
義臣之功
in saving the lost and succouring the desperate,
存亡繼絕,
rescuing the weak and executing the violent.
救弱誅暴.

5a.) Honest ministers' achievements are
貞謙之功
in rejecting selfishness to establish the public. [155]
廢私立公.

6a.) Worthy knights' achievements are
賢士之功
that enemy nations beware of them.
敵國憚之.

7a.) Wise knights' achievements are
智士之功
when operations arrive to manage
事至而治
and when troubles arrive to respond.
難至而應.

8a.) [Courageous knights' achievements are][156]
[勇士之功]

in that their four borders are not invaded.
四境不侵.

---

[155] *Hánfeizǐ* (VI Yôudù) 22. *MWD Jingfâ* (Dàofâ) 43, 7b; (Sì-Dù) 51, 44a; reject the selfish (private) to establish the public qusi ér lìgong 去私而立公.

[156] Cf. viii-d. I reconstruct 8a) as 'Courageous knights', to match the list above, from the third line of 6a) on 'Worthy knights'.

9a.) Eloquent knights' achievements are
辯士之功
in undoing resentments and resolving difficulties.
釋怨解難.

10a.) Faithful ministers' achievements are
信臣之功
in correctness and not altering speech (*honesty*).
正不易言.

11a.) The Sage Man's achievements are
聖人之功
in establishing control in darkness so that[157]
定制於冥冥
requests are attained, desires obtained,
求至, 欲得,
words heard, conduct followed.
言聽, 行從.

The near relate to him, the far give allegiance,
近親, 遠附,
illumination pervades the four quarters.
明達四通.
Internally he has a rule to check himself.[158]
內有挾[=揆]度.
Only then does he have the means to assess men.
然後有以量人.

1b.) For the rich:
富者:
he see what they give
觀其所予
to know their humanity.
足以知仁.

---

[157] This definition of the Sage recalls the Night Walker of iii-b; xix-a. *Chunqiu Fánlù* (VI-19 Lì Yuánshén) 38b: The lord values sitting in darkness to illuminate others' position, abiding in shadow to face the light. Lì points out 'light' and 'darkness' here have identical sound (míng 冥/明).
[158] I follow Lù Diàn in reading:'examines and assesses' (kuídù 揆度 for jiádù 挾度).

2b.) For nobles:
　貴者：
　he sees what they undertake
　觀其所舉
　to know their loyalty.
　足以知忠.

3b.) [For the great:]
　［大者］：
　he sees that seniors don't defer to juniors,
　觀其大長不讓少,
　nobles don't defer to commoners,
　貴不讓賤,
　to know their propriety.
　足以知禮.

4b.) For the successful:
　達［者］：
　he sees what they do not do
　觀其所不行
　to know their righteousness.
　足以知義.

5b.) For the poor:
　貧者：
　he sees what they do not take
　觀其所不取
　to know their honesty.
　足以知廉.

6b.) For commoners:
　賤者：
　he sees what they do not contrive
　觀其所不爲
　to know their worth.
　足以知賢.

7b.) For appointees to office and deputies in government:
　受官任治：
　he sees what they shun and choose
　觀其去就
　to know their wisdom.
　足以知智.

8b.) [For soldiers:
[兵者：
he sees that] under pressure they are not scared
觀其]迫之不懼
[to know their courage.]
[足以知勇.]

9b.) [For diplomats:
[使者：
he sees that] their mouths are sharp and
language skillful
觀其]口利辭巧
to know their eloquence.
足以知辯.

10b.) [For ministers:
[臣者：
he sees that] in their work they do not dissemble
觀其]使之不隱
to know their sincerity.
足以知信.

11b.) [For the Sage:
[聖者：
he sees him] fathom depths and observe the heavens
觀其]測深觀天
to know his sagacity.
足以知聖.

d) The Sage's Rule
His ranks will not lose precedence,
第不失次,
his principles will not mutually conflict.
理不相舛.
When the near are blocked in, the distant closed out,
近塞遠閉,
prepared at the prime, his revolution will be completed.
備元變成.

Illumined in operations, he knows how to divide.
明事, 知分.
Reckoning by numbers, alone he will act.
度數, 獨行.

Lacking the Way rulers
無道之君
Trust and employ the trifling and paltry.
任用幺麼.
They move in confusion and obscurity.
動即煩濁.
When they have the Way rulers
有道之君
trust and employ the brave and virile.
任用俊雄.
They move in illumined clarity.
動則明白.

These two are first:
二者先：
fix your plainstuff, establish clarity.
定素立白.
In a trio with illumination arising,
蓡[=參?]明起
energy and blood will mutually minister.
氣榮相宰.

Superiors will join their tallies,
上合其符
subordinates will check their substance and timing.
下稽其實時.

When a ruler welcomes men with virtue,
君遇人有德,
gentlemen will arrive at his gate.
君子至門.
If without speaking he has goodfaith,[159]
不言而信,
myriad people will closely rally to him.
萬民附親.
If he encounters men with violence and arrogance,
遇人暴驕,
myriad people will be alienated and drift away.
萬民離流.
Superiors and subordinates will be mutually suspicious,
上下相疑,
turning circles day and night in mutual antagonism.
復而如環日夜相撓.

---

[159] Cf. *MWD Jingfǎ* (Mínglǐ) 58, 70b.

When remonstrances are not accefpted,

諫者弗受,

those who speak endanger their persons.

言者危身.

[The ruler] will be without recourse to hear of his excesses,

[君]無從聞過,

so great ministers will be hypocritical and disloyal.

故大臣偽而不忠.

So, if men's ruler cherishes his people as sons,

是以爲人君親其民如子者,

unsummoned they will come.

弗召自來.

He will be called illuminated.

故曰有光.

At the end he will have a fine name.

卒於美名.

If he does not give but exacts,

不施而責,

does not endow yet seeks relationships,

弗受[=授]而求親,

it means there will be catastrophe.

故曰有殃.

In the end he will be accursed.

卒於不祥.

Now, elders in serving their ruler

夫長者之事其君也

attune and harmonise with him.

調而和之.

Knights in pure honesty

士於純厚

guide and reform him.

引而化之.

The Under-Heaven will love him,

天下好之,

his Way will be daily followed.

其道日從.

So in the end he will necessarily triumph.

故卒必昌.

Now, when small-minded men serve a ruler,
夫小人之事其君也,
they strive to cover his lights,
務蔽其明,
block his hearing, exploit his awe,
塞其聽, 乘其威,
use his dynamic to burn men.[160]
以灼熱[=勢灼?]人.
The Under-Heaven will hate him.
天下惡之.

His evils become daily more ill-fated.
其崇日凶.
So, in the end he will necessarily fail,
故卒必敗,
disaster will reach his lineage men.
禍及族人.

This is ruler and ministers' revolution,
此君臣之變,
rule and disorder's division.
治亂之分.
It is prosperity versus destruction's barrier and bridge,
興壞之關梁,
nation and household's archway.
國家之閡也.
Disloyalty and obedience, profit and harm
逆順利害
from this issue and are born.
由此出生.

The only thing without study in which you may have ability
凡可無學而能者
is just sleep and eating.[161]
唯息與食也.

---

[160] I read 'hot' (rè 熱) as 'dynamic' (shì 勢) and reverse order to 'use his dynamic to oppress men' yǐ shì zhuó rén 以勢灼人 in place of 'by scorching heat men' yǐ zhuó rè rén 以灼熱人). Guǎnzǐ (LXVII Míngfǎ Jiě) 343: 'for fear of the ruler's awesome dynamic.' -yǐ wèi zhǔ-zhī wēiShì-yě 以畏主之威勢 也. Wèi Qǐpéng 1992: MWD Hé Yīnyáng 130n22 conflates 'dynamic' (shì 埶=勢) and 'hot' (rè 熱).
[161] Mèngzǐ (VIIa Jìnxin-a, 15 Liángzhi, liángnéng) 298: That in which men without study are capable is innate ability.

94

So the First Kings transmitted the Way
故先王傳道
for mutual emulation and allegiance.
以相效屬也.

Worthy rulers adhere to complete law so
賢君循成法
their subsequent generations will be long-lasting.
後世久長.
Indolent rulers do not follow it so
惰君不從
their present generation will be exterminated and lost.
當世滅亡.

vii. NEARING COLLAPSE (Jìndié 近迭第七)

This is a warning to hào on the imminent danger of conquest by Qín, but the chief finger of blame is pointed inwardly. Qín is not mentioned by name yet the direction of the threat beyond doubt. Its theme is comparable to Mâwángdui's 'Destruction'.[162] The salient line is a blunt call to the king (vii-b):

> Publicly to apologize to the Under-Heaven
> for yielding to an enemy nation.

There is only one known scenario that can fit these words. Young military theorist Zhào Kuò (趙括) was the son of great general Zhào She (趙奢). Duped by Qín agents, King Xiàochéng (r. 265-245) replaced Lián Po and appointed Zhào Kuò commander. This was opposed by his mother and ailing veteran Lìn Xiangrú who mocked this as nepotism, in an iconic metaphor, "like sticking down the tuning-struts to play the zither." Adaptative policies are required as are different modes in music. Sons may not be like fathers. Comparable resort to musical metaphor characterises *Héguanzî* (iii-a, ix-c, xvii-f), where adaptive modulation is contrasted with the inflexibility of adherence to the precedents of fixed modes.

Zhào She's widow, who had experience serving her late husband, knew her brash son was unfit for command. She therefore petitioned against his appointment, but was ignored. Her protest coincides with *Héguânzî*'s strictures against hereditary privilege and denunciation of the king's policies.[163]

The outcome was Zhào's army entrapment by Qín general Baí Qî (白起 d. 257) at Chángpíng (長平, near Gaopíng in southeast Shanxi) in 260 BC. Qín reportedly immolated Zhào's army of close to half a million soldiers on the spot.[164] This fits the pointed remark against murder of surrendered troops. (vii-a) A shrine with statues of the unfortunate general and his wife was erected at the site in the Táng dynasty. Two 'bone pits' (gûkeng) from the battle were excavated at Yônglù village in 1995. (Plates 23-25)

---

[162] *MWD* Jing fâ (Wánglùn) 55.

[163] *Shîjì* (LXXXI Lièzhuàn, Zhào She) dì-408a: Like sticking down tuning struts to play a sè zither. Ruò jiaozhù ér gûsè 若膠柱而鼓瑟.

[164] *Shîjì* (XLIII) dì-301a. cf. *Hánfeizî* (I Chu jiàn Qín) 5.

'Man and arms' here reverse the order of Vergil's classic opening "arma virumque..." to the *Aeneid*. Righteous response to oppressive rule through the populist agency of Heaven was sanctioned by Mencius (Ia.5). Wú Qî (ca. 440-361), who led Jìn (from which Zhào was to split) to victory over Qín, had listed the four martial virtues as "the Way, righteousness, propriety and humanity."[165]

Héguan Zî defines 'arms' as propriety, righteousness, loyalty and goodfaith, four virtues important in war, among others discussed elsewhere (vi-b, xv-b). His purpose, like that of Confucius, is not pacifist but to impress upon the general to view war, never for its own sake, but only in terms of moral values.

This, and three subsequent chapters (ix,xiv-xv), name the interlocutors as Héguan Zî as teacher and Páng Zî as disciple. The Páng clan of Páng Huàn (ca. 300, xix) and general Páng Xuan (fl. 250, xvi) belonged to a martial lineage in Zhào of which the latter's dates make a plausible match.

a) Prioritise Man and Arms

Páng Zî asked Héguan Zî saying:

龐子問鶡冠子曰:

> In the Sage Man's Way, what has priority?
> 聖人之道, 何先?

Héguan Zî said:

鶡冠子曰:

> Prioritise Man.
> 先人.

Páng Zî said:

龐子曰:

> In man's Way, what has priority?
> 人道, 何先?

Héguan Zî said:

鶡冠子曰:

> Prioritise Arms.
> 先兵.

Páng Zî said:

龐子曰:

> Why do you put aside Heaven and prioritise Man?
> 何以舍天而先人乎?

---

[165] *Wúzî* 吳子 (I). *Simâfâ* 司馬法 (I). Sawyer 1993: 126, 207.

Héguan Zî said:
鶡冠子曰:

Heaven is high and hard to know.[166]
天高而難知.
It has good fortune that may not be requested.
有福不可請.
It has disasters that may not be avoided.
有禍不可避.
If your law is Heaven, you will be harsh.
法天, 則戾.

Earth is wide and deep,
地廣大深厚,
thick and with much profit, yet scarcely awesome.
多利, 而鮮威.
If you take your law from Earth, you will be disgraced.
法地, 則辱.

The seasons rise and settle.
時舉錯.
They alternate without uniformity.
代更無一.
If your law is the seasons, you will equivocate.
法時, 則貳.

These three may not be used
三者不可以
to establish reforms and implant customs.
立化樹俗.
So, the Sage Man does not take them as laws. (*i.e. models*)
故, 聖人弗法.

Páng Zî asked saying:
Shady and sunny (yinyáng), what about them?
龐子曰:陰陽, 何若?

Héguan Zî said:
鶡冠子曰:

Divine spirits' awesome luminaries with Heaven join.
神靈威明與天合.
Gouméng ('*Hook Spike*', *the springtime god*) moves into action
勾萌動作

with Earth together.
與地俱.

---

[166] cf. xiii-a: 'Heaven is high yet may be known.'.

98

Shade and sunshine, cold and warmth
陰陽寒暑
with the Seasons arrive.
與時至.
These three, if by the Sage Man kept, are governed,
三者聖人存則治,
If lost are disordered.
亡則亂.
For this reason, I prioritise man.
是故, 先人.

The rich become proud, the noble complacent.
富則驕, 貴則嬴.
Arms in one hundred years are not once used,
兵者百歲不一用,
but may not for one day be forgotten.
然不可一日忘也.
For this reason, the human Way prioritises arms.
是故, 人道先兵.

Páng Zî said:
龐子曰:
　　Prioritisation of arms, why is this?
　　先兵, 奈何?

Héguan Zî said:
鶡冠子曰:
　　Arms are propriety, righteousness, loyalty, and goodfaith.
　　兵者禮, 義, 忠, 信也.

Páng Zî said:
龐子曰:
　　I would like to hear about arms' righteousness.
　　願聞兵義.

Héguan Zî said:
鶡冠子曰:
　　When the Way is lost,
　　失道,
　　some dare as commoners to oppose the noble.
　　故敢以賤逆貴,
　　If unrighteous,
　　不義,
　　Some dare as the small to invade the great.
　　故敢以小侵大.

Páng Zî said:
龐子曰:

In practice, what is to be done?
用之奈何?

Héguan Zî said:
鶡冠子曰:

If conduct is perverse, prohibit it.
行枉, 則禁.
If it reverts to the correct, leave it.
反正, 則舍.
For this reason, not killing men who have surrendered[167]
是故, 不殺降人
is what rulers of the Way extol.
主道所高.

Nothing is more valuable than contractual obligations.
莫貴約束.

To gain the Earth by losing goodfaith,
得地失信,
the Sage King will not rely.
聖王弗據.
To betray one's word or break a contract,
倍言負約,
Everybody will have excuses.
各將有故.

---

[167] *MWD Jingfǎ* (Wánglùn) 55, 60a, killing men who have surrendered lù xiángrén 戮降人 will ultimately doom yourself. Assuming a date of writing post-260 BC, this must serve as a rebuke to Qín for the mass slaughter of Zhào's capitulated troops at Chángpíng.

b) Imminent Overthrow

He whose arms are strong

兵強者

will first 'get his will in the Under-Heaven'.[168]

先'得意於天下'.

Now, taking what is seen to equate to what is not seen,

今以所見合所不見,

surely it can hardly be so.

蓋殆不然.

Now, a great nation's arms conversely are crushed

今大國之兵反詘

and speeches are exhausted.

而辭窮.

Its prohibitions do not prevent,

禁不止,

Its orders are not enacted.

令不行.

What is the cause?

之故何也?

Héguan Zî said:

鶡冠子曰:

If you wish to know the future, examine the past.

欲知來者察往(wâng).

If you wish to know the ancient, examine the present.

欲知古者察今.

He who selects the men to employ is king (wáng).

擇人而用之者王,

He who employs men without[169] selection is doomed (wáng).

用人而[=無]擇之者亡.

This is how 'counter rhythm' is generated.[170]

逆節之所生.

---

[168] Contrast *Lâozî* (XXXI): He who delights in killing men may not get his ambition in the Under-Heaven. Cf. fn 170, below. Here Héguan Zî in person expresses doubt about his nation's prospects in combating Qín's power.

[169] I read 'without' wú 無 for 'and' ér 而.

[170] 'Counter rhythm' (nìjié 逆節) is a phrase first found in the tale of Goujiàn of Yuè and the recovery of his kingdom from Wú with the counsel of Fàn Lî. *Guóyû* (XXI Yuèyû- xià) 1-5. *Guânzî* (XLII Shì 'Dynamics') 252. *MWD* Shíliù-jing (Wánglùn 'Doom Thesis') 55, 59b x2.

The unworthy's encroachment on the worthy's mandate
不肖侵賢命
is termed 'usurpation'.
曰凌.

The hundred clans not daring to speak of their mandate,
百姓不敢言命
is termed: 'conquest'.
曰勝.

Just now what you asked,
今者所問,
you should take care not to say.
子慎勿言.

Now, if a land is great, the nation rich,
夫地大國富,
people many, arms strong, it is called: sufficient.[171]
民眾兵強, 曰足.

When knights have super-abundant force,
士有餘力
yet cannot first 'get their ambition in the Under-Heaven',[172]
而不能以先 '得志於天下' 者,
their ruler is unworthy and his actions arrogant to excess.
其君不賢而行驕溢也.

---

[171] *Shangjun Shu* (I Qiángguó) plans for national wealth and strength.

[172] *Lâozî* (XXXI): He who delights in killing men may not get his ambition in the Under-Heaven. Fu lèsha rén-zhê zé bùkê dézhì yú Tianxià –yî. 夫樂殺人者則不可得志於天下矣. Cf. fn 166, above.

If unworthy, he will be unable to practice non-contrivance (*wúwei*)[173]

不賢則不能無爲

and may not induce others by it.

而不可與致焉.

If arrogant, he will 'make light of the enemy'.[174]

驕則輕敵.

'Making light of the enemy',

輕敵,

he with his intimates takes counsel

則與所私謀

on what they do not know how to contrive.

其所不知爲.

He employs those who are not strong

使非其在力

to overcome those who they cannot match.

欲取勝於非其敵.

He does not reckon a life-time's disasters

不計終身之患,

but rejoices in momentary pleasures.

樂須臾之說.

For this reason, a nation's ruler, covering his faults,

是故國君被過,

listens to slanders and libels in the Under-Heaven.

聽之謗醜於天下,

and wise councillors suffer impostors' denunciations

而謀臣負濫首之責

from enemy nations.

于敵國.

---

[173] 'Non-contrivance' (wúwei) is reserved for the virtuous ruler in the present work.

[174] *Lǎozǐ* (LXIX): No disaster is greater than making light of the enemy, Huò mò dà-yú   qingdí 禍
莫大於輕敵.

Enemy nations denounce them, so they are dismissed.[175]
敵國乃責, 則卻.
Dismissed remonstrators are ashamed of their weakness.
卻則說[=諫?]者羞其弱.
Myriad commoners' honesty
萬賤之直
cannot undo one noble's crookedness.
不能撓一貴之曲.

A nation bearing spiritual wounds,
國被伸[神?]創,
When provoked goes to war.
其發則戰.
War causes innocent people
戰則是使元元之民
to go forth to die for evil ministers' wrong policies.
往死邪臣之失薊[=策?]也.

When errors are generated by superiors,
過生於上,
the (unjustly) incriminated die among subordinates.[176]
罪死於下.
Enemies externally conspire with the barons.
讎既外結諸侯.

Their accumulated crimes are in danger of overturning the state shrine.
畜其罪則危覆社稷.
The generation's lord paralysed,
世主懾懼,
with cold heart in isolation stands.
寒心孤立.
If he does not attack to punish these men,
不伐此人,
two nations' troubles will not be resolved.[177]
二國之難不解.

---

[175] *Shǐjì* (LXXXI) dì-408a: Zhào She's biography relates how Qín agents conspired to persuade Zhào's king to dismiss his most competent general Lián Po for Zhào Kuò.

[176] This remarkable couplet on unjust incrimination recurs in iv-d and viii-b. It must express personal trauma.

[177] xiii-b has a similar couplet: Consequently, the Under-Heaven is cold with fearful heart, and men's ruler in isolation stands. Shìgù Tiānxià hánxīn ér rénzhǔ gūlì 是故天下寒心而人主孤立. The next couplet, urging punitive action against collaborators, recurs in xii- d on Wú (Jiangsu) and Yuè (Zhèjiang). Yuè was conquered but in 473 BC recovered and annexed Wú. (Cf. Gou Jiàn, Dramatis Personae, above.)

If the ruler does not immediately reverse,
君立不復,
repent his former schemes and erroneous counsels,
悔曩郵[=猷?]過謀,
alter plans and change officers,
徙計易濫[=監?],
his head will be insufficient to cover it.
首不足蓋.

For their accumulation's weight,
以累重,
He should annihilate their houses and exterminate their lineages,
滅門殘疾族,
publicly apologize to the Under-Heaven
公謝天下
for yielding to an enemy nation.
以讓敵國.

Unless it is so,
不然則,
warfare's Way will not end,
戰道不絕,
and the nation's wounds will not cease.
國創不息.

Great indeed is its undiagnosed harm,
大乎哉夫弗知之害
Sad indeed is its disastrous extremity.
悲乎哉其禍之所極.
This is due to reliance on the nobility,
此倚貴,
Alienation from the Way and deficiency in humanity.
離道少人[= 仁].

Naturally it is to be condemned.
自有之咎也.
For this reason, before the army releases its chariot brakes,
是故, 師未發軔,
His arms will collapse.
而兵可迭也.

Now, great nations' rulers
今大國之君
Do not harken to the first Sages' Way
不聞先聖之道
But instead serve hosts of ministers.
而易事群臣.

They lack the illumined help of great calculation
無明佐之大數
And corrupt governance with fragmented wisdom.
而有滑正之碎智.
They reverse justice when enacting it,
反義而行之,
Oppose virtue by leading it.
逆德以將之.

Their arms will be crushed and speeches exhausted,
兵詘而辭窮,
their orders will not be enacted,
令不行,
their prohibitions will not prevent.
禁不止.
How is this sufficient to wonder at?
又奚足怪哉?

c) Law's Degrees

Páng Zî said:
龐子曰:
What is the corruption of governmental wisdom?
何若滑正之智?

Héguan Zî said:
鶡冠子曰:
When Law's predictions are not employed,
法度無以,
intuition is speculative.
遂意爲摸.
The Sage Man accords with numbers and complies with Law
聖人按數循法
Yet still finds them incomplete.
尚有不全.
For this reason, unless a man makes a hundred his laws,
是故人不百其法者,
he cannot contrive to be Under-Heaven's master.
不能爲天下主.

Now, if you lack calculation and self-adapt,
今無數而自因,
lack Law and self-suffice,
無法而自備,
altogether without superior Sages' monitoring,
循無上聖之檢,
yet decide by your own lights,
而斷於己明,
in human employments however well-prepared,
人事雖備,
how will you emulate an hundred-selves person?
將尚何以復百己之身乎.

A ruler in wisdom unillumined
主知不明
from his nobles contrives the Way,
以貴爲道,
from his ideas contrives Law,
以意爲法,
dragged along by the times to insult his generation.
牽時誑世.

Suppressed subordinates deceive superiors,[178]
迮下蔽上,
employees and operations go both awry.
使事兩乖.

Nourishing evil, he promotes mistakes.
養非, 長失.
From tranquillity he contrives disturbance,
以靜爲擾,
from security he contrives danger.
以安爲危.

So among the hundred clans, homes are troubled, men aggrieved.
百姓, 家困, 人怨.
What disaster is greater than this?
禍孰大焉?

---

[178] *MWD* (Jiŭ-Zhŭ 'Nine Rulers') 6; 31 have this exact line; iv-a, fn 101, has it in couplet Form; ix-e.

Like this, defeated and in flight on that day
若此者, 北走之日
will he know his mandate is doomed.
后[=後?]知命亡.

Páng Zî said:
龐子曰:
In human employments, the hundred laws, what of them?
以人事, 百法, 奈何?

Héguan Zî said:
鶡冠子曰:
Cangjié created Law.
蒼頡作法.
He invented writing from the sexagenary calendar (jiâzî)
書從甲子
to complete bureaucratic administration.[179]
成史李官.

If Cangjié had not taught the Way,
蒼頡不道,
if not for Cangjié,
然非蒼頡,
writing and ink would not have arisen.
文墨不起.

If not for Law's codification in documents,
縱法之載於圖者,
to instruct the mind and express ideas,
其於以喻心達意,
promotion of the Way's meaning
揚道之所謂
would only occupy one tenth.
乃纔居曼之十分一耳.

---

[179] Qín's First Emperor named his great dictionary of unified script *Cangjié Pian* in honour of Cangjié. The sexagenary cycle (jiâzî 甲子) runs the ten 'heavenly stems' tiangan (from jiâ) against twelve 'earthly branches' dìzhi (from zî) overlappingly to make the sixty days of the calendar. 'Calligraphy' (shufâ 書法) combines the two characters 'writing' (shu) and 'Law' (fâ). Shèn Dào 慎到 in (**80**) claims Cangjié was before Páoxi (Fúxi), i.e. before the Yellow Emperor (Thompson 1979: 143, 279).

So, he who knows the hundred Laws
故知百法者,
is an outstanding hero,
桀雄也
as if spanning the formless,
若隔無形,
he will make such the still non-existent
將然未有者
with the knowledge of a myriad men.
知[=智]萬人也.

Without the knowledge of a myriad men,
無萬人之智者,
his knowledge would be unable to perch
智不能棲
at his generation of study's pinnacle.
世學之上.

Páng Zî said:
龐子曰:
I have been favoured by your stern teaching,
得奉嚴教,
and received its lessons for some time!
受業有閒[=聞?]矣!

To disregard his teacher's counsel
退師謀言
your disciple will be ever more afraid.
弟子愈恐.

MID SCROLL

viii. SAVING MYRIADS (Duòwàn 度萬第八)

Héguan Zî now attacks the perversion of true governance by 'savage law' (mêngfâ) and predicts trouble or 'revolutionary change' (biàn) ahead. This chapter, like the preceding, seems directed against Qín and inhumane legalism as the potential nemesis of Zhào. *Xúnzî* (XVI) makes a comparable criticism of authoritarian policies in pre-unification Qín.

Héguan Zî argued (vii-b) that Zhào's recent debacle stems from its adoption of tyrannical policies. Now he warns Páng Zî of drought induced by moral disruption. Unjust punishments provoke heavenly wrath manifested by denial of rain. "Gods are wet" implies they weep and so withhold rain. The dialectical generation of fire and water as opposites has a cousin in *Zhuangzî* (XXVI) which asserts "water's centre has fire."

A Messianic Sage, as yet un-named, will establish utopia (cf. xviii-a), promulgating governance by 'Five Governances', a term cited, but never explained, in an excavated 'Yellow Emperor' scroll (viii-c, d; *MWD* Shíliù-Jing (Wû-Zheng) 65, 91b cf. iii-c; iv-a>e passim):

1) **reformative**, embodied by the Augustans of high antiquity;
2) **bureaucrative**, embodied by Divine Luminaries of the emergent order;
3) **educative**, embodied by Sage founders of the three classic dynasties;
4) **adaptative**, embodied by baron-kings of the present Warring States;
5) **operative**, embodied by hegemons of the Spring and Autumn period.

a) Savage Laws
Páng Zî asked Héguan Zî, saying:
龐子問鶡冠子曰:
> The Sage with gods counsels.
> 聖與神謀.
> The Way is with men completed.
> 道與人成.
>
> I wish to hear how to fathom gods
> 願聞度神c
> and cogitate victory's essentials.[180]
> 慮成之要.
> How about it?
> 奈何?

---

[180] Cf. xii-d: "Heaven may not be counseled with, Earth may not be cogitated with."

Héguan Zî said:

鶡冠子曰:

Heaven is divinity,

天者神也,

Earth is form.

地者形也.

Earth is wet, yet fire is generated from it.

地濕, 而火生焉.

Heaven is dry, yet water is generated from it.[181]

天燥, 而水生焉.

When Laws are savage and penalties unfair,

法猛刑頗,

the gods are wet (with weeping).

則神濕.

When gods are wet,

神濕,

Heaven does not generate water.

則天不生水.

When keys are fixed but modes inverted,[182]

音故聲倒,

forms will be dessicated.

則形燥.

When forms are dry, Earth will not generate fire.

形燥則地不生火.

When water and fire are not generated,

水火不生,

shade and sunshine will lack means to generate energies.

則陰陽無以成氣.

Degree and measure will lack means to achieve control,

度量無以成制,

the Five Conquests (agents) will lack means to generate dynamics.

五勝無以成執 [=勢].

---

[181] Excavated bamboo book *Guodiàn Chûmù Zhújiân*: (Tapìyi Sheng Shuî) 125: Grand Unity begets water. Water returns aided by Grand Unity and by this creates Heaven. *Hànshu* (Wû-Xíng Zhì, shàng): Heaven by one begets water. Earth by two generates fire… *Shàngshu* (*Zhoushu*: Hóngfàn) has the same sequence.

[182] Cf. iii-a: Five keynotes are for tuning. Five modes are for precedents. Music is the metaphor for governance.

Myriad beings will lack the means to complete their species,
萬物無以成類,
the hundred enterprises will be entirely disrupted.
百業俱絕.
Myriad lives will all be frustrated.
萬生皆困.
They will jostle about in confusion. Who knows the reason?
濟濟混混. 孰知其故?

Heaven and man have the same design,
天人同文,
Earth and man have the same principles.
地人同理.
The worthy and unworthy differ in ability.
賢不肖殊能.
所失甚少,
Thus, highest sagacity may not be confused,
故上聖不可亂也,
lowest idiocy may not be debated.
下愚不可辯也.

Shade and sunshine are energy's governors,
陰陽者氣之正也,
Heaven and Earth are form and spirit's governors.
天地者形神之正也.
The Sage Man is virtue's governor,
聖人者德之正也,
Law's edicts are the four seasons' governors.
法令者四時之正也.

So, if one man's justice is lost 'here',
故, 一義失此,
a myriad perhaps will be disordered 'there'.[183]
萬或亂彼.
Though what is lost be very little,
所失甚少,
what is spoiled will be very much.
所敗甚眾.

---

[183] *Mèngzǐ* (II Gongsun Chôu-shàng) 2 Hàorán-zhi qì: If by enacting one injustice or killing one innocent I could get the Under-Heaven, I would not do it.

What I mean by 'Heaven'
所謂天者
is not this blue-grey energy called Heaven.[184]
非是蒼蒼之氣之謂天也.
What I mean by 'Earth'
所謂地者
is not this round-clump of soil called Earth.
非是膞膞之土之謂地也.

What I mean by 'Heaven'
所謂天者,
refers to its making the suchness of things
言其然物
and unconquerablity.[185]
而無勝(朕)者也.
What I mean by 'Earth'
所謂地者
refers to its equalization of things
言其均物
So, they may not be disordered.
而不可亂者也.

Keynotes are their counsels,
音者其謀也,
Modes are their operations.
聲者其事也.
Keynotes are Heaven's five luminaries (*planets*),[186]
音者天之三[=五?]光也,
Modes are Earth's five offices.
聲者地之五官也.

When form and spirit are attuned,
形神調,
life's principles are cultivated.
則生理脩.

---

[184] *Hánshi Waìzhuàn* (IV) 172: Guân Zǐ's response to Duke Huán of Qí: What I mean by Heaven is not the blue-grey Heaven. Kings of the hundred clans contrive Heaven...

[185] *MWD* (Jiǔ-Zhǔ) 30: Yi Yîn said: "The *Record* says: 'Only Heaven conquers. All things are conquered." Zhì yuè: 'Weí Tian shèng. Fán wù yôu shèng.' 志曰惟天勝凡物有勝. 377n26 reads 'trace' (zhèn 朕) for 'conquest' (shèng 勝). *Huaínánzî* (XV 'Arms' Strategy' Binglyuè) 3a: All things have traces (are conquered), only the Way has no traces (is unconquered). Fán wù yôu zhèn= shèng? Weí Dào wúzhèn= shèng? 凡物有朕=勝? 惟道無朕=勝?

[186] I read ' five' (wû 五) for ' three' (san 三) luminaries, as in planets, to match the pentatonic scale. Cf. viii-c.

113

b) Trouble Ahead

Now when life's reproduction betrays its root,
夫生生而倍其本,
its virtues are monopolized by the self.
則德專己.
If knowledge lacks the Way,
知無道,
above, it will disorder the Heavenly Way,
上亂天文,
below, destroy Earthly principles,
下滅地理,
in the centre, disrupt human harmony.
中絕人和.

When governance is subverted from end to beginning,
治漸終始,
so on listening, nothing will be heard,
故聽,而無聞,
on looking, nothing will be seen.
視,而無見.
In plain daylight there will be darkness.
白晝而闇.

You have righteousness but lose emotive reality.
有義而失諡[=情?].
Losing reality, you are confused.[187]
失諡[=情?],而惑.
You demand from men what they lack,
責人所無,
compel men to do the impossible.
必人所不及.

Making histories of the bygone,
相史於既,
you do not exhaust your love.
而不盡其愛.
Constricted by past achievements,
相區於成,
you do not search out substance (*facts*).
而不索其實.

---

[187] I read (yì 諡) here as 'reality' (qíng 情). Defoort 1997: 29 takes it as 'posthumous titles' (shì) and sees an attack on Qín's decree in 221 abolishing such titles: "The neglect of official posthumous rewards in the form of titles causes, according to the author, real political confusion." However, in ix-e their use is denied only to the unworthy.

Empty names are honoured,
虛名相高,
pure white is taken as black.
精白爲黑.
Motion and rest in turn revolve,
動靜組轉,
spirits cut off, turn to rebel.
神絕,復逆.
When channels and energies are not of a kind,
經氣不類,
forms become divorced from their correct names.
形離正名.
When the five energies lose governance,[188]
五氣失端[=政],
the four seasons are not completed.
四時不成.

When errors are generated by superiors,
過生於上,
the incriminated die among subordinates.[189]
罪死於下.
When a generation is about to peak,
有世將極,
it charges and gallops about seeking disaster.
驅馳索禍.
It opens the door to flee from good fortune.
開門逃福.
The worthy and good are made a joke.
賢良爲笑.
Fools run the nation.
愚者爲國.

When heavenly censure is first revealed,
天咎先見,
calamity and harm come together.
菑害並雜.
From reliance on dynamics[190] omens are generated.
人埶[=任勢?]兆生.

---

[188] The five energies are presumably the five agents (elements). I read duan (端) here as taboo avoidance for zhèng (正), as previously.

[189] This exact couplet on unjust incrimination of subordinates recurs in iv-d and vii-b.

[190] Cf. *MWD Jingfǎ* (Guóci 45) 13a-b x2; Shíliù-jing (Guan 62) 86b-87a x2: rénshì 人埶 all in a negative sense. It appears to mean unbridled resort to force. (see Appendix I).

Who knows their limits?[191]
孰知其極?
'He who sees sun and moon
見日月者
is not considered keen-sighted.
不爲明.
He who hears thunder peals
聞雷霆者
is not considered of sharp-hearing.'[192]
不爲聰.
He who only after events happen deliberates
事至而議者
cannot prevent trouble's occurrence.
不能使變無生.

So, he who is expert at handling troubles
故,善度變者
looks to his root.
觀本.
If his root is adequate, they will be exhausted.
本足,則盡.
If inadequate, his virtue will necessarily be thin,
不足,則德必薄,
his arms necessarily depleted.
兵必老.

Who can with poor talent[193]
其執[=孰?]能以褊材
contrive to protect virtue and universal justice?
爲褒德博義者哉?
Though you be culturally skilled and martially resolute
其文巧武果
but still treasons do not cease,
而姦不止者,
they spring from your root being inadequate.
生於本不足也.

So, if the ruler is ambivalent in governance,
故,主有二政,
subjects are ambivalently controlled.
臣有二制.

---

[191] *Lâozǐ* (LVIII) has this question on the alternations of good and bad fortune.
[192] *Sunzǐ Bīngfǎ* (IV Xíng).
[193] I read shú (孰) 'who?' for zhí (執) 'hold' here. Cf. Wells 2001: 61-71.

When subjects will not work for him,
臣弗用,
the ruler cannot employ them.
主不能使.
When subjects are determined to die,
臣必死,
their ruler cannot prevent them[194]
主弗能止.

c) The Sage Messiah (cf. xviii-a Song of the Primal Sage)

Therefore, the Sage King alone sees
是以聖王獨見
to rule official appointments.
故主官以授.
Elders internally
長者在內
harmonise externally.
和者在外.
When elders contrive offices,
夫長者之爲官也,
internally there will be correct justice,
在內則正義,
externally it will be firmly protected.
在外則固守.
Law's application will be fair.
用法則平.
Law for men is rooted in no harm.
法人本無害.

In the governance of Heaven and Earth
以端天地
ordinances issue from one source[195]
令出一原
and are propagated in all directions.
散無方.

---

[194] Cf. *Lâozî* (LXXIV): When people do not fear death, why with death threaten them?

[195] Guânzî (LXXIII Guóxù) 359: Strong nations have one aperture, lost nations four. Shang jun Shu (III Nóngzhàn 'Farming and War') 10: when people see that superiors' profit from one hole issues, they work as one, mín jiàn shànglì-zhi cóng yi-kong chu-yê, zé zuò yi 民見上利之從壹空出也則作 壹. *Lyûshì Chunqiu* (XVII.7 Bù'èr) 16a: as if issuing from one hole, rú chu hu yi-xuè-zhê 如出乎一 穴者. *MWD* Shíliù-Jing (Chéngfâ) 72 123b: all issuing fromone hole, jie yuè yi-kong 皆閲一空.

The reformer of the myriad things
化萬物者
is ordinances.
令也.
Protector of the united Way,
守一道,
controller of the myriad things, is Law.
制萬物者,法也.

Law is what protects internally,
法也者守內者也,
ordinances are what control externally.[196]
令也者出制者也.
Now, Law does not defeat truth,[197]
夫法不敗是[=正],
ordinances do not harm principles.
令不傷理.

So, gentlemen will get to be honoured,
故君子得而尊,
small men will get to be prudent:
小人得而謹:
both together will get completion.
胥靡[不]得以全.

The gods will be prepared in mind,
神備於心,
the Way prepared in material form.
道備於形.
Men with them will complete their model,
人以成則,
knights will make them their guideline.
士以爲繩.

Arrayed seasons in sequence of energies
列時第氣
will be appointed according to name.
以授當名.
So, Law will be set up, shade and sunshine modulated.
故法錯, 而陰陽調.

---

[196] For parallelism and sense, I read 'externally' (wai 外) for 'control' (zhì 制).

[197] I take 'rectitude" (shì 是) here as a taboo avoidance for 'correct' (zhèng 正).

Phoenix is the Quail Fire bird. (*constellation of the south*)

鳳凰者鶉火之禽.

It is sunshine's (yáng) essence.[198]

陽之精也.

Unicorn is the Dark Hollow beast. (*constellation of the north*)

騏麟者元[=玄]枵之獸.

It is shade's (yin) essence.[199]

陰之精也.

Myriad people are virtue's essence.

萬民者德之精也.

If virtue can activate them,

德能致之,

their essences will altogether arrive.[200]

其精畢至.

Páng Zî said:

龐子曰:

To induce them, how can it be done?

致之奈何?

Héguan Zî said:

鶡冠子曰:

Heaven and Earth, shade and sunshine,

天地陰陽,

take their portents from the body.

取稽於身.

---

[198] Pankenier 2013: 197 notes the planet Jupiter in the Fire Bird constellation signaled the dynastic victory in battle of King Wû of Zhou over Shang. The equation of phoenix with Fire Bird has been ascribed to the Yí culture of southwest Sìchuan.

[199] Quail Fire is Chúnhuô, the south star; Dark/Prime Hollow, Xuán/Yuánxiao, the north star, otherwise associated with Dark Warrior. *Huaínánzî* (IV) 11b: Zodiac Horse [south sign] generates unicorns… Jiànmâ sheng Qílín…建馬生麒麟… See Figure 1, above.

[200] These beasts' appearance was believed to signal a political augury. *Lúnyû* (IX-8): Master said: 'Phoenix does not come, Yellow River puts forth no map. I am finished.' *Chunqiu*, Duke Ai (494-468) of Lû: 14th year (481), spring: West Hunt, caught unicorn. Xishôu huò lín 西狩獲麟. Zuôzhuàn: Confucius, seeing it, said: 'It is a unicorn' and took it. The annals, whose editorship is attributed to Confucius, end with this chapter. He died two years later. Cf. Gentz 2005: 227-254 on messianic reading of this passage in the Gongyáng commentary. Mencius (*Mèngzî* II-13) expected Heaven to send down a Sage King every five hundred years.

So, he will promulgate the Five Governances (*cf. viii-d*)
故布五正[=政]
To serve the Five Luminaries (*planets*).[201]
以司五明.

Ten transformations and Nine Ways,
十變九道,
their signs from the body start[202]
稽從身始.

Five tones and six pitchpipes,
五音六律,
their signs from the body issue.
稽從身始.

Five fives make twenty-five
五五二十五
to organize the Under-Heaven.
以理天下.
Six sixes make thirty-six
六六三十六
to contrive the year's format.
以爲歲式.
(*In 221, Qín divided the Under-Heaven into thirty-six commanderies/ provinces. Six was made the primal number. Shîjí VI, year 26, 42a*)

Energies from gods are born,
氣由神生,
the Way from gods is completed.
道由神成.

Only the Sage Man can
唯聖人能
correct their keynotes, tune their modes.
正其音調其聲.

---

[201] *MWD* Shíliù-jing (Wû-Zheng) 65, 91b: Promulgate the Five Governances to serve the Five Luminaries. Huáng 2004: 147, 153 cite 要篇 五正之事 不足以至之. Cf. xv-a.

[202] Lù Diàn commented: Great Yû from his voice made 'semi-tones', from his body made measurements. *MWD* Shíliù-jing (Wû-zhèng) 91a: It starts from his body…

So, his virtue above returns to Grand Purity,
故其德上反太清,
below reaches Grand Tranquillity,
下及泰寧,
in the centre reaches myriad souls.[203]
中及萬靈.

Fat dew will descend,
膏露降,
white cinnabar shoot forth.
白丹發.
Wine springs will issue,
醴泉出,
crimson flowers grow.
朱草生.
All portents will combine[204]
眾祥具.

So, a myriad mouths will declare
故萬口云
the imperial system's divine reformation and
帝制神化
lucky stars' radiant influence.
景星光潤.

By culture he will disarm the Under-Heaven's armies.
文則寢天下之兵.
In the war of the Under-Heaven's armies
武則天下之兵
none can withstand him.
莫能當.
Far from near, manifest from invisible,
遠之近,顯乎隱,
great from small, multitudes from few:
大乎小, 眾乎少:
none but from the subtle take their start.[205]
莫不從微始.

---

[203] 'Return' (fân 反) resembles 'reach' (jí 及). Lâozî (XXXIX), absent from Guodiàn ca. 300 BC Lâozî:
Heaven got unity to be pure (qing), Earth got unity to be tranquil (níng). Gods got unity to be magical
(líng), valleys got unity to be filled (yíng), myriad things got unity to live (sheng), baron-kings got unity
to be the Under-Heaven's governors (zhèng). Guânzî (XLIX Neìyè) 271: He mirrors great purity
(qing), observes great brilliance (míng)...

[204] Lâozî (XXXII): Heaven and Earth will join together to send down sweet dew. Huaínánzî (VIII
Bênjing) 1b: on the lucky auguries of Grand Purity's start.

[205] Xúnzî (V Fei Xiàng 'Against Appearances') 72: So it is said: From the near know the distant, from
the one know myriads, from the subtle know the manifest...

So, all that by getting him will be achieved
故得之所成
may not be exhaustively described.
不可勝形.
All that by losing him will be ruined
失之所敗
may not be exhaustively named.
不可勝名.

From here on,
從是往者,
you, sir, cannot exhaustively enquire about it.
子弗能勝問.
It is also beyond what I can express.
吾亦弗勝言.
In all questions of importance,
凡問之要,
desire near knowledge to become far sighted,
欲近知而遠見,
from one to fathom myriads.
以一度萬也.

Without the desire for it, a lord
無欲之君
may not participate in its undertakings.
不可與舉.
If worthies are not employed by him,
賢人不用,
he cannot cause them to make the nation profit[206]
弗能使國利.
This is most important.
此其要也.

d) Five Governances
Páng Zî said:
龐子曰:
I venture to ask about the Five Governances.
敢問五正.

---

[206] *Mèngzî* (Ia.1) disapproved a ruler's wish to "profit his kingdom." Lù Diàn expresses puzzlement at Pheasant Cap's approbation of 'desire'. He cites *Mèngzî*, *Lâozî* and *Zhuangzî* on controlling desires, with *Guíguzî* on exploiting desires in others.

Héguan Zî said:
鶡冠子曰;
　　There is the divinely **Reformative**,
　　有神化,
　　there is **Bureaucrative** governance,
　　有官治,
　　there is **Educative** governance,
　　有教治,
　　there is **Adaptative** governance,
　　有因治,
　　there is **Operative** governance.
　　有事治.

Páng Zî said:
龐子曰:
　　I wish to hear their forms.
　　願聞其形.

Héguan Zî said:
　`鶡冠子曰:
　　The divinely Reformative is in the future,
　　神化者於未有,
　　Bureaucrative governance is at the Way's root,
　　官治者道於本,
　　Educative governance is at the self,
　　教治者脩諸己,
　　Adaptative governance does not alter customs,
　　因治者不變俗,
　　Operative governance corrects at the periphery.
　　事治者矯之於末.

Páng Zî said:
龐子曰:
　　I wish to hear of their operations.
　　願聞其事.

Héguan Zî said:
鶡冠子曰:
　　The divinely Reformative
　　神化者
　　settles Heaven and Earth,
　　定天地,
　　anticipates the four seasons, controls shade and sunshine,
　　豫四時,拔陰陽,
　　shifts cold and heat.
　　移寒暑.

It corrects streams, unites the living.
正流並生.
Myriad beings are not harmed,
萬物無害,
Myriad species are complete and entire.
萬類成全.
Its name is embodied by the energy of Augustans.[207]
名尸氣皇.

Bureaucrative governance
官治者
takes as teachers the shady and sunny,
師陰陽,
responds to what is yet to be.
應將然.
Earth will be tranquil, Heaven clear.
地寧天澄.
A multitude of good will come home to it.
眾美歸焉.
Its name is embodied by Divine Luminaries.
名尸神明.

Educative governance
教治者
ordains the four seasons' operations,
置四時事,
achieves compliance with the Way.
功順道.
Its name is embodied by worthy Sages.
名尸賢聖.

Adaptative governance
因治者
summons worthy Sages,
招賢聖,

---

[207] 'Embodied', literally 'encorpsed', shi 尸 means the 'corpse' impersonated by an actor at funerals. It likely embraced the practice of spirit-possession by mediums. 'Its name is embodied by Divine Luminaries' in the following verse recurs in xi-a, and three times with variation as 'with Divine Luminaries embodying governance' yǔ shénmíng tǐ zhèng 與神明體正 in ix-b x2 and ix-g. *Zhuangzǐ* (VII Ying Dìwáng, 'Fit for Emperors and Kings') 307: Non-contrivance is named as 'embodiment'. Wúweí míng shi. 無爲名尸. Cf. Seaman 1987: 12ff.

makes a Way of mind technique,[208]
而道心術,
respects employments to generate harmony.
敬事生和.
Its name is embodied by baron-kings.[209]
名尸后(=侯?)王.

Operative governance summons humane Sages
事治者招仁聖
so the Way is known from them.
而道知焉.
It gathers their essence to herd spirits,
苟精牧神,
divides offices, completes insignia.
分官成章.
Its teaching is bitter, its profits distant.
教苦, 利遠.
Law's system is generated from it.
法制生焉.

Law causes people
法者使
to reject self for the sake of the public.[210]
去私就公.
It shares knowledge, unifies admonishments,
同知,壹警,
So all have common motives.
有同由者也.
It condemns conduct that is selfish,
非行私,
Causing men to join together and share.
而使人合同者也.
So, ultimate governance is not by this.
故,至治者弗由而[=是?].
Its name is embodied by duke hegemons.[211]
名尸公伯[=霸].

---

[208] 'Mind technique' (xinshù 心術) covers quasi-Daoist meditational practices. Cf. ix-x. *Guânzî*: (XXXVI-XXXVII Xinshù; XXXVIII Báixin; XLIX Neìyè).

[209] 'Baron-kings' (hóuwáng) date from the fourth century when barons began to call themselves kings. It occurs five times in *Lâozî* (XXXII, XXXVII, XXXIX 3x). Otherwise, it is used in 221 by Qín Shî Huángdì (*Shîjì* VI: Year 26) dì-43a.

[210] *Hánfeizî* (VI Yôudù) 22. *MWD* Jing fâ (Dàofâ 43) 7b; (Sì-Dú 51) 44a: reject the selfish (private) to establish the public qusi, ér lìgong 去私而立公. Cf. vi-c.

[211] Five Duke Hegemons ruled in turn during the *Chunqiu*, 'Spring and Autumn Annals', period (770-476) which followed the collapse of royal Zhou's central power.

ix. ROYAL AXE (Wángfu 王鈇第九)

Nine, being the highest digit, odd 'sunny' (yáng) number and homonym for 'long-lasting' (jiû 久) symbolizes the universe. Here Pheasant Cap introduces us to the 18,000-year series of the Complete Ninth (Chéngjiû 成鳩), nine written as 'dove' (jiu) bird. This auspicious ninth chapter presents a transcendental blueprint for the Complete Ninth's mandate by which they will realize divine justice on Earth. Its endorsement of 'one lineage' (zú) implies a dynasty, though it ends: "what does it matter from what clan he is?" It may imply nine thousand years of past nine Heavenly Augustans are to be matched by a future series of Earthly Augustans with equal longevity.[212]

According to received lore, primeval Sage Kings were not succeeded by offspring but abdicated to the most worthy, as Yáo abdicated to Shùn (xiii-b). Thus, in an ideal world like Plato's Republic, "the superior worthy becomes Heaven's Son." Yet the lesson ends with an escape-clause allowing a hereditary monarch, though unworthy, to avoid doom if he "receives teaching." (xi-b)

The royal axe (i-a,-b, ix-f), like the Roman fasces, is the symbol of mandate and punitive empowerment. This text uniquely preserves five punctuation marks, perhaps showing its importance to imperial rule. We see five new virtues: sincerity, goodfaith, adaptation, illumination, and unity. The terminology 'Heaven's melodies' (tianqû 天曲) and 'Solar numerology' (rìshù 日術=數) is unique. Their solar calendrical scheduling correlates seasons with five notes and bi-months with six whole-tones. Concern is shown to protect the environment and myriad beings. Yet their draconian penalties, centralized organization and references to war, are closer to Qín than utopia. (ix-c)

The regional control system attributed to seventh century Qí premier Guân Zhòng has a similar calendar. He employs the same term 'warehouser' (sèfu 嗇夫), title of district officer under Zhou, used here (ix-c).[213] Qín tombs, excavated at Shuîhûdì (Yúnmèng, Húbeî) from 1973, have yielded a host of bamboo documents detailing the administration, legal jurisdiction, religious observances and personal life of imperial Qín's 'warehouser' officialdom.[214] 'Warehousing' as a verb is used by Lâozî as a metaphor for 'accumulation of virtue', and governance as here. (ix-b)[215]

---

[212] Cf. *Shîjì* (VI Bênjì) Qín Shíhuáng year 26, 221 BC, on the three grades of 'Augustan'.

[213] *Guânzî* (XLI Wû-Xíng) 243-244. (IV Lìzhèng, 'Shôuxián') 10-11; (XXXIX Junchén- shàng) 162 'sèfu'.

[214] Lewis 2014: 195-205. Yates 1995: 331-365. Qiu Xigui 1981: 226-302. Gao Mîn 1979: 185-200.

[215] *Lâozî* LXIX. *Lyûshì Chunqiu* (II.3); *Hánfeizî* (XX Jiê Lâo).

a) The Complete Ninth

Páng Zî questioned Héguan Zî, saying:

龐子問鶡冠子,曰:

> The Grand Superior Complete Ninth's Way,
>
> 泰上成鳩之道,
>
> one clan will use for 18,000 years
>
> 一族用之萬八千歲
>
> to have the Under-Heaven.[216]
>
> 有天下.
>
> Their arms being strong,
>
> 兵強,
>
> for generations they may not be usurped,
>
> 世不可奪,
>
> with Heaven and Earth they will be preserved.
>
> 與天地存.
>
> Eternal and absolutely beyond compare,
>
> 久絕無倫,
>
> all marvel in wonder at them.
>
> 齊殊異之.
>
> 'Things' are inadequate to describe them
>
> 物不足以命
>
> because they are mutually removed from them and not the same.
>
> 其相去之不同也.
>
> In this generation there are none who do not speak of
>
> 世莫不言
>
> inculcating morals and instituting reforms.
>
> 樹俗立化.
>
> What Way do they alone practice
>
> 彼獨何道之行
>
> to implement these?
>
> 以至於此?

---

[216] Lù Diàn cites a 'Chronicle' (Zhuàn): When Heaven and Earth were first established, Heaven's Augustan Unity was called Heavenly Soul (Tiānlíng). He ruled for 18,000 years. Lìdài Shénxiān Tóngjiàn (I:1.3a): Heavenly Augustan took the hexagenary symbols (ganzhi 干支) he had created and set them on months and days times to record their order and cyclical return... Heavenly Augustan was in the world 18,000 years.

Héguan Zî said:

鶡冠子曰:

He of the Complete Ninth clan is Heavenly:[217]

彼成鳩氏天:

so none can increase his height or elevate his soul.

故莫能增其高尊其靈.

Páng Zî said:

龐子曰:

What do you mean 'of Heaven'? What is he like,

何謂天? 何若,

that none can increase his height or elevate his soul?

而莫能增其高尊其靈?

Héguan Zî said:

鶡冠子曰:

Heaven is sincerity, the sun is its virtue (*rewards*).[218]

天者誠,其日德也.

The sun sincerely comes out, sincerely goes in.

日誠出,誠入.

At south and north it has its poles.

南北有極.

So, none but take it as Law's model.

故,莫弗以爲法則.

Heaven is faithfulness, the moon is its form (*penalties*).

天者信,其月刑也.

The moon faithfully dies, faithfully is born.

月信死,信生.

It ends then has a beginning.

終則有始.

So, none but by it contrive governance.

故,莫弗以爲政.

---

[217] At this point the text has a 'punctuation mark' (jù 句). Such marks rarely survive in received classical texts but are seen in excavated manuscripts.

[218] The following four quatrains from 'Heaven is sincerity' to 'necessity (bì 必) is Heaven's mandate' are close to *MWD* (*Jīngfǎ*: Lùn) 53, 50b. Cf. iii-a; x-a fns 247-248. Appendix I. According to tradition, mentioned in *Wèiliáozî* (I) ca. 300 BC, the Yellow Emperor conquered by 'punishments and rewards' xíngdé 刑德, here equated with moon and sun, also with bad and good omens. Ref. Sawyer 1993: 230-232, 242-243.

Heaven is luminary, the stars are its signs:
天者明,星其稽也:
its constellations are not disorderly.
列星不亂.
Each in precedence moves.
各以序行.
So, great and small are all in it manifested.
故,小大莫弗以章.

Heaven adapts to the seasons,
天者因時,
they are its model.
其則也.
The four seasons according to their names
四時當名
succeed each other and do not clash.
代而不干.
So, there is nobody that does not take it as necessity.[219]
故,莫弗以爲必然.

Heaven unifies by making Law uniform:[220]
天者一法其同也:
front and rear, left and right,
前後,左右,
past and present are naturally so.
古今自如.
There are none who do not take it as constant.
故莫弗以爲常.

Heaven is sincerity and faithfulness.
天誠信.
Its illumination is based on unity.
明因一.

It will not for the multitude of fathers change unity.[221]
不爲眾父易一.

---

[219] *MWD Jingfǎ* (Lùn) 53, 50b: Necessity is Heaven's mandate, Bì-zhê Tian-zhi mìng-yê. 必者天之命也.

[220] Cf. *Mòzǐ* (XII Shàngtóng-zhong) on 'equality' (tóng).

[221] *Lǎozǐ* (XXI) 'multitude of fathers' (zhòng fù 眾父) appears synonymous with 'hundred fathers' in ix-g. It is more respectful than 'multitude of men' (zhòngrén) in xii-d, xvii-e.

So, none can with it contend for precedence.
故,莫能與爭先.
Changeable unity is not unity.
易一非一.
So, it may not be elevated or increased.
故,不可尊增.
The Complete Ninth gets unity,
成鳩得一,
so none but aspire to be controlled by it.
故莫不仰制焉.

b) His System and Signs
Páng Zî said:
龐子曰:
I wish to hear of their system.
願聞其制.

Héguan Zî said:
鶡冠子曰:
The Complete Ninth's system
成鳩之制
with Divine Luminaries embodies governance.
與神明體正.
Its divine illumination plumbs the depths
神明者下究
and ascends to the limits.
而上際.
It is able to warehouse myriad things
克嗇萬物
yet not be satiated.
而不可猒者也.
It universally pervades, everywhere shines,
周泊遍照,
returning with Heaven and Earth to consummate.[222]
反與天地總.

---

[222] Lâozî (LIX): To govern men and serve Heaven, there is nothing like warehousing. Now just warehousing means early submission. Early submission means heavy accumulation of virtue. MWD Jing fâ (Lùn) 53,48a: with Heaven and Earth consummated yû Tiandì zông 與天地總.

So, it can contrive for the Under-Heaven to plan.
故能爲天下計.
Illumined in foreknowledge,
明於蚤識,
from afar it clarifies beyond doubt
逢曰[=逺白?]不惑

salvation and doom's omens,
存亡之祥,
security and danger's signs.
安危之稽.

Páng Zî said:
龎子曰:
I wish to hear of its signs.
願聞其稽.

Héguan Zî said:
鶡冠子曰:
If you set the foundations insecurely:-[223]
置下不安,
the super-structure may not be supported.
上不可以載.
When piled adequately,
累其足也,
a superstructure that does not stand erect has never existed.
其最高而不植局者未之有也.
It discerns human realities,
辯於人情
researches things' principles,
究物之理.
Assesses by Heaven and Earth.
稱於天地.
Its dismissals and appointments will not be endangered.
廢置不殆.
It researches mountains and streams
審於山川
for transport and stations,
而運動舉錯,
inspecting that living things are unharmed,
有檢生物無害,
contriving to be as their father and mother.
爲之父母.
Nothing is trampled on.
無所躪蹂.

---

[223]   At this point the received text has a 'punctuation mark' (jù 句).

Humane in taking and giving,
仁於取予,
fully prepared to teach the Way,
備於教道,
concise in speech and discourse,
要於言語,
faithful in contractual agreements.
信於約束.
What has been agreed will not be usurped.
已諾不專.

Its delights and angers are not excessive,
喜怒不增,
its arms are not martial,
其兵不武,
it implants to contrive customs.
樹以爲俗.
Its reforms issue from this.
其化出此.

Páng Zî said: I wish to hear how
龐子曰:願聞
his humane realism and things' principles
其人情物理
warehouse the myriad things,
所以嗇萬物,
with Heaven and Earth to consummate,
與天地總,
with Divine Luminaries to embody governances's Way?
與神明體正之道.

Héguan Zî said:
鶡冠子曰:
The Complete Ninth's Way has never departed from
成鳩氏之道未有離
Heaven's Melody and Solar Numbering.
天曲日術[=數]者.
Heaven Melody illumines and is easy to follow,
天曲者明而易循也,
Solar Numbering is concise and easy to implement.
日術[=數]者要而易行也.

c) Control by Commanderies and Districts

Páng Zî said:

龐子曰：

>I wish to hear of Heaven's Melody and Solar Numbering.
>
>願聞天曲日術.

Héguan Zî said:[224]

鶡冠子曰：

>To control cities and organize the capital
>
>其制邑理都
>
>employ supervisors.
>
>使曈習者.
>
>Five households make a quintet,
>
>五家爲伍,
>
>each quintet has an elder for it.
>
>伍爲之長.
>
>Ten quintets make a hamlet,
>
>十伍爲里,
>
>each hamlet appoints an officer.
>
>里置有司.
>
>Four hamlets make a district,
>
>四里爲扁,
>
>each district has an elder.
>
>扁爲之長.
>
>Ten districts make a township,
>
>十扁爲鄉,
>
>each township appoints a teacher.
>
>鄉置師,
>
>Five townships make a county,
>
>五鄉爲縣,
>
>each county has a warehouser to govern it.
>
>縣有嗇夫治焉.
>
>Ten counties make a commandery (province),
>
>十縣爲郡,
>
>having a minister to protect it.
>
>有大夫守焉.
>
>Their mandate is officialdom's bureaucracy.
>
>命曰官屬.

---

[224] *Guânzî* (XX Xiâokuang) 220-224, and *Guóyû* (VI Qíyû) 4-7, describe in similar terms the pyramidal organization of seventh century BC reformer Guân Zhòng, premier of Qí to Hegemon King Huán. Each has differences in names and detail, but both start from the unit of five households and divide the state into twenty-one districts. *Héguanzî* lacks their description of recruitment and promotion by 'Triple Selection' (San- Xuân).

Commandery ministers withdraw to manage their assigned
counties,
郡大夫退脩其屬縣,
warehousers withdraw to manage their townships,
嗇夫退脩其鄉,
township teachers withdraw to manage their districts,
鄉師退脩其扁,
district elders withdraw to manage their hamlets,
扁長退脩其里,
hamlet officers withdraw to manage their quintets,
里有司退脩其伍,
quintet elders withdraw to manage their households.
伍長退脩其家.

In employments, they admonish and correct,
事相斥正,
in their dwellings, they mutually inspect.
居處相察,
going out and coming they mutually supervise.
出入相司.
Fathers with fathers speak of righteousness,
父與父言義,
sons with sons speak of filialty.
子與子言孝.
Elders speak of goodness,
長者言善,
the young speak of respect.
少者言敬.
From dawn to dusk they mutually inculcate these
旦夕相薰蒸以此 kind and filial
tasks. 慈孝之務.

If there is any shift or move,
若有所移徙去就,
household with household mutually receives,
家與家相受,
men with men mutually hand over.
人與人相付.
Absconders and stolen property
亡人姦物
have nowhere to disappear or escape.
無所穿窬.

This is humane realism and things' principles.
此其人情物理也.

If in a quintet men are unreasonable and
伍人有勿故
disobey superiors' orders,
不奉上令,
if there is excess or deficiency
有餘不足
in their dwellings' circumstances,
居處之狀,
and do not always report to the hamlet officer:
而不輒以告里有司:
it means a disorderly household.
謂之亂家.
It incriminates the quintet elders equally.
其罪伍長以同.

If in a hamlet there are those
里中有
who do not respect elders or are unkind to the young,
不敬長慈少,
if they exceed their class or differ from the multitude,
出等異眾,
unheeding father and elder brother's teaching,
不聽父兄之教,
if they receive or hear anything
有所受聞
which they do not entirely report to the district elder:
不悉以告扁長:
it means a disorderly hamlet.
謂之亂里.
It incriminates its officer and implicates his household.
其罪有司而貳其家.

If a district does not punctually
扁不以時
comply by action with instructions,
循行教誨,
if it receives or hears anything
受聞
which it does not entirely report to the town teacher,
不悉以告鄉師,
it means a disorderly district.
謂之亂扁.
It incriminates its district elder and implicates his household.
其罪扁長而貳其家.

If a township does not punctually
鄉不以時
comply by action with instructions,
循行教誨,
if it receives or hears anything
受聞
which it does not entirely report to the county warehouser,
不悉以告縣嗇夫,
it means a disorderly township.
謂之亂鄉.
It incriminates the township teacher and implicates his household.
其罪鄉師而貳其家.

If a county warehouser does not punctually
縣嗇夫不以時
comply by action with instructions,
循行教誨,
if he receives or hears anything
受聞
which he does not entirely report to the commandery,
不悉以告郡,
if good deeds are not publicized,
善者不顯,
it is mandated as 'covering up the light'.
命曰蔽明.

If evil is hidden,
見惡而隱,
it is mandated as 'subordinate complicity.'
命曰下比,
It means a disorderly county:
謂之亂縣:
execution of the warehouser without reprieve.
其誅嗇夫無赦.

If a commandery minister does not comply
郡大夫不以
by action with instructions,
循行教誨,
if he receives or hears anything which, though factual,
受聞,雖實,
has any errors or omissions
有所遺脫

which he does not entirely report to the premier of the nation,
不悉以教柱國,
it means a disorderly commandery:
謂之亂郡:
execution of the commandery minister without reprieve.
其誅郡大夫無赦.

If the premier of the nation does not govern,
柱國不政,
so subordinates' real feelings are not by superiors heard
使下情不上聞
and superior's real feelings are not by subordinates followed,
上情不下究,
it means negligence in governance:
謂之綠政:
execution of the premier of the nation,
其誅柱國
annihilation of family and extermination of clan.
滅門殘疾[=族?].

If the chief magistrate
令尹
does not adjust the seasons in accord with Earth,
不宜時合地,
harming the hundred clans,
害百姓者,
it means disordering the Under-Heaven,
謂之亂天下:
dismemberment of the chief magistrate
其軫令尹
and exposure of his body.
以狥.

This is the means of warehousing things.
此其所以嗇物也.

d) Solar Reporting Periods

Heaven employs four seasons
天用四時.
Earth uses five agents ('elements').
地用五行.
Heaven's Son holds unity
天子執一
to sit on the central axis.
以居中央.

He modulates by five keynotes (terms),
調以五音,
governs by six pitchpipes (*bi-monthly periods*),
正以六律,
organizes by graded numbers,
紀以度數,
reigns by penalties (*forms*) and rewards (*virtues*).
宰以刑德.

From root to tip,
從本至末,
he proceeds by the 'ten heavenly stems' (*jiayi, ten-day week*).
第以甲乙.

Heaven starts from New Year's day (*of solar year*),
天始於元,
Earth starts from the new moon. (*lunar months*)
地始於朔.
The four seasons start from the calendar.
四時始於歷.

So, households and hamlets use five days (*5 x 72 = 360*).
故家里用提.
District elders use ten days (*10 x 36 = 360*).
扁長用旬.
Township teachers use fifteen days (*15 x 24 = 360*).[225]
鄉師用節.
County warehousers use months (*30 x 6 = 360*).
縣嗇夫用月.
Provincial ministers use forty-five day energy periods
(*45 x 8 = 360*).
郡大夫用氣分.

---

[225] The twenty-four 'solar nodes' of fifteen days is still used by farmers, adjusted to coincide with solstices and equinoxes. Cf. *Huaínánzî* III-6ff. Needham 1956: 404. Bodde 1975: 28ff.

These extend to the premier of the nation
所至柱國
who uses the six pitchpipes.
(60 x 6 = 360 i.e. bi-monthly periods)[226]
用六律.

Hamlets every five days report to the district,
里五日報扁,
Districts every ten days report to the township,
扁十日報鄉,
Townships every fifteen days report to the county,
鄉十五日報縣,
Counties every thirty days report to the commandery,
縣三十日報郡,
Provinces every forty-five days report to premier of the nation.
郡四十五日報柱國.

The premier of the nation every sixty days
柱國六十日
has an audience with Heaven's Son.
以聞天子.
Heaven's Son every seventy-two days despatches an envoy
天子七十二日遣[=遣]使
to encourage those who have achievements,
勉有功,
and punish those who have not complied:[227]
罰不如:
this is how he with Heaven and Earth's consummates.
此所以與天地總.

---

[226] Six Pitchpipes (liù-lyù 六律) represent the whole tones in the octave from Yellow Bell I, Great Gathering (D), Maidens Washing I, Flowery Festival (F#), Level Rule (G#) to Non-satiation (A#). These tones were paired with the odd numbered months in six bi-monthly periods. Calendars in Lǐjì (Yuèlìng) and *Lyûshì Chunqiu* (Jì I.12) pair the twelve months with this overlapping series of six yáng whole-tones and six yin whole-tones, calculated by the cycle of perfect fifths. Prince Zhu Zàiyù in late Míng famously discovered the method of equal temperament to calculate them as twelve equal semi-tones within the octave, overcoming the discrepancy of the Pythagorean comma but his method was not adopted by state ritual. The year of 6 x 60 = 360 days would fit the primacy given by the First Emperor to the number six. (*Shǐjì* VI, year 26, 42a)

[227] A 'punctuation mark' (jù 句) survives in the received text. *Guânzǐ* (XLI Wǔ-Xíng) 243-244 similarly divides the year into 5 x 72-day periods.

Subordinate's realities are every sixty days
下情六十日
once to superiors reported (*60 x 6 = 360 days*).
一上聞.
Superiors' favours are every seventy-two days
上惠七十二日
once for subordinates reviewed. (*72 x 5 = 360 days*)
一下究.

These are Heaven's Melody and Solar Numbering.
此天曲日術也.

e) Reformation of Customs

So, the unworthy do not lose their baseness
故不肖者不失其賤
and the worthy do not lose their luminance.
而賢者不失其明.

Superiors enjoy their good-fortunes and emoluments
上享其福祿
and an hundred employments are rationalised.
而百事理.

Actions of treachery do not profit.,
行畔者不利.
So, no one can diminish his strength.
故,莫能撓其強.

Consequently, he can rule in fullness and not overflow.[228]
是以能治滿而不溢.

---

[228] 'To hold fullness and not overflow' was a general concern of the elite. Cf. *Xiaojing, Xúnzǐ* (XXVIII Yòuzuò) 593. A sacred vessel in the ancestral was pivoted to overturn when filled beyond a certain point as a warning.

He restrains the great and is not injured.
縮大而不芒.
Heaven's Son is centred and correct.
天子中正.

If envoys dare to alter messages,
使者敢易言,
if the noble enlarge their areas for profit,
尊益區域使利,
if they suppress subordinates or deceive superiors: (*Cf. iv-a, vii-c*)
逼下蔽上:
their penalty is beheading or chastisement without reprieve.
其刑斬笞無赦.

When officials teach harshly with virtue slight,
諸吏教苦德薄,
invade or violate the hundred clans,
侵暴百姓,
they are always dismissed and not employed.
輒罷毋使.

When corrupt officials disorder government
汙官亂治
by disobeying orders or breaking the Law,
不奉令犯法,
their guilt is increased.
其罪加.

The people are profited but do not take profit,
民利而不取利,
they are rotated and do not take precedence.
運而不取次.
So, the four quadrants follow him,
故四方從之,
Just fearing to be last to arrive.
唯恐後至.

Consequently, rotating Heaven's wefts are spread,
是以運天而維張,
Earth is broad and virtues displayed.
地廣而德章.
The Under-Heaven is at peace and happy.
天下安樂.

It will set up annual bestowal of prosperity,
設年予昌,
Assigning to each in uniformity,
屬各以一,
Seasonally regulating the most superior.
時典最上.

If a worthy does not accord with the chief magistrate,
賢不如令尹,
the chief magistrate holds a hearing.
令尹以聞.
The first, and second time, he demotes his office.
壹再削職,
The third time, he does not reprieve.
三則不赦.

Governance by not overstepping offices
治不踰官
causes officials and clerks not to err.
使史李不誤.
Public markets are contrived fairly.
公市爲平.

The living do not rejoice,
生者不喜,
the dead are not resentful.
死者不怨.

Men get what they desire,
人得所欲,
the nation has no revolutions.
國無變故.
Publicly rewarded achievers will have
著賞有功
virtues (blessings) extending to the third generation.
德及三世.

A father convicted of crime
父伏其辜
will not get created a posthumous title[229]
不得創謐.

---

[229] Posthumous titles were used for revered ancestors in remembrance services. The First Emperor abolished all posthumous titles on the grounds that they involved juniors passing judgement on their seniors.

Operations begin from one and two
事從一二,
Throughout all ages they will not be subverted.
終古不勃.

He reckons that to do good in a township
彼計為善於鄉,
is not as good as to do good in a hamlet;
不如為善於里
to do good in a hamlet
為善於里
not as good as to do good in a household.
不如為善於家.

Consequently, those who do good
是以為善者
May get advancement.
可得舉.
Those who do evil
為惡者
May get executed,
可得誅.

None dare to make a way of one day's good;
莫敢道一旦之善,
All for a lifetime's good contrive to aim.
皆以終身為期.

Customs do not lose precedence.
素無失次.
So, reforms are established
故,化立
and the generation has no evils.
而世無邪.

When reforms are established and morality complete,
化立俗成,
the young share with their peers.
少則同儕.
Elders share with friends,
長則同友,
travellers share provisions.
遊敖同品.

In prayers and sacrifices they share good-fortune,
祭祀同福,
in death and life they share love.
死生同愛.
In disaster and catastrophe, they share worries,
禍災同憂,
in their dwellings they share pleasures.
居處同樂.

In action and work they share harmoniously.
行作同和.
In mourning and celebration they share rites,
吊賀同雜[=禮?],
in weeping they share grief.
哭泣同哀.

Their joys are sufficient for mutual encouragement.
驩欣足以相助.
Sagely admonitions are sufficient for mutual restraint.
聖謀[=牒?]足以相止.

In peace, they mutually exercise.
安平相馴.
Army brigades mutually protect.
軍旅相保.
In night battles, they are sufficient for mutual trust.
夜戰,則足以相信.
In day battles, they are sufficient for mutual support.[230]
晝戰,則足以相配.

Internally, they prohibit violence,
入,以禁暴,
Externally, they 'correct' those who lack the Way.
出,正無道.

Consequently,
是以,
their arms can march across to execute and punish
其兵能橫行誅伐
and none will dare resist.
而莫之敢禦.

So, their penalties are set up but not applied.
故其刑設而不用.
They do not dispute yet authority is weighty.
不爭而權重.

Chariots and armour are not deployed,
車甲不陳,
yet Under-Heaven they have no match!
而天下無敵矣!

If they lose the Way,
失道,
commoners will dare to defy the noble.
則賤敢逆貴.

Under injustice,
不義,
the small will dare encroach on the great.[231]
則小敢侵大.

Once the Complete Ninth appears,
成鳩既見,
as superior generations' successor,
上世之嗣
he who has lost the Way's achievements is doomed for
失道亡功[=功亡?]
distorting its root and destroying virtue's model.
倍本滅德之則.

So, he will contrive an undecaying nation
故,爲之不朽之國
by settling positions securely.
定位牢.
In prayer he will summon demons and gods.
祭使鬼神.

---

[230] This whole passage on communal cooperation closely parallels *Guânzî* (XX Xiâokuang) 123.
[231] cf. *Hánfeizî* (VI Yôudú) on using heavy penal law to prevent such infractions.

On abdication, he will say:

亶[禪?]曰:

'Augmented compasses are not circular.

'增規不圓.

'Expanded set-squares are not square.'

'增矩不方.'

[*Heaven circular and Earth square, symbols of perfect forms, have their limits. See also xi-a, xviii-b.*]

So, they set examples to future generations

夫以效末傳

for sons and grandsons.

之子孫.

Only this may be held,

唯此可持,

only this may be undertaken.

唯此可將.

Those who undertake it nourish good-fortune,

將者養吉,

those who abandon it are ill-omened.

釋者不祥.

Abdication wil be the fulfillment of sacrifice,[232]

墠[=禪?]以全犧,

governance is the fasting of illumination.

正[=政?]以齋明.

At the four seasons we worship him

四時享之

by libations as household king

祀以家王

to contrive divine sustenance.

以爲神享.

---

[232] I read 'terrace-platform' (shàn 墠) here in the sense of 'abdication' (shàn 禪).

Ritual spirit tallies are
禮靈之符
stored in the ancestral temple
藏之宗廟
as seals to validate (*'correct'*) them.
以璽正諸.

So, in subsequent generations
故,其後世之
preservation of his teaching will be entire[233]
保教也全!

When ears and eyes do not function,
耳目不營,
you use your mind undividedly.
用心不分.

You will not look at strange things
不見異物
nor deviate from sacrificing selfishness,
而遷捐私.
Inwardedly discriminating,
於內哲,
You will be steadfast in what you protect.
固於所守.

f) Primal Renaissance

He will restart a renewal
更始逾新
from the superior prime to contrive his era.
上元爲紀.

His successors will undertake in excellent benevolence,
其承嘉惠,
in equal height, unaltered,
相高,不改,
to abdicate generation by generation in entirety.
亶[=禪?]昭穆具.
(*Generations in a lineage were enshrined in alternating 'sunny and shady', zhaomù, sides of their ancestral temple.*)

---

[233] At this point the received text has a 'punctuation mark' jù 句.

Summoned knights are first pledged to him.
招士先結之.
After entry do not unpledged.
後入,弗解.
They know the ultimate's extent.
此知極之至也.

Páng Zî said:
龐子曰:
I wish to hear why they do not alter
願聞所以不改
or restart renewal of the Way.
更始逾新之道.

Héguan Zî said:
鶡冠子曰:
The Complete Ninth means
成鳩所謂
getting the Royal Axe's transmission.
得王鈇之傳者也.

Páng Zî said:
龐子曰:
What is meant by the Royal Axe?
何謂王鈇?

Héguan Zî said:
鶡冠子曰:
The Royal Axe is not one generation's weapon.[234]
王鈇者非一世之器也.
In death it follows life,
以死遂生,
from the centre it controls the exterior.
從中制外.
Its teaching,
之教也,
subsequent generations will complete,
後世成,
extending to grandchildren as one.
至孫一.

---

[234] This develops the opening line of i-a, and i-b above.

Spirit feathers will be arrayed,[235]

靈羽理,

tallies daily ordered.

符日循.

The clever will not dare spoil it.[236]

功[巧?]弗敢敗.

It will sustain enterprises, research administrations,

奉業,究制,

maintain governance, guard the interior.

執正,守內.

The stupid will not dare abolish it.

拙弗敢廢.

Towers and pavilions will be erected[237]

樓閣與旱[=興建?],

by the new to continue the old.

以新續故.

Through the four seasons their foundation will be efficacious,

四時執[=勢/設?]效,

responding securely, not over-bearing.

應錮不駿[=峻?].

If the empress gets to enter the temple,

后得入廟,

doubts will disturb the succession.

惑爽不嗣.

It would mean burning (*promiscuity?*).

謂之焚(=婪?).

The ancestral mandate would be falsified in the generation,

祖命冒世,

ritual succession discontinued.

禮嗣弗引.

If employment of constants is not observed in the harem,

奉常弗內,

spirits would not eat offerings.

靈不食祀.

---

[235] 'Spirit feathers are arrayed' líng yǔ lǐ 靈羽理 may refer to the long pheasant feathers used in temple ritual dances and spirit possession trances. Cf. Seaman 1987: 12ff on spirit medium cults.

[236] I read 'achievement' (gong 功) as 'clever' (qiǎo 巧) to contrast with 'stupid' (zhuó) 拙, below.

[237] From the initial graph and profile of the following three which appear to make no sense, I tentatively reconstruct: 'towers and pavilions will be erected' lóugé xing jiàn 樓閣興建for this impenetrable line lóucuò yǔhàn 樓剒與旱.

If, in his household, a king did not raise sacrifices,
家王不舉祭,
then Heaven would send down censure.
天將降咎.
The Augustan gods would not be feasted.
皇神不享.
Then there would be no alternative
此所以不改
to restarting a renewal of the Way. (*i.e. revolution*)
更始逾新之道也.

g) Utopian Society

So, when the ruler has no alien ideas,
故,主無異意,
the people's heart will not shift.
民心不徙.
With Heaven he joins his model:[238]
與天合則:
for a myriad years there will be united commonality.
萬年一范.
Then the near will relate to his goodness,
則近者親其善,
the far will yearn for his virtue,
遠者慕其德,
and there will be no end.
而無已.

Consequently, his teachings will not tire,
是以,其教不猒,
their usage will not wear out. (*cf. iv-a; xii-d*)
其用不弊.
So, he will enable his borders to unite the four seas
故能疇合四海
and contrive one household.
以爲一家,
So the barbarians of myriad nations
而夷貉萬國
will all by seasons come and pay homage at his court.
皆以時朝服.
He will promote a succession so none will dare
致績而莫敢
to compete by adding or subtracting.
效增兔.

---

[238] 'Punctuation mark' (jù 句) survives in received text.

Hearers will transmit by translation
聞者傳譯
to come and home to his righteousness.
來歸其義.
None can change his moral customs or alter his teachings.
莫能易其俗移其教.
So, universal awe will be established and not invaded.
故共威立而不犯.
It will flow afar and not be abolished.
流遠而不廢.

This is the innate Augustan and inner God's Law.[239]
此素皇內帝之法.
It is what the Complete Nine grasps to transcend gradations.
成鳩之所枋以超等.
Generation by generation it may not be usurped.
世世不可奪者也.
Its achievements daily increase and monthly grow.
功日益月長.
So, he can with Heaven and Earth be preserved for ever.
故能與天地存久.
This is how he with Divine Luminaries
此所以與神明
embodies governance's technique.
體正之術也.

He does not depend on knights and scribes or
不待士史
Cangjié's invention of writing.
蒼頡作書.
So, in after generations none can speak his censure.
故,後世莫能云其咎.
I never heard of anyone, not with
未聞,不與
Way's virtue plumbed,
道德究,
Who yet can contrive excellence.
而能以爲善者也.

Páng Zî said:
龐子曰：
In this manner, are antiquity and modern Ways the same?
如是古今之道同邪？

---

[239] 'Augustan God' (Huáng Dì) is the self-canonisation adopted by the Qín's First Emperor which became synonymous with 'Emperor'. Cf. *Guânzî* (XVII Bingfâ): 94.

Héguan Zî said:

鶡冠子曰：

> Antiquity is indeed through us (*individuals wô*)
>
> 古者亦我
>
> caused to become ancient.
>
> 而使之久.
>
> Multitudes are indeed through us
>
> 眾者亦我
>
> caused to become multitudes!
>
> 而使之眾耳!
>
> Why take them as different?
>
> 比異哉?
>
> If your type is good
>
> 彼類善
>
> then for myriad ages you will not be forgotten.
>
> 則萬世不忘.
>
> If your Way is evil,
>
> 道惡,
>
> then disaster will reach your person.[240]
>
> 禍及於其身.
>
> What is strange about it?
>
> 尚奚怪焉.

Páng Zî said:

龐子曰：

> From modern operations
>
> 以今之事
>
> we observe antiquity's Ways.
>
> 觀古之道.
>
> Boats and chariots mutually communicated,
>
> 舟車相通,
>
> clothing was of the same colours,
>
> 衣服同采,
>
> words and language were mutually understood.
>
> 言語相知.[241]

---

[240] Cf. *MWD* Wáng Lùn 62a; Mínglî 72a.

[241] *Lâozí* (LXXX) on the golden age: People were serious about death and did not travel far. Though they had chariots and boats, there was nowhere to ride them. Though they had armour and weapons, there was nowhere to deploy them. This anticipates or reflects Qín unification.

We demarcate Earth to guard it
畫地守之,
and cannot mutually transgress.
不能相犯.
Different rulers and alien elders
殊君異長不能相使,
cannot mutually employ.
不能相使.
When offensive words pass the ears,
逆言過耳,
arms and armour are mutually readied.
兵甲相李[=理].
The hundred fathers,[242] mothers and children
百父母子
are not not easily led.
且未易領.

But, according to what you said,
方若所言,
they will not be separated from the central kingdom's rule.
未有離中國之正也.
Rural enterprises from their borders did not issue forth,
邱第之業, 域不出著,
their dwellings did not join eaves.
居不連垷.

Yet you say:
而曰:
"The Complete Ninth clan will universally enclose
成鳩氏周闔
"the four seas in one household.
四海爲一家.
"Barbarians of a myriad nations will come to pay court."
夷貉萬國莫不來朝.
Will this in fact be reality?
其果情乎?

---

[242] 'Hundred fathers' (baîfù) appears to be synonymous with 'multitude of fathers' (zhòng fù), in ix-a, simply meaning 'elders.'

Héguan Zî said:
鶡冠子曰：
　　When tigers and wolves kill a man,
　　虎狼殺人，
　　crows and flies from above,
　　烏蒼從上，
　　worms and maggots from below gather on him.
　　蟲蛾從下聚之．

　　These six are different species,
　　六者異類，
　　yet they simultaneously converge.
　　然同時俱至者何也．
　　Why? What they desire is the same.[243]
　　何也?所欲同也．

　　From this we observe that
　　(cf. xiii-b, xvii-b; Shèn Dào; Zhuangzî XVII)
　　由是觀之
　　those who have mankind's name
　　有人之名
　　share the human reality of feelings.
　　則同人之情耳．
　　How may it not be so?
　　何故不可乎?

　　Heaven's degrees and numbers in action
　　天度數之而行
　　within unity are not less,
　　在一不少，
　　In myriads no more multitudinous.
　　在萬不眾．
　　It is the same with a forest's trees.
　　同如林木．

　　Accumulated in a silo, grain
　　積如倉,粟
　　whether in pecks or piculs distributed,
　　斗石以陳，
　　or in pints stored, has no loss.[244]
　　升委無失也．

---

[243] This alarming picture seems as if it could contain an oblique reference to Zhào's situation facing its six rival states at the close of the Warring States period.

[244] *Héguanzî* reconciles the contradiction between division and wholeness, multiplicity and unity. *MWD* Jing fǎ (Dàofǎ) 43, 5a: When operations are like straight trees: though many as a silo's grains, whether in bushels and pecks supplied, or in feet and inches laid out, there is nowhere to let escape their spirit.

Open lands divided among people
列地分民
are indeed still one!
亦尚一也耳!

The hundred fathers, mothers and children,
百父母子,
how can they increase or decrease it?
何能增減?

Other rulers, different elders,
殊君異長,
Again, how will they subtract from or add to it?
又何出入?

If he is able in government to unify
若能正一
myriad nations within shared boundaries,
萬國同極,
His virtue extending to the four seas,
德至四海,
Again, who would be sufficient to exceed him?
又奚足闔[=蓋]也?

Páng Zî said:
龐子曰:

In fact, it is necessarily credible.
果必信然.

Shade and sunshine dissipate and scatter
陰陽消散
Over three hundred and sixty days,
三百六十日,
each reverting to the old (*in the solar cycle*).
各反其故.
Heaven and Earth are meticulous.
天地踽踽.
Where is there room for doubt?
奚足以疑?

The Sage Man is high and great.
聖人高大.
Internally he feels out shallow from deep,
內揣深淺,
far- from short-sighted principles.
遠近之理.
If demons and gods once go wrong,
使鬼神一失,
they cannot be revived.
不復息也.

By Heaven and Earth protected,
天地相蔽,
until now he is still present,
至今尚在.
Face to face in outstanding action.[245]
以鉦面達行.

It is fitting indeed!
宜乎哉!
That the Complete Ninth should have 18,000 years!
成鳩之萬八千歲也!

Whoever gets this Way,
得此道者,
what does it matter from which clan he is
何辯誰氏
or the employed nation,
所用之國,
if the Under-Heaven profits?
而天下利耳?

---

[245] 'Face to face' (zhèngmiàn 鉦 = 正面) is a special expression that recurs at the close of xii-d. There, it is used of Guân Zhòng (eminent premier to hegemon Duke Huán of Qí) meeting the Three Kings of antiquity on equal terms. Its addition of the metal classifier to zhèng (金＋正＝鉦) may be another taboo avoidance of Qín Shî Huángdì's personal name.

x. GRAND EXPANSE (Taìhóng 泰鴻第十)

We are party here to a dialogue between gods, comparable to those in the Mâwángdui Yellow Emperor texts. Grand Unity is the source of the lineage of Nine Augustans to which Grand Augustan requests initiation. 'Grand Expanse' might also be translated 'grand flood', reflecting the idea of heavens composed of water, recalling the Greek word 'galaxy' for 'Milky Way'.

Again, we find reference to self-cultivation: "love your essence to nourish energy" and "formless inner governance." Heaven, Earth and mankind are harmonised in a cosmo-political system transmitted by Nine Augustans. The Ninth Augustan, whose coming is awaited, concludes the series of the Complete Ninth (ix-g). 'Great community/ equality' (dàtóng 大同) is a Mohist-sounding term adopted by the Confucian Ritual Record for social utopia. Here it is the complement of compliant love (shùn'aì 順愛). The Way and its virtue are prominent, again with play on the pun 'virtue' with 'getting' or winning (dé. See: v-d, ix-g, x-a, xii-c, d, xviii-a,-b).

Five agents are generated in sequence by season with Grand Unity at centre. The concluding passage on modulation of flavour, display of colour, and correction of note must be code for foods, clothes and ranks.

a) The Teaching of Grand Unity
Grand Unity will set up great community's system,
泰一者執[=設/執?]大同之制,
to modulate the Grand Expanse's energies,
調泰鴻之氣,
to govern the Divine Luminaries' positions.
正神明之位者也.
So, the Nine Augustans receive his transmission
故九皇受傅[=傳?]
to seek their suchness's generator.
以索其然之所生.

The transmission means getting Heaven and Earth's explanation.
傅謂之得天之解.
The transmission means getting Heaven and Earth's start.
傅謂之得天地之所始.
The transmission means the Way to get the Way's constant.
傅謂之道,得道之常.
The transmission means the Sage Man.
傅謂之聖人.

The Sage Man's Way
聖人之道
with divine illumination is mutually gotten.
與神明相得.
So it is called Way's virtue.
故曰道德.

From subtle beginnings and barren starts,
邻(希)始窮初,
getting the same issue,[246]
得齊之所出,
the Nine Augustans have different systems
九皇殊制
yet their governances all emulate him,
而政莫不效焉,
So, he is called Grand Unity.
故曰泰一.

Grand Augustan asked Grand Unity, saying:
泰皇問泰一曰:

    Heaven, Earth and Man
    天地人
    of these three, which is the most urgent?
    事三者孰急?

Grand Unity said:
泰一曰:

    Love your essence to nourish spirit.
    愛精養神.
    Inner governance is the means of ascending Heaven.[247]
    內端=正者所以希[=升?]天.
    Heaven is where divine illumination is rooted.
    天也者神明之所根也.

    It distills and reforms four seasons,
    醇化四時,
    kneads and moulds formlessness,
    陶埏無形,

---

[246] *Lâozî* (I): These two are of the same issue but different names. There is sustained play here on 'getting' (得) and 'virtue' (德), both pronounced dé.

[247] I read 'erect' (duan 端) as taboo for 'governance' (zhèng 正); 'scarce/subtle' (xi 希) as 'ascend' (sheng 升). Cf. iv-e, fn 117: Heavens it, Earths it, Mans it; xiv-a, fn 313; xvii-f, fn 341. *MWD Jingfǎ* Liù-fen 49, 28b. Shíliù-Jing (Bingróng) 71, 116b. *Mèngzî* (II) 1. *Guóyǔ* (XXI) 1-2.

Carves and inlays the still unsprouted,
刻鏤未萌,
sculpts and designs what is about to be.[248]
離[=雕?]文將然者也.

Earth receives Heaven's evolutions
地者承天之演
entirely sustaining it by tranquillity.
備載以寧者也.

I will inform you:
吾將告汝:
Divine Luminaries' ultimates are
神明之極
Heaven, Earth and human employments.
天地人事.
These three return to unity.
三者復一也.

To set up and place ministers righteously
立置臣義
is what is meant by the four models.
所謂四則.

Disseminate to the eight winds, (*compass points*)
散以八風,
examine by the six co-ordinates. (*up, down, left, right, front, back*)
揆以六合.
Work by four seasons,
事以四時,
drain to the eight extremities (*directions*).
寫[=瀉]以八極.

Shine by the three lights (*sun, moon, stars*),
照以三光,
herd by penalties and rewards.
牧以刑德.
Adjust by the five keynotes (*terms*),
調以五音,
govern by the six pitchpipes (*bi-monthly periods*).
正以六律.

---

[248] I read 'sculpts and designs' (diaowén 雕文) for 'separates patterns' (liwén 離文).

Divide by grades and numbers,
分以度數,
display by the five colours (*to indicate ranks*).
表以五色.
Alter by the two energies (*day and night*),
改以二氣,
extend to south and north.
致以南北.

Equalize by the new and full moon,
齊以晦望,
receive by the luminaries'calendar (*360-day year*).
受以明歷.

The sun, faithfully rising, faithfully setting,[249]
日,信出,信入,
north and south having poles,
南北有極,
is measure's sign.
度之稽也.

The moon, faithfully dying, faithfully being born,
月,信死,信生,
advancing and retiring with constancy,
進退有常,
is number's sign.
數之稽也.

Stars do not disorder their motions,
列星不亂其行,
exchanging places but not encroaching,
代而不干,
they are position's signs.[250]
位之稽也.

Heaven illumines by three (*sun, moon and stars*) to fix unity.
天明三以定一.
So, myriad things all arrive!
則萬物莫不至矣!
Three seasons (*spring, summer, autumn*) produce and grow,
三時生長.

---

[249] Cf. ix-a, fn 221ff. above. *MWD Jingfa* (Lùn) 53, 49b. See Appendix I, below.
[250] Cf. *MWD Jingfa* (Lùn) 53, 49a-b.

One season (*winter*) kills and punishes.

一時煞刑.

The four seasons being fixed,

四時而定,

Heaven and Earth are finished[251]

天地盡矣.

b) The Divine Sage

Now, things at their start totter and wobble.

夫物之始也傾傾.

Having attained their being, flourish.

至其有也,錄錄.

Having achieved their complete forms,

至其成形,

they stand erect and correct.

端端王王[=正正?].

Without subtracting or adding,

勿損勿益,

infants and youth go on their own feet

幼少隨足

to follow teachers' customs.

以從師俗.

Do not change the Heaven-born,

毋易天生,

do not disperse Heaven's simplicity.[252]

毋散天樸.

Self-suchness is pure,

自若則清,

motion muddies it.[253]

動之則濁.

The Divine Sage steps up to the succession's position

神聖踐承翼之位

with Divine Augustans joined in virtue.

以與神皇合德.

---

[251] Cf. iv-a. *MWD* Jing fǎ (Lùnyue) 57, 66a.

[252] 'Simplicity' (pú) is goodness in the rough, 'the uncarved block.' *Lǎozǐ* (XXVIII): Constant virtue is sufficient (zú). Return home to simplicity. Simplicity dispersed then makes vessels. Sages used them to make officials and leaders.

[253] *Lǎozǐ* (XV): Who can the muddied through stillness gradually purify? Shú néng zhuó yǐ jìng- zhi xú qing? 孰能濁以靜之徐清?

According to plan, correct and erect,
按圖,正端,
he extends without limit.
以至無極.

Two rulers, four inducers (*day and night, four seasons*)
兩治,四致
make spaces for stops and rests.
閒以止息.
They assign seasons, separate energies
歸時離氣
to complete myriad enterprises.
以成萬業.
Once coming, once going,
一來,一往,
to observe the weighing scales dipping and rising.
視衡低(?)仰.

The five offices and six bureaux
五官六府
in making divisions have the Way
分之有道
without hook and without string.
無鈎無繩.
If chaos were undivided,
渾沌不分,
the Great Image would not be completed,[254]
大象不成,
employments would lack the axioms (*warps*) of Law.
事無經法.

Essence and spirit mutually at odds
精神相薄
will injure the hundred clans.
乃傷百族.
When spirit and energy mutually support,[255]
偷[=神?]氣相時[=持?],
then success may be established.
後功可立.

---

[254] *Lǎozǐ* (XXXV): Grasp [=erect?] the great image (dàxiàng), the Under-Heaven will go to you. Zhí [= shě] Dàxiàng, Tiānxià wǎng.

[255] I read 'spirit' shén 神 for 'steal' 偷 tou: shéqì xiangchí 神氣相持 to fit the prior pairing 'essence' + 'spirit' jingshén 精神 > 'spirit' + 'energy' shénqì 神氣.

First fix their profits,
先定其利,
waiting for things of themselves to arrive.
待物自至.
If you habitually proceed by Law,
素次以法,
things on arrival always comply.
物至輒合.
Law is Heaven and Earth's governing instrument.
法者天地之正器也.

If application of Law is incorrect,
用法不正,
prime virtue will not be complete.
元德不成.
Superior Sages with Heaven and Earth contact,
上聖者與天地接,
binding the six co-ordinates so that they are not undone.
結六連而不解者也.

For this reason, he who has the Way to be 'South Facer' (*king/emperor*)
是故,有道南面
maintains governance to protect the Divine Luminaries.
執政以衛神明.
Between left and right, front and rear,
左右前後,
in tranquillity he rests at the central axis.
靜侍中央.

He opens the source flowing to the oceans.
開原流洋.
In essential subtlety he goes and comes.
精微往來.
The tottering and wobbling, awry and tangled,
傾傾,繩繩,
inwardedly he supports by threads,
內持以維,
outwardly he ties by cables.
外紐以綱.

Acting by rational principle's dynamics,
行以理執,[=勢]
he connects end to start.
紀以終始.

He joins in unity different appointments
同一殊職
to establish as enlightened officials.
立爲明官.

c) Commonality
In five-fold commonality's four seasons,
五范四時,
Each by species mutually follows.
各以類相從.
Flavour's prime produces colours,
昧(=味?)元生色,
Keynote and mode mutually balance.
音聲相衡.

In the east quadrant (*springtime*)
東方者
myriad things are set up.
萬物立止焉.
So, they are tuned to **sol** (zhi).
故調以徵.

In the south quadrant (*summer*)
南方者
myriad things flower and feather.
萬物華羽焉.
So, they are tuned to **la** (yû).
故調以羽.

In the west quadrant (*autumn*)
西方者
myriad things are completed and displayed.
萬物成章焉.
So, they are tuned to **re** (shang).
故調以商.

In the north quadrant (*winter*)
北方者
myriad things are recorded and stored.
萬物錄臧焉.
So, they are tuned to **mi** (jiâo/jué).
故調以角.

The centre is Grand Unity's position.
中央者太一之位.
The hundred gods look up to his control there.
百神仰制焉.
It is tuned to **do** (gong).
故調以宮.

The Way from him contrives leadership.
道以爲先.
He lifts and supports divine illumination,
舉載神明,
Flowery Heaven above is raised by him,
華天上揚,
his root issues from the Yellow Bell (*'middle C'*).
本出黃鍾.

He starts from the east quadrant.
所始爲東方.
The myriad beings just flourish.
萬物唯隆.
Trees and flowering things in the Under-Heaven
以木華物天下
is entirely due to the agency of Wood.
盡木也.
It is made to occupy the east to govern springtime.
使居東方主春.

The illumination of things in the Under-Heaven
以火照物
is entirely due to the agency of Fire.
天下盡火也.
It is made to occupy the south to govern summer.
使居南方主夏.

The cutting down of things in the Under-Heaven
以金割物天下
is entirely due to the agency of Metal.
盡金也.
It is made to occupy the west to govern autumn.
使居西方主秋.

The flooding of things in the Under-Heaven
以水沉物天下
is entirely due to the agency of Water.
盡水也.
It is made to occupy the north to govern winter.
使居北方主冬.

The superiority of the great capital of the Under-Heaven
上爲大都天下
is entirely due to the agency of Soil.
盡土也.
It is made to occupy the central axis.
使居中央.

The protection of Earth Under-Heaven
守地天下
is all entirely due to men.
盡人也.
By Heaven's Son they contrive governance.
以天子爲正.

He modulates their energies
調其氣
to harmonises their flavours (*foods*).
和其味.
He listens to their sounds
聽其聲
to correct their forms.
正其形.
He refers to the past to observe the present,
迭往觀今,
so livelihoods may be pursued.
故業可循也.

If head and tail change direction,
首尾易面,
Earth's principles will be divorced from its warps.
地理離經.
Usurped love[256] will bring about disorder.
奪愛令亂.
Above it obliterates Heaven's design,
上滅天文,
rational principles may not be known,
理不可知,
divine illumination will lose coherence.
神明失從.

---

[256] 'Usurped love' (duó'ai 奪愛) must indicate love that is forced and so not genuine.

Design and rationality are mutually illuminating,
文理者相明者也,
colours and flavours are mutually complementary,
色味者相度者也,
foliage and flowers are mutually completing.
藻華者相成者也.

Multitudes through individuals become multitudinous,
眾者我而眾之,
So they may be united in the commonality of real feeling.
故可以一范請(=情?)也.
Under consensual love's government,
順愛之政,
different races mutually communicate.
殊類相通.
Under forced love's government,
逆愛之政,
those of the same race mutually doom.
同類相亡.

So, the Sage Man establishes Heaven as his father,
故聖人立天爲父,
founds Earth as his mother.[257]
建地爲母.
His commonality does not strive to make others
范者非務使
say they are necessarily the same.
云必同.
Knowing unity, he aims to cause unity in men.
知一期以使一人也.
His commonality is placed in Heaven and Earth's interval
氾錯之天地之閒
And everyone is covered by its harmony.
而人人被其和.
Harmony is formless but has flavour.
和也者無形而有味者也.
Equality and harmony is humane benevolence,
同和者仁也,
mutual accomodation is righteousness.
相容者義也.
The humane and righteous in enjoyments share.
仁義者所樂同.

---

[257] *MWD* Shíliù-jing (Guótóng) 66: By Heaven contrive fatherhood; by Earth motherhood.

Each can share the joy in
名[=各?]也能同所樂
formless internal governance.[258]
無形內政.
So the Sage, knowing the divine recipe,
故聖,知神方,
modulates in formlessness
調於無形
and all things without exception follow.
而物莫不從.

Heaven bestows luxuriant blossoms
天受[=授?]藻華
to contrive divine illumination's root.
以為神明之根者也.
Earth bestows seasons
地受[=授?]時
to contrive myriad things' source.
以為萬物原者也.

The Divine Sage is meticulous in rational principle.
神聖詳理.
He hates to part from control of mandate's levers.
惡離制命之柄.
He collects and scatters flowery essence
斂散華精
to comfort Earth and honour Heaven.[259]
以慰地貴天者也.

He modulates flavours, displays colours, corrects modes
調味章色正聲
to fix Heavenly, Earthly and human operations.
以定天地人事.
The three are perfected in this!
三者畢此矣!

---

[258] Music and joy (Yuè/lè 樂) are synonymous. *Mòzǐ* (XXXII) condemns music but *Mèngzǐ* (II-2.4) urges King Huì of Liáng: to share musical pleasure with his people, -yǔ mín tong yuè/lè 與民同樂.

[259] As alternative reading to 'honour' (guì 貴), Lù Diàn gives 'accusing/blaming' (zé 責), which he compares the former to Chán (Zen) "shouting at Buddha and cursing Patriarchs."

168

xi. GRAND RECORD (Tàilù 泰錄第十一)

Abiding in Grand Unity, the Nine Augustans are the Sage King, empowered like Plato's philosopher king (Republic 8). His 'commonality' plan (fàn 范= 笵/範) for the Under-Heaven is based on the promise of 'flavour's energy,' food and justice. Internally, he cultivates the three-fold Daoist triad of spirit, essence and energy (qì). The hereditary principle should not determine rank. Heaven's Son is to be the 'highest worthy,' and the next worthy dukes, and so on. The teacher Is to be ruler and student subject. Implementation relies on the advent of a 'god emperor' (dì 帝). As a concession to hereditary kingship, doom can be avoided by heeding the advice of worthies.

Philosophically, the most interesting is the first section's description of parallel universes, visible and invisible, with a third human dimension like that of Plato's heavenly 'Idaeas' mirrored in material form.

a) Grand Unity
The (Nine Augustans) enter to order the Grand Expanse's interior,
入論[=倫?]泰鴻之內,
exit to observe the Divine Luminaries' exterior.
出觀神明之外.
They found their system in Grand Unity's bosom
定制泰一之衷
to become things' paragons.
以爲物稽.

Heaven's nine expanses,
天有九鴻,
Earth's nine continents,
地有九州,
Grand Unity's Way,
泰一之道,
the Nine Augustans' transmission:
九皇之傅[=傳?]:
in reality was complete at the Grand Start's finish.
請[=情?]成於泰始之末.

(Grand Unity) observes detailed operations
見不[=其?]詳事
at names and principles' exterior,
於名理之外,
makes commonality from the formless,
范無形,

tastes the flavourless,[260]
嘗無味,
to demand that in which name and principle join.
以要名理之所會.

Commonality is flavour (food)'s governor,
范者味之正也,
Flavour is energy's father and mother,
味者氣之父母,
essential subtlety is Heaven and Earth's start.
精微者天地之始也.

Not seeing in form his peer,
不見形巘[=孿?],
the Under-Heaven render praises unto him.
而天下歸美焉.
His name embodies Divine Luminaries.
名尸神明者.
He is the Great Way's governor[261]
大道是[=正?]也.

He determines action to accord with ideas,
夫錯行合意,
upholds justice rooted in humanity.
扶義本仁.
He accumulates obedience to complete
積順之所成
what the first kings generated.
先聖之所生也.

He who practices his Way has his name,
行其道者有其名,
he who works in his service has his achievements.
爲其事者有其功.

---

[260] *Lâozî* XXXV: The Way's speech is bland oh! Without flavour. Dào-zhi chukôu xi dàn xi qí wúwèi.
道之出口兮淡其無味.

[261] Lù Diàn notes zhèng (正) as a variant for shì (是) here. I take shì here as another case of Qín taboo avoidance for Qín First Emperor's name, though the taboo is not observed in the preceding verse, unless it was re-amended there. Cf. viii-a: 'governor' zhèng (正).

So, Heaven and Earth are completed from primal energy,[262]
故天地成於元氣,
myriad things ride on Heaven and Earth.
萬物乘於天地.
The Divine Sage rides on Way's virtue
神聖乘於道德
in order to plumb its principles.
以究其理.
The superior Sage and August Heaven are that
若上聖皇天者
on which first kings rested their awesome power
先聖[=王?]之所倚威
to establish their mandates.
立有命也.
So, induction of rule is from the self.
故致治之自在己者也.

He who attracts the high is high.
招高者高.
He who attracts the low is low.
招庳者庳.
So, to complete form unalterably is degree,
故成形而不變者度也,
Not apart from oneself yet present in others are impressions.[263]
未離己而在彼者狎[=押?]漚也.
Deployed structures, established rules,
陳體,立節,
for a myriad generations unchanging,
萬世不易,
are Heaven and Earth's positions.
天地之位也.

---

[262] Lù Diàn notes some editions have 'nothing' (wú 无) for 'prime' (yuán 元). 'Six' (liù 六) and 'dark/mysterious' (xuán 玄) are possible readings. Cf. *Zhuangzǐ* (I Xiaoyáoyóu): rides Heaven and Earth's governance to tune the six energies' metamorphoses. *Zuǒzhuàn* (Zhaogong 1" year). Dǒng Zhòngshū: *Chunqiu Fánlù* (IV-6 Wáng Dào) 25: When the King is correct, primal energy is harmoniously compliant. Wáng zhèng zé yuánqì héshùn 王正則元氣和順; (XVII-78 Tiandì-zhi xíng) 95: as primal energy flows to skin and pores. Ruò yuánqì-zhi liú pímáo còulǐ-yê. 若元氣之流皮毛腠理也. Defoort 1997: 84. *Yǒnglè Dàdiǎn* (1974, 3) 1a5 inserts a long passage here but omits 'energy' (qì 氣) which is needed to complete the rhyme. (see Postscript II)

[263] Literally 'bubble' (漚). I take 'bubble' as a seal stamp (ya 押)'s mark or impression. Lù Diàn takes it somewhat fancifully as *Lièzǐ* (II)'s 'seagull lover' (xiá'ou 狎鷗). Defoort 1997: 85 remarks the phrase is omitted from *Yǒnglè Dàdiǎn* (1974, 3) 1a6. She renders it: "Hence, what doesn't change after the completion of a shape is measure: it is what is present there, without having left itself."

The division of things, attachment of names,
分物,紀名,
cultured Sagacity and illumined discrimination
文聖明別
are the Divine Sage's complements.
神聖之齊也.
The Law of Heaven resident on Earth
法天居地
rejects the square to set up the circle.[264]
去方錯圓.
It is the Divine Sage's mirror.
神聖之鑒也.

Images are interpreted to name things,
象說名物,
"achieve success and finish the job."[265]
成功遂事.
The invisible and visible's inseparability
隱彰不相離
is the Divine Sages' teaching.
神聖之教也.

So, flows divide and divinity is born,
故流分而神生,
motion ascends and illumination is born.
動登而明生.
Illumination is seen, forms are completed,
明見,而形成,
forms completed, achievements kept.
形成而功存.

So, cultured design is how to divide things.
故,文者所以分物也.
Principles are the means to attach names.
理者所以紀名也.

Heaven and Earth are equal in operation
天地者同事
yet have separate realms.
而異域者也.

---

[264] On the circle and square, cf. ix-e, xviii-b.
[265] *Lǎozǐ* (XVII). Cf. iii-b, xi-b, xvi.

Without compasses yet circular
無規圓者
are Heaven's designs.
天之文也.
Without set-square yet square
無矩方者
are Earth's principles.
地之理也.

Heaven complies with design to move,
天循文以動,
Earth complies with principle to create.
地循理以作者也.
The two factors are divine Law.
二端者神之法也.

b) The Divine Sage's Reforms

The Divine Sage's human mandate
神聖之人后[=命?]
before Heaven and Earth was honoured.
先天地而尊者也.
After Heaven and Earth he was born, (*Cf. xviii-b*)
後天地生,
yet knows Heaven and Earth's start;
然知天地之始;
before Heaven and Earth perishes,
先天地亡,
yet knows Heaven and Earth's end.
然知天地之終.

His Way embraces them,
道包之,
So he can know and predict them.
故能知度之.
He honours and gives them importance
尊重焉
so he can alter and move them.
故能改動之.
His numerology illumines them
敏[數?]明焉
so he can control and determine them.
故能制斷之.

Essential spirit is what things value most greatly.
精神者物之貴大者也.
Inner sagacity is essential spirit's source.
內聖者精神之原也.
Nothing is greater than it,
莫貴焉,
So there are none who do not look up to its control.
故靡不仰制焉.

Control (abstinence) is how he guards essence
制者所以衛精
and uplifts spirits to induce energy.
擢神致氣也.
He secludes himself so it does not leak,
幽則不洩,
simplifies so is undistracted.
簡則不煩.
Undistracted, thus his essence is illumined and pervades.
不煩則精明達.
So, he can employ the worthy and able,
故,能役賢能,
deploy Divine Luminaries.
使神明.
A hundred reforms follow and
百化隨而
transform from end to start.
變終始.

Consequently, in anticipation,
從,而豫,
Divine Luminaries accumulate essential subtlety
神明者積精微
and holistic excellence's completion.
全粹之所成也.
The Sage's way and divine method
聖道神方
are requisite's utmost.
要之極也.
Imperial control-system and divine reformation
帝制神化
are good-order's aim.
治之期也.
So, teachers become lords,
故,師爲君,
students become subjects (ministers).
而學爲臣.

The superior worthy becomes Heaven's Son,
上賢爲天子,
lesser worthies become the three dukes,
次賢爲三公,
The high become barons.
高爲諸侯.
He changes families to make kings,
易姓而王,
he does not by ancestral registry make rulers.
不以祖籍爲君者.
He desires equality to unite the good in peace.
欲同一善之安.

He has Heaven and Earth's motions in his breast:
彼天地動作於胸中:
only then are operations completed externally.
然後事成於外.
Myriad things go out and in from him:
萬物出入焉:
only then are living things unharmed.
然後生物無害.

He opens and closes the four seasons,
闔闢四時,
withdraws and shifts shade and sunshine.
引移陰陽.
Resentments are submerged by his purification of things.
怨沒澄物.
'The Under-Heaven consider it 'spontaneous'.[266]
天下以爲自然.
This is how the Divine Sage transcends multitudes.
此神聖之所以絕眾也.

Sagacity's source is divine design.
聖原神文.
It has signs that may not be seen.
有驗而不可見者也.
So, when extraordinary men may be seen,
故,過人可見,
transcendent men will not be far off.
絕人未遠也.

---

[266] *Lâozî* (XVII): I achieve success and finish the job: the hundred clans all call me 'spontaneous' (self-so/natural; zìrán 自然)! (Hàn) Dông Zhòngshu: *Chunqiu Fánlù* (XIII, 57 Tónglèi Xiangdòng) 76: They call it natural. Actually, it is not natural. Someone causes it to be so. Cf. iii-b, xi-a, xvi.

Divine Luminaries are the means by which races are joined.
神明所以類合者也.
So Divine Luminaries firmly tie their bonds.
故神明鋼結其紘.
Every race, born and complete,
類類,生成,
will employ unity inexhaustibly.
用一不窮.
Shadow follows form,
影則隨形,
echo responds to sound[267]
響則應聲.
So, form and sound
故形聲者
are the Heaven and Earth's teachers.
天地之師也.

The four seasons' achievements,
四時之功,
shade and sunshine cannot alone contrive.
陰陽不能獨爲也.
The Sage King does not lose their root or tip,
聖王者不失本末,
So, Divine Luminaries end and start in him.
故,神明終始焉.

He altogether commands the eight winds and
卒令八風
triple luminaries' transformations,
三光之變,
regulates energy's inconstant causes.
經氣不常之故.
Where does he not command reality and oversee principle in them?
孰不詔請[=情]都理焉?

So, his divine soul's awesome illumination
故神靈威明
above transforms the luminaries
上變光
fast or slowly, leisurely or urgently.
疾徐緩急.

---

[267] Cf. *MWD Jingfã* (Mínglî) 58, 76a.

In their midst he moves energies
中動氣
that kill and maim in destruction and disasters
煞 傷 毀 禍
below on Earth.
下在地.

So, Heaven and Earth, shade and sunshine (*yin and yáng*)
故天地陰陽之
receive mandates and take their image
受命取象
from the Divine Luminaries' efficacy.
於神明之效.
This has already been shown!
既已見矣!

Heaven is whence energy universally issues,
天者氣之所總出也,
Earth is principle's inexorability (*necessity*).
地者理之必然也.

So, the Sage Man issues it from Heaven,
故聖人者出之於天,
harvests it on Earth.
收之於地.

In Heaven[268] and Earth, as shade and sunshine,
在天地若陰陽者,
he is the shrine of dry and wet.
杜[=社]燥濕.

His Law's righteousness
以法義
according to the times shifts.
與時遷焉.
When these two are by the Sage Man kept,
(Yônglè Dàdiân: 'these three' 三者.)
二者聖人存,
there will be good government.
則治.

---

[268] Here the 1407 *Yônglè Dàdiân* (1974, 3) 1b, 8-2a4 inserts a long passage which I take as an attempt to sanctify Yônglè's usurpation. See: Postscript II, below. Cf. Defoort 1997: 86-87, 214-15; Wells 2013: 63-64, 79.

As for the ancestrally recorded
及至乎祖籍之
hereditary succession of rulers,
世代繼之君,
a person though unworthy,
身雖不賢
yet 'a south facer' proclaimed 'the loner',[269]
然南面稱寡,
will not after all be doomed
猶不果亡者
if he can receive teaching
其能受教乎
from Way-possessing knights.
有道之士者也.

Otherwise, the ability to maintain his lineage temples
不然而能守宗廟
and keep safe his nation and house
存國家者
has never existed.
未之有也.

---

[269] 'South Facing' (nánmiàn 南面) refers to the view from the King's position, symbolized by the northern Pole Star. 'Loner' (guârén 寡人) is the ruler's self-deprecating title. Here, as we hear again in Study Problems (xv-a), the essential role of the teacher in guiding the ruler is emphasized.

BOTTOM SCROLL

xii. GENERATIONS OF ARMS
(Shìbing 世兵第十二)

This chapter analyses historical conflicts. It links illumined Law with the tactically efficacious subtle Way, recalling Goujiàn intrigues to recover his throne of Yuè. The positive endorsement it gives to the desperate act of Cáo Mò, patriotic general of Lû, who held up Duke Huán of Qí at a conference to recover territory. It foreshadows an attempt in 227 on the life of Qín King Zhèng, future First Emperor Shîhuángdì, by assassin Jing Ke, on behalf of Yàn's Crown Prince Dan. Yet this work betrays no knowledge of that attempt.

Prince Dan had grown up as hostage in Zhào with Zhèng, and later been mistreated himself as hostage in Qín. In Simâ Qian's account, Prince Dan cites the example of Cáo Mò when plotting to assassinate Zhèng. The Cáo Mò narrative here suggests a similar sense of desperation, reflecting the current mood of Zhào in the face of the Qín threat.

The reported suicide of defeated Yàn general Jù Xin, in 242 BC, is the last dateable event here, and a year before the defeat of Zhào's final coalition of five kingdoms against Qín. Héguanzî's appended criticism of his suicide as useless has the poignancy of contemporaneous reference. Equally, the ironic comment on the futile sacrifice of altruistic Shen Túdí (Cf. xiii-a) contrasts with sanctification of protest martyrdom by Lyû Bùweí and Zhuang Zî.[270] By contrast, the suicide in 227 of Yàn general Fán, who donated his head to Jing Ke for use in gaining an audience with Qín King Zhèng in his assassination attempt, would no doubt have gained hearty approbation.

The chapter concludes with a 'Rhapsody of the Hero' whose affinities with Jiâ Yì's Owl Rhapsody (see Postscript I) led to suspicions of plagiarism or forgery. Both share materials with *Zhuangzî*, yet *Héguanzî*'s concern is national recovery and activation of positive dynamics. Jiâ Yì, by contrast, bemoans his own fate in mock seriousness. He confesses to consulting 'books of prognostication' and converse with the bird of ill omen which cannot speak. He asks the owl: will it be 'later or sooner'? This too has a near parallel here: "Quick or slow have their mandates." (xii-d) Could he be satirizing *Héguanzî*?

---

[270] Cf. *Hánfeizî* (XIX Shìxié) mocks Jù Xin's reliance on oracles to predict victory. *Zhuangzî* (XXVI) 944, (XXIX) 988. *Lyûshì Chunqiu* (XIX-1 Lísú) 2a.

a) Dynastic Revolutions

The Way has predictive numerology,
道有度數,
So, Divine Luminaries may interact.
故神明可交也.

Things have mutual conquests,
物有相勝,
So, water and fire may be applied.
故水火可用也.
They have east, west, south, and north
東西南北
So, forms and names may be trusted.
故形名可信也.

The Five Emperors (*of prehistory*) were before,
五帝在前,
The Three Kings (*of Xià, Shang and Zhou*) afterwards.
三王在後,
Superior virtue had then already decayed!
上德已衰矣!
Arms and knowledge together arose[271]
兵知俱起.

The Yellow Emperor had a hundred battles,
黃帝百戰,
Chiyóu [his arch-foe] had seventy-two.
蚩尤七十二.
Yáo attacked Yôutáng,
堯伐有唐,
Great Yû (of Xià) subdued the Yôumiáo.
禹服有苗.

Heaven does not transform its constants,
天不變其常,
Earth does not change its model.
地不易其則.

Shade and sunshine do not disorder their energies,
陰陽不亂其氣,
Birth and death do not swap their positions.
生死不僾其位.

---

[271] *Zhuangzǐ* (X Quqiè): Intelligence (zhì) is contention's weapon.

The Triple Luminaries do not alter their usages,
三光不改其用,
Divine Luminaries do not shift their Laws.
神明不徙其法.

Winning and losing are not separately deployed,
得失不兩張,
Victory and defeat are not separately established.
成敗不兩立.
What is meant by worthy or unworthy
所謂賢不肖者
from antiquity to the present are one.
古今一也.

Gentlemen are not not slothful,
君子不惰,
True men are not tardy.
真人不怠.
They are never seen to be for ever poor and base.
無見久貧賤.

According to the Bamboo Books,
則據簡之,
Yi Yîn (*premier to King Tang of Shang*) had been a publican,
伊尹酒保,
Taìgong (*premier to King Wû of Zhou*) had butchered oxen.
太公屠牛,
Guânzî (*premier to Duke Huán of Qí*) had worked in a tannery,
管子作革,
Baîlî Xi (*premier to Duke Mù of Qín*) had been an official slave.[272]
百里奚官奴.

When the seas' interior had been laid waste and disordered,
海內荒亂,
They were established as their generation's teachers,
立爲世師,
none but as Heaven and Earth excellent in counsel.
莫不天地善謀.
They were as sun and moon unresting
日月不息

in completing the four seasons.
迺成四時.

---

[272] Allan 1981/2016: 149ff on Taìgong Wàng. The first two kings founded the Shang and Zhou dynasties respectively, the two dukes were hegemons in the Spring and Autumn period. Their brilliant premiers were recruited as commoners. See Dramatis Personae; Table II.

They refined their practice like gods.
精習象神.
Who says he is capable of this?
孰謂能之?
Through habit they perfected their application.
素成其用.
They had fore-knowledge of causation.
先知其故.

King Tang was able from seventy square lî
湯能以七十里
to (overcome and) banish the tyrant Jié.
放桀.
King Wû from a hundred square lî
武王以百里
attacked and punished the tyrant Zhôu.
伐紂.

Knowing unity, they were not vexed
知一不煩
by a thousand tactics and myriad turns.
千方萬曲.
Whatever is mixed up becomes all the same,
所雜齊同
victory's ways are not only one.
勝道不一.

The wise plan for entirety.
知者計全.
An enlightened general does not ignore timing
明將不倍時
and cast away advantage.
而棄利.
The courageous knight does not fear to die
勇士不怯死
and obliterate his name.
而滅名.

If you wish to surpass ultimate virtue's excellence,
欲喻[=逾]至德之美者,
your cogitations will not be with your desires identical.
其慮不與欲同.

If you desire to experience the Nine Heavens' heights,
欲驗九天之高者,
in action you will not disregard emotive reality.[273]
行不徑請(=情).

For these reasons, the loyal minister does not put first his own person
是以,忠臣不先其身
nor put last that of his ruler.
而後其君.

With trepidation in mind, alone he stands
寒心孤立
in suspense before the mandate.
懸命.

b) Cáo Mò's Heroism
When generals in the wilderness battle,
將軍野戰,
then nations are wasted and their people exhausted.
則國弊民罷.

When cities are besieged,
城守則
people eat men and grill their corpses.
食人灼骸.
If his plan fails, his nation will be reduced, his ruler confined
計失,其國削主困
and made the Under-Heaven's laughing stock.
爲天下笑.

He who holds the nation's plans may he not be careful?
持國計者可以無詳乎?
Indeed, there are mistaken plans,
固有過計,
there are trials and experiments.
有嘗試.

---

[273] 'Disregard reality' jìngqíng 徑情 echoes *Zhuangzǐ* (I Xiaoyáoyóu): he passes by never approaching human reality/feelings, jìngtíng bùjìn rénqíng 徑庭不近人情.

For this reason, Cáo Mò as Lu's general with Qí thrice battled
是以曹沫爲魯將與齊三戰
and lost land of a thousand lî.[274]
而亡地千里.

Supposing Master Cáo had not planned for posterity,
使曹子計不顧後,
but had cut his throat and died,
刎頸而死,
then he would not have avoided
則不免爲
his army's defeat and generals' capture.
敗軍擒將.
Master Cáo considered that
曹子以爲
to have his army defeated and generals captured
敗軍擒將
would not be courage.
非勇也.
To have his nation reduced and its name obliterated
國削名滅
Would not be wisdom.
非智也.
To have his person dead and the ruler endangered
身死君危
Would not be loyalty.
非忠也.

Now, dead men's employment is unable
夫死人之事者
to extend men's longevity.
不能續人之壽.
So he withdrew and with Lû's ruler plotted.
故退與魯君計.
When Duke Huán convened the barons,
桓公合諸侯,
Master Cáo by one sword's service
曹子以一劍之任
held hostage Duke Huán at the altar's summit.
劫桓公壇位之上.

---

[274]The story of Cáo Mò (alias Cáo Jù) is also told by Lû Lián in a letter to the Yàn general in 284 who is besieging Jímò, the last city of Qí still to hold out. After reading the letter, Yàn lifts the siege. *Zhànguó Cè* (XIII Qí Cè: 3). Caldwell 2014: analyses a newly excavated bamboo manuscripts from Chû, 'Cao Mie's Battle Array', in which Cáo Mò/Miè advises Duke Zhuang of Lû (r. 693-662) on strategy.

His complexion's colour did not alter,
顏色不變,
his speech energy was not awkward.
辭氣不悖.
In three battles all that had been lost
三戰之所亡
was in one day recovered.
一旦而反.
The Under-Heaven was shaken and moved,
天下震動,
the four neighbor states were startled and terrified,
四鄰驚駭,
his name was transmitted to later generations.
名傳後世.
If he had put reliance on small shame,
扶杖於小愧者,
his great work would not have been achieved.
大功不成.
So, Master Cáo Mò rejected rage and fury's mind-set
故曹子去忿悁之心
to establish a lifetime's achievement.
立終身之功.
He cast away small anger's shame
棄細忿之愧
to establish succeeding generations' fame.
立終身之功.
So, Master Cáo is considered a man who knew timing,
故,曹子爲知時,
Lǔ's ruler is considered a man who knew men.
魯君爲知人.

c) Jù Xin's Suicide
Jù Xin as Yàn's general,
劇辛爲燕將,
with Zhào battled and his army was defeated.
與趙戰軍敗
Jù Xin cut his own throat,
劇辛自剄,
Yàn by this lost five cities.
燕以失五城.
Making himself a criminal, he contrived disaster's gate.
自賊以爲禍門.
His personal death imperilled his ruler.
身死以危其君.
His name and substance were both obliterated.
名實俱滅.

This meant being a loser.
是謂失.
It was not a recovery plan,
此不還人之計也,
It was not outstanding talent's strategy.
非過材之莉[=策?]也.

Now, he, who gets the Way,
得道者
Strives to be without great losses.
務無大失.
Common men strive to have small excellences.
凡人者務有小善.
Small excellences accumulate hatred and desire.
小善積惡欲.

If you have many hatreds, you will not accumulate virtue.
多惡,則不積德.
If it is not accumulated, there will be many troubles.
不積則多難.
If there are many troubles, there will be confusion.
多難,則濁.
If there is confusion, there will be no wisdom.
濁則無知.

If you have many desires, you will not have breadth.
多欲則不博.
If you do not have breadth, you will have many worries.
不博則多憂.
If you have many worries, you will be befouled.
多憂則濁.
Befouled, you will not have wisdom.
濁則無知.
Desires and hatreds are wisdom's clouding.
欲惡者知之所昏也.

Now, he who forces the incapable,
夫強不能者
Slaughters them.
傡[=戮?]之.
This means disgrace.
其言辱.
Indeed Jù Xin's ability was outstanding
是劇辛能絕
But the King of Yàn did not know men.
而燕王不知人也.

d) The Rhapsody of the Hero[275]

Formerly, he who excelled in battle
昔善戰者
Raised troops from his followers,
舉兵相從,
Deployed by the five agents,
陳以五行,
Battled by the five keynotes.
戰以五音.

Pointing to Heaven's zenith,
指天之極,
He with the gods is in equal position.
與神同方.

In every category born complete,
類類生成,
His employment of unity is inexhaustible.
用一不窮.
'Openly he contrives Law,
明者爲法,
The subtle Way is what he practises.'[276]
微道是行.

Evenly he crosses, advances and retires,
齊過進退,
Triangulating with Heaven and Earth.
參之天地.

'He issues from the substantial to charge the vacuous',[277]
出實觸虛,
Capturing generals and breaking armies.
禽將破軍.

He shoots forth like an arrow,
發如鏃矢,
Moves like thunder and lightning.
動如雷霆,

---

[275] Verses that follow may be compared with Jiâ Yì's 'Owl Rhapsody'. See: Postscript I, below.

[276] This couplet occurs in *Guóyû* (XXI Yuèyû-xià): Míng-zhê weí fâ, weí Dào shì xíng 明者爲法微道是行; *MWD* Shíliù-jing (Guan) 62; (Xingzheng) 69. Zhang Shùnhuì 1988: 40ff on forged *Shàngshu*: Dà Yû Mò: The Way's heart is subtle, men's hearts are dangerous. Dàoxin weí wei, rénxin weí weí 道心惟微人心惟危; *Xúnzî* (XXI Jiêbì) 439.

[277] *Sunzi Bingfâ* (VI Xushí): He avoids the substantial and pounds the vacuous.

With ferocious speed he pounds the vacuous,
暴疾擣虛,
Rumbling like a collapsing wall.
殷若壞牆.

'His dynamics are urgent, his rhythms short.'[278]
執[=勢]急節短,
His application does not slacken.[279]
用不縵縵.
He shuns where one would die
避我所死
To go where we will live.
就吾所生.
He urges on our supporters[280]
趨吾所時[?持]
To aid where we will conquer.
援吾所勝.

So, his knights will not be repelled,
故士不折北,
His troops will not be surrounded.
兵不困窮.

He who gets this Way
得此道者
Drives recruited townsfolk.[281]
驅用市人.

He rides the flow to go,
乘流以逝,
With the Way soaring and gliding.
與道翱翔.
Soaring and gliding, he gives and takes.
翱翔授取,
Securely grasping, firmly holding.
錮據堅守.

---

[278] *Sunzǐ Bingfǎ* (V Shì, 'Dynamics') line 14. Here we see another case of 'dynamics' shì 勢 miscopied, in this case as 'hold' zhí 執. Jiǎ Yì's Qwl Rhapsody, by contrast, lacks any positive conceptualization of dynamics as here. (Postscript I).

[279] This distinctive line yòng bù mànmàn 用不縵縵 recurs in iv-a; and with variation in ix-g.

[280] As above, I read 'season' shí 時 as 'support' chí 持.

[281] Cf. 'untrained multitudes' xvii-e. *Shǐjì* (XCII Lièzhuàn, Huáiyin Hóu) dì-438b Hán Xìn quotes: This is what is called 'driving townsfolk to war'. Suôweì 'qu shìrén, ér zhàn-zhī. 所謂驅市人而戰之.

Exhaling and inhaling, halting and altering.
呼吸鎮移,
With the times he shifts and contrives.
與時更爲.

Once ahead, once behind,
一先一後,
Musical notes and semi-tones together play.
音律相奏.
Once right, once left,
一右一左,
His Way has nothing impossible.
道無不可.

He receives numbers from Heaven,
受數於天,
Settles positions on Earth,
定位於地,
Completes names for men.[282]
成名於人.

He whose time has arrived,
彼時之至,
How may he be turned back?
安可復還,
How may he be contended with?[283]
安可控搏?
Heaven and Earth are not biased
天地不倚
In setting up to await the able.
錯以待能.

Calculations and numbers mutually exploit,
度數相使,
Shade and sunshine mutually attack.
陰陽相攻.
Death and life each other support,
死生相攝,
Energy and awe are mutually destructive.
氣威相滅.

---

282 *MWD* Shíliù-jing (Lìmìng) 61, 78b: We receive mandate from Heaven, settle positions on Earth, complete names among Men.
283 Lù Diàn explains kòngbó 控搏 as 'stop' (zhî 止). Jiâ Yì's 'Owl Rhapsody' Fúniâo Fù (see below) writes it as kòngtuán 控團 which Lî Shàn, curiously, glosses 'loving life'.

Void and substance to each other adapt,
虛實相因,
Win or lose they float suspended.
得失浮縣
Arms by dynamics conquer:
兵以勢勝:
Timing is not constantly deployed.
時不常使.

Early or late, contracting or expanding,
蚤晚絀贏,
Opposites are mutually bred and born.
反相殖生.
Revolutions and reforms are inexhaustible.
變化無窮.
How will they all be told?
何可勝言?

'Water shot forth goes dry,
水激則旱,
Arrows shot forth go far.'[284]
矢激則遠.
Essence and spirit turn and twist,
精神回薄,
Shaken and stirred they spin around.
振蕩相轉.

Slow or fast have mandates:
遲速有命:
You must centre on threes and fives.[285]
必中三五.
Gathering and scattering, dispersal and growth.
合散消息.
Who understands their timing?
孰識其時?

---

[284] Lyûshì *Chūnqiū* (Lân XVI Quyóu) 16b against uncontrolled anger has the same couplet in reverse order; (Zhòngqiu VIII-2 Lùnwei) 4b: water thrown on water scatters. *Wénzî* (IX Xiàdé) 75: So when water is agitated, waves arise. When energy is disorderly, wisdom becomes clouded... *Huaínánzî* (VIII Bênjing) 11a; (XV Binglyuè) 11b: energy agitated explodes in anger.

[285] Three levels: Heaven, Earth, Man and Five Directions with centre; or 'triangles and squares'. *Hánfeizî* (VIII Yángquán) 32: 'three and five' canwû 參伍. Cf. vi-a.

The Ultimate Man abandons things,
至人遺物,
Alone with the Way conjoined.
獨與道俱.
Loosing and urging, he deputises mandates,
縱驅委命,
With the times he goes and comes.
與時往來.
Fullness and decay, death and life,
盛衰死生,
Who knows their dates?
孰識其期?
Sternly and most candidly,
儼然至湛,
Who knows his faults?
孰知其尤?

'Disaster is what good-fortune leans on.
禍乎福之所倚.
Good-fortune is where disaster lurks.'[286]
福乎禍之所伏.
Disaster and good-fortune are as if intertwined.
禍與福如糾纏.
In chaos mixed and shattered,
渾沌錯紛,
Their appearance is as one.
其狀若一.
To unravel their form and appearance,
交解形狀,
Who knows their model?
孰知其則?
Murky and vague, without a face,
芴芒無貌,
Only the Sage Man determines their meaning.
唯聖人而後決其意.
They spin and flow, remove and shift,
斡流遷徙,
Certainly without break or rest.
固無休息.
Where there are endings, there are beginnings:
終則有始:
'Who knows their limits?'[287]
孰知其極?

---

[286] *Lâozî* (LVIII).
[287] *Lâozî* (LVIII).

A one-eyed net may not be used
一目之羅不可
To catch sparrows.
以得雀;
A caged bird
籠中之鳥
Vainly peeks through but will not get out.
空窺不出.

The multitude of men just obey,
眾人唯唯,
How can they determine an outcome of disaster or good-fortune?
安定禍福?

Sorrow and joy gather at the gate,
憂喜聚門,
Luck and ill-luck share borders.
吉凶同域.
Loss turns into gain,
失反爲得,
Victory turns into defeat.
成反爲敗.

Wú (Jiangsu) was great, its arms powerful,
吳大兵強,
King Fuchai was nevertheless surrounded.
夫差以困.
Yuè (Zhèjiang) perched at Kuaìji,
越棲會稽
Goujiàn became hegemon of his generation.
勾踐霸世.
(*Goujiàn of Yuè suffered for years under Fuchai before final triumph.*)

The penetrating man takes the big view,
達人大觀,
So he sees the possibilities.
乃見其可.
Round wheel or square brake,
橢枋一術,
How could one technique be sufficient for driving?
奚足以游?
From past ages until the present,
往古來今,
In their operations, who was without fault?
事孰無郵[=尤?]?

Shùn had unfilialty, (*cf. Shèn Dào* **49**)
舜有不孝,
Yáo had unkindness.
堯有不慈.
King Wén was handcuffed and shackled,
文王桎梏,
Guân Zhòng was captured and imprisoned.
管仲拘囚.

Yang-ya without end,
坱軋無(?)垠,[288]
Who hammers it out?
孰錘(?)得之?

Ultimate virtue is unselfish,
至得無私,
It sails like an untied boat:[289]
泛泛乎若不繫之舟.
The able cross over by it,
能者以濟,
The incapable are overturned in it.
不能者以覆.

Heaven may not be counseled with,
天不可與謀,
Earth may not be cogitated with[290]
地不可與慮.

The Sage Man sacrifices things, (*cf. iv-c*)
聖人捐物,
Following principle to give or reject.
從理與舍.
The multitude of men are defiled,
眾人域域[=掝掝?],[291]
Oppressed by cravings and desires.
迫於嗜欲.

---

[288] *Chŭcí* (XII: Zhao Yînshì, 'Summoning a Recluse'): The cicada cries oh! 'yang oh ya'. Huìgu míng xi, yang-xi ya, 蟪蛄鳴兮坱兮軋. Jiâ Yì's Owl Rhapsody has yang-ya wúyín 坱軋無垠. See Postscript I, fn 378.

[289] *Zhuangzǐ* (XXXII, Liè Yùkòu): 1040. The expression used here is 'unselfish' wúsi 無私, not 'without self' wújî 無己 as there. Cf. Owl Rhapsody, Postscript I, below.

[290] Páng Zî in viii-a asks: The Sage with gods counsels, the Way by humanity is completed. I wish to hear how to fathom the gods and cogitate on completion's essentials.

[291] Cf. *Xúnzî* (III) 40: receive men's defilement, shòu rén-zhi yùyù 受人之掝掝.

193

Small knowledge establishes biases,
小知立趨,
Lovers and haters are self-preoccupied.
好惡自懼.

Boasters die for power,
夸者死權,
Self-esteemers vie for appearance.
自貴矜容.
Valiant knights sacrifice themselves for fame,
列士徇[=殉?]名,
Greedy fellows sacrifice themselves for wealth. (*cf. Zhuangzî VIII*)
貪夫徇[=殉?]財.

Ultimate universality is unbounded.
至博不給.
In knowing the times, where is the shame?
知時何羞?
The unworthy are bound by vulgar custom,
不肖繫俗,
The worthy strive for the times.
賢爭於時.

If Goujiàn of Yuè had not been held captive,
勾踐不官,
Two nations would not be settled.[292]
二國不定.
If King Wén had not been confined,
文王不幽,
King Wû would not have attacked (and conquered Shang).
武王不正.

Petty causes and trifling tribulations,
細故裂蒯,
How are they sufficient to cause doubt?
奚足以疑?
Operations completed and desires gained,
事成欲得,

Again, how are they sufficient to boast about?
又,奚足夸?

---

[292] Goujiàn recovered his throne from Wú and annexed it in 473 to become Hegemon. The phrase 'two nations' recurs in vii-b. where the context appears to be Zhào under threat from Qín.

A thousand words, myriad explanations,

千言萬說,

In the end what reward are they?

卒賞謂何?

If Guân Zhòng had not been disgraced and shamed,

管仲不羞辱,

His name would not be with the great worthies.

名不與大賢.

His achievements would not be with the Three Kings

功不得與三王

To meet face to face fit![293]

鉦面備矣!

When virtue flourished,

德之盛,

mountains had no paths or foot tracks,

山無徑跡,

marshes had no bridges.

澤無橋梁.

---

[293] 'Three Kings' refers to founders of Xià, Shang and Zhou dynasties. 'Face to face' zhèngmiàn 鉦=正面 is a special expression, used also at the close of ix-g, where it is applied to the Complete Ninth's appearance.

xiii. PREPARED KNOWLEDGE
(Beìzhi 備知第十三)

This chapter is the most 'Daoist' in Graham's definition of primitivist but asserts the positive value of knowledge. It laments the loss of human emotive reality, the innocence of the primordial age, like that of *Lâozî* and *Zhuangzî*, the classic Graeco-Roman golden age or biblical garden of Eden. Graham understood it to glorify a state of 'anarchy' (1989: 311).

Profit is presented, in Mencian mode, as contrary per se to righteousness (*Mèngzî* I a.1). Yet it is not profit itself that is denounced but corrupt and coercive rule. 'Daoist saints' and suicide are ridiculed. The Sage must prepare himself by combining knowledge in employment of human psychology, 'knowing men' (zhirén 知人), to unite his generation. Many historical figures are those from the previous chapter, namely martyrs, unscrupulous ministers, evil kings and sagacious heroes. Its theme matches *Zhuangzî*'s Abdicating Kingship (XXVIII) but takes an opposite stand on 'righteous' suicide.

In this potted Chinese history, loyal and wise subjects, who foresaw danger and dared to warn and admonish their rulers, paid the ultimate penalty for their good advice. Wû Zîxu (d. 494) of Chû was a bi-generational case. He got help from neighbouring Wú to avenge his father's unjust execution. Following victory, he exhumed the king of Chû's corpse to inflict a posthumous scourging. Years later, Wû Zîzu's ignored warnings to the king of Wú, about a resurgent Yuè, led to his own suicide before Yuè's invading army crushed Wú. [294]

Not mentioned is the most famous of all suicide martyr heroes, Qu Yuán (d. ca. 300 BC) of Chû, who, like Wû Zîxu, became a river god commemorated with annual dragon-boat races. Qu Yuán is believed to have drowned himself in Mìluó river, near Chángsha, after Qín captured his King Huaí (328-299). A century later, in exile at Chángsha, Jiâ Yì (201-169), author of Owl Rhapsody (see Postscript I, below), also composed an elegy to Qu Yuán.

In opposition to the hereditary principle, this chapter accuses dynastic founders Tang of Shang and Wû of Zhou of ordering executions simply to enable their family's seizure of power. This 'heretical' charge was refuted by Dông Zhòngshu (ca. 179-104) on grounds of filial obedience to their father Heaven. Dông claimed that 'principle' demands the overthrow of rulers who 'lack the Way'. He even used this to justify Qín's overthrow of Zhou and placed it on a par with Qín's own overthrow by Hàn in 206 BC.[295]

---

[294] *Shîjì* (LXVI Lièzhuàn:Wû Zîxu) 372-374.

[295] *Chunqiu Fánlù* (VII) 25.

a) A Corrupt World

Heaven is high yet may be known,[296]
天高而可知,
Earth is great yet may be presided over:
地大而可宰:
myriad things rest in them.
萬物安之.
Human feeling, where is it to be found?
人情安取?

Recluses Bóyí and Shúqí
伯夷叔齊
were able not to rob,
能無盜,
yet unable to cause men not to suspect them.
而不能使人不意已.

Shen Túdí considered his generation
申徒狄以爲世
polluted and uninhabitable,
溷濁不可居,
so on his back loaded a rock
故負石
and cast himself into the Yellow River.[297]
自投於河.
He did not know water's
不知水中之
disorder was even more extreme.
亂有逾甚者.

When virtue flourished,
德之盛,
mountains had no paths or foot tracks,
山無徑跡,
marshes had no bridges.
澤無橋梁.

---

[296] Contrast vii-a: Heaven is high and hard to know.

[297] In *Mòzǐ* fragments (*Taìpíng Yùlǎn*: Zhenbâo, bù-1) 802, Shen Túdí (申徒狄) petitions the Duke of Zhou, probably Dàn regent to King Chéng (r. 1055-1021), for promotion of worthy commoners, citing precious gems' origin in humble soil. This matches a bamboo strip on promotion of worthies recovered from a mid-Warring States tomb in 1958 at (Hénán) Xìnyáng, Chángtáiguan. Li Xueqin 1994: 341-344. *Zhuangzǐ* (XXVI Waìwù) 944 places Shen under King Tang (r. ca. 1675-1646), founder of Shang; (XXIX Dàozhí) 988: Shen petitioned but was ignored and his body eaten by fish and turtles. *Chûcí* (Bei Huífeng) and *Hánshi Waìzhuàn* I) 31 incongruously place Shen Túdí after Wû Zîxu (d. 494).

197

There was no going and coming,
不相往來,
boats and chariots did not communicate.[298]
舟車不通.
Why was this?
何者？
Its people were like infants.
其民猶赤子也.

Having intelligence was not used for
有知者不以
mutual cheating and enslavement.
相欺役也.
Having strength was not used
有力者不以
mutually to make servants and masters.
相臣主也.

And so, birds and sparrows nests might be peered down into,
是以鳥鵲之巢可俯而窺也,
deer, in herds living, might be followed and tied up.[299]
麋鹿群居可從而係也.
When generations become corrupt,
至世之衰,
fathers and sons plot against each other,
父子相圖,
elder and younger brother are mutually suspicious.
兄弟相疑. Why is this?
何者？

Their reformation, being weak,
其化,薄,
they proceed from mutually having contrivance.
而出於相以有爲也.

So, contrivance spoils it.
故,爲者敗之.

Ordering disorders it.[300]
治者亂之.

---

[298] This view of the 'Golden Age' is comparable to *Lâozî* (LXXX). Cf. ix-g.

[299] *Zhuangzî* (IX Mâtí 'Horses' Hooves') and Wénzî: Shànglî have versions of this couplet.

Huaínánzî: XIII Fànlùn has the first line. *Lyûshî Chunqiu* VI-5: Mínglî has a version of the next verse: When disorder's reformation came … zhì luàn-zhi huà… 至亂之化…

Spoiled, there are factions,
敗,則儞,
disordered, there is fawning.
亂,則阿.
When there is fawning, principle is cast away.
阿,則理廢.
When there are factions, righteousness is not established.
儞[=佣?],則義不立.

b) Promotion of the Worthy

Yáo transmitted to Shùn the Under-Heaven. (*on merit, not birth*)
堯傳舜以天下.
So, those who love righteousness consider Yáo wise.
故,好義者以爲堯智.
Those who love profit consider Yáo foolish.
其好利者以爲堯愚.
Kings Tang and Wû banished and executed
湯武放弑
to profit their sons. (*founding the Shang and Zhou dynasties*)
利其子.
Those who love righteousness consider them lacking in the Way,
好義者以爲無道,
yet lovers of profit consider them worthy.
而好利之人以爲賢.

Those generations did not transmit to the worthy,
彼世不傳賢,
so there was banishment of lords.
故有放君.
Rulers loved factions and distortion,
君好儞阿,
so there was assassination of rulers.
故有弑主.
Now, banishment and assassination occur
夫放弑之所加
where doomed nations are present.
亡國之所在.
I have never seen anyone happily
吾未見便樂而
and peacefully live there.
而安處之者也.

---

[300] Cf. *Lâozî* (XXIX) 122; (LXIV) 108: He who contrives it, spoils it. He who holds, loses it. Weízhê baì-zhi, zhí-zhê shi-zhi. 爲者敗之,執者失之.

Now, he who abides in danger to subvert peace
夫,處危以妄安
pursues grief to diminish joy.
循哀以損樂.
So, nations will have shroud-less funerals,
是,故國有無服之喪,
army-less arms.
無軍之兵.
This may be foreseen.
可以先見也.

For this reason, Jizî fled.[301]
是故箕子逃.
(Jizî, uncle to Zhôu Xin, corrupt last king of Shang whom he
admonished unsuccessfully. He later advised King Wû, Zhou dynasty
founder ca. 1122.)
But (Nán'gong Wàn) fought Chóu Mù.[302]
而搏仇牧.
(In 682 Nán'gong Wàn assassinated Duke Mín of Sòng and killed loyal
minister Chóumù.)

Shang Róng was imprisoned
商容拘
(Music master who tried to reform king Zhôu Xin of Shang.)
and Jiân Shú wept.[303]
商容拘而蹇叔哭.
(Jiân Shú warned Duke Mù of Qín against attacking Zhèng in 628 but
was ignored, and Qín's army annihilated.)

Formerly, when someone climbed high,
昔之登高者,
men below on his behalf trembled,
下人代之凌,[304]
hands and feet for him sweated.
手足爲之汗出.
The man above would then
上人乃
start to grasp the bending branches
始搏折枝
and hasten to hold onto the trunk.
而趨操木.

---

[301] *Shàngshu*, Hóngfàn. *Shîjì* (XXXVIII Sòng Shìjia) 263a: Weizî Kai.
[302] *Shîjì* (XXXVIII Sòng Shìjia) dì-264c: Mín'gong 11ᵗʰ year.
[303] *Zuôzhuàn*, Xîgong 32ⁿᵈ year.
[304] "Trembling 凌 is written here with the 'heart' (xin) radical.

Those who would correct are executed.
止[=正?]之者僇.
Consequently, the Under-Heaven is cold with fearful heart,
是故,天下寒心,
and men's ruler in isolation stands.[305]
而人主孤立.

In the present generation those who remain on the side
今世之處側者
are all traitorous ministers.
皆亂臣也.
Their knowledge is sufficient to make the ruler not succeed,
其智足以使主不達,
their words are sufficient to corrupt government,
其言足以滑政,
their parties and cliques sufficient to suit their own interests.
其朋黨足以相甯於利害.

Formerly, King Tang employed Yi Yîn, (*an ex-publican*)
昔,湯用伊尹,
Zhou employed Taìgong Wàng. (*Grand Duke Jiang, an ex-butcher*)
周用太公.
Duke Mù of Qín employed Baîlí Xi, (*an ex-herdsman*)
秦用百里,
Chû employed Shen Biao (*in 505, Shen got Qín help to save Chû from Wú*),
楚用申麃,
Duke Huán (r. 685-643) of Qí employed Guân Zhòng (*great reformer*).[306]
齊用管子.

What caused these various premiers
此數大夫之所
to be exalted in their generation
以高世者
is the same reason that causes all doomed kingdoms'
皆亡國之
loyal ministers to die.
忠臣所以死也.

---

[305] The same couplet recurs in vii-b.
[306] These are historical examples of highly talented individuals of low social status promoted to high office with spectacularly successful results. Ref. Allan 2018/2016, passim.

For this one observes, (cf. ix-g; xvii-b. Shèn Dào, *Zhuangzî* XVII)
[由]是觀之,
it is not that their wisdom and ability had difficulty in coping,
非其智能難與也,
it was the times' mandate which could not reach them.
乃其時命者不可及也.

It is not only like this.
唯無如是.
Times have those whom they reach and seek out,
時有所至而求,
times have those whom they reach but reject.
時有所至而辭.
Mandates have those they reach but shut out,
命有所至而闔,
mandates have those they reach and open for.
命有所至而闢.
Worthies do not necessarily get their times,
賢不必得時也,
the unworthy do not necessarily lose their mandate (*i.e. their life*).
不肖不必失命也.

Consequently, worthies protect their times
是故,賢者守時
and the unworthy protect their mandates (*their own lives*).
而不肖者守命.
The present generation does not lack those with Shùn's conduct:
今世非無舜之行也:
it does not know Yáo's precedent. (*in abdicating to Shùn*)
不知堯之故也.
It does not lack King Tang and Wû's operations,
非無湯武之事也,
it does not know Yi Yîn and Taìgong's precedents (*in giving wise counsel*).
不知伊尹太公之故也.

Feìzhòng and Wùlaí got King Zhôu Xin of Shang's profits
費仲惡來得辛紂之利
but did not know Wû of Zhou would rebel to punish him.
而不知武王之伐之也.
Ministers Bîgan and Wû Zîxu loved to make loyal admonitions
比干子胥好忠諫
but did not know their ruler would murder them.
而不知其主之煞之也.

202

Feìzhòng and Wùlaí may be said to know psychology!

費仲惡來者可謂知心矣!

But they did not know operations.

而不知事.

Bîgan and Wû Zîxu may be said to know operations!

比干子胥者可謂知事矣!

But they did not understand psychology.

而不知心.

The Sage Man is of necessity with both fully prepared.

聖人者必兩備.

Only then can he entirely unite his generation.

而後能究一世.

xiv. ARMED CAMPAIGNS
(Bingzheng 兵政[=征]第十四)

From its content and by reference to Mâwángdui essays like 'Ruler's Campaigning', this chapter's title must be 'armed campaigns', though it is written as 'armed government'.[307] Héguan Zî explains how man by understanding dialectical laws of nature can adapt them by balance (quán) and dynamics (shì) to his own advantage. This attention to dynamics and the five agents has affinities with *Sunzî Bingfâ* (V). Páng Zî's opening question on warfare parallels Mencius, who advised compliance with "Heaven's timing, Earth's advantages and Human togetherness" (cf. iv-e, xvii-f),[308] but adds rewards and punishments.

All stems from human endeavour through six phases: Worth > Sagacity > Way > Law > Divinity > Illumination, before going to war. This recalls step by step preparations prior to committal to war in Confucius' *Analects*, *Guânzî*, and Mâwángdui 'Yellow Emperor' scrolls.[309]

a) Dynamics of Nature

Páng Zî asked Héguan Zî saying:
龐子問鶡冠子曰:
> To implement arms' laws,
> 用兵之法,
> 'Heaven them, Earth them, and Man (*humanize*) them.'[310]
> 天之,地之,人之.
> Rewards urge to battle, punishments compel multitudes.
> 賞以勸戰,罰以必眾.
>
> Though these five have already been planned,
> 五者已圖,
> if the Nine Barbarians use them,
> 然九夷用之
> victory is not necessitated.
> 而勝不必者.

---

[307] Cf. *MWD* Shíliù-jing (Junzheng 君正=征) 47.

[308] *Mèngzî* (Iib.1 Gongsun Chôu-xià, Dé Dào duozhù): Heaven's timing, Earth's advantages, Human cooperation, Tianshí, Dìlì, Rénhé 天時地利人和. Xúnzî (XV Yì Bing) 283: unify the people. *Guóyû* (XXI Yuèyû-xià) 1-2. *MWD* Shíliù-jing (Bingróng) 71: If arms are not formed by Heaven, arms may not move. If they do not take law from Earth, arms may not be positioned. If penal law is inhuman, arms may not win.

[309] *Lúnyû* (XIII Zîlù) 29. *Guânzî* (IV Lìzheng, Qi-guan) 12-13. *MWD* Shíliù-jing (Junzheng).

[310] Cf. iv-e, fn 117: Heavens it, Earths it, Mans it…; x-a, fn 246; xvii-f, fn 341. *Mèngzî* (Iib. 1 Gongsun Chôu-xià, Dé Dào duozhù). *MWD* Shíliù-jing (Bingróng) 71. *Guóyû* (XXI Yuèyû-xià) 1-2.

Why is this?
其故何也?

Héguan Zî said:
鶡冠子曰:
Things have life (physics).
物有生.
So, metal, wood, water, fire and soil:
故金木水火未[=土]:
when applied, exercise mutual control.
用,而相制.

Have you never seen, for example, a gate-beam?
子獨不見夫閉關乎?
If leant-to, a housewife will shift it.
立而倚之,則婦人揭之.
If laid flat then, without selection by physique,
仆而措之,則不擇性,
Anyone can lift
it by the middle.
而能舉其中.
If one were to hold its extremity,
若操其端,
Even a champion could not raise it off the earth.
則雖選士不能絕地.

The gate-beam is still one body,
關尚一身,
yet heaviness or lightness differ:
而輕重異之者:
dynamics cause them to be so. (*cf. Lièzî: 6 Lìmìng 215. Shizî: Guângzé 12.*)
埶[=勢]使之然也.

Now, from the gate-beam to speak,
夫,以關言之,
where there are things, dynamics are present!
則物有,而埶在矣!
Though the Nine Barbarians use them,
九夷用之,
they will not necessarily conquer because
而勝不必者
they have not fathomed things' life. (physics)
其不達物生者也.
When you fathom things' life,
若達物生者,
these five are as one!
五尚一也耳!

205

Páng Zî said:

龐子曰：

> To make the five into one, how can this be done?
>
> 以五爲一奈何？

Héguan Zî said:

鶡冠子曰：

> Heaven cannot make early into late.
>
> 天不能以早爲晚．
>
> Earth cannot make high into low.
>
> 地不能以高爲下．
>
> Man cannot make male into female.
>
> 人不能以男爲女．
>
> Rewards cannot motivate the incompetent to succeed.
>
> 賞不能勸不勝任．
>
> Punishments cannot compel the impossible.
>
> 罰不能必不可．

b) Balance and Dynamics

Páng Zî said:

龐子曰：

> To achieve success, how is it done?
>
> 取功,奈何？

Héguan Zî said:

鶡冠子曰：

> Heaven cannot compel men,
>
> 天不能使人，
>
> men cannot compel Heaven.
>
> 人不能使天．
>
> Adapt to things' suchness,
>
> 因物之然，
>
> failure and success are stored in it.
>
> 而窮達存焉．
>
> These two derive from balance and dynamics.
>
> 之二也在權在埶．
>
> From balance in production of materials
>
> 在權故生財
>
> you will have super-abundance of wealth.
>
> 有過富．
>
> From dynamics in use of arms
>
> 在埶故用兵
>
> you will have super-abundance of victories.
>
> 有過勝．

Material production comes from
財之生也
labour in Earth and obedience to Heaven.
力之於地,順之於天.
Arms' victories come from
兵之勝也
compliance with the Way and union with men.
順之於道,合之於人.

Those who do not understand
其弗知者
take rebellion as obedience,
以逆爲順,
take disasters as success (*profit*).
以患爲利.

By taking rebellion as obedience,
以逆爲順,
their wealth becomes poverty.
故其財貧.
By taking disasters as success,
以患爲利,
their troops will be captured.
故其兵禽.

Formerly, those who knew the times
昔之知時者
by the Way were vindicated.
與道證.
Those who did not know them
弗知者
were in danger from the Divine Luminaries.
危神明.

What the Way dooms,
道之所亡,
what Divine Luminaries defeat,
神明之敗,
what being may sustain their injuries?
何物可以留其創?

So it is said:
> 'The Way oh! The Way oh!
> 故曰道乎道乎!
> By Divine Luminaries mutually protected!'[311]
> 與神明相保乎!

Páng Zî said:

龐子曰:
> How do they mutually protect?
> 何如而相保?

Héguan Zî said:

鶡冠子曰:
> Worth generates sagacity,
> 賢生聖,
> Sagacity generates the Way,
> 聖生道,
> the Way generates Law,[312]
> 道生法,
> Law generates divinity,
> 法生神,
> Divinity generates luminaries,
> 神生明,
> Divine Luminaries are campaigning's tip.[313]
> 神明者正之末也.
> Tips are fed from their roots.
> 末受之本.
> For this reason, they mutually protect.
> 是故相保.

---

[311] *Zhuangzî* (XXV Kèyì): The pure unadulterated Way is just by divinity guarded.

[312] *MWD Jingfǎ* (Dàofǎ) 43, 1a: The Way generates Law.

[313] As elsewhere, Héguan Zî affirms the primacy of human action, yet connects it to 'Divine Luminaries' who are absent from *Lâozî*. Guânzî (XLIII Zhèng) 254 expounds a five- fold progression: penalties > governance > law > virtue > Way. *Shangjun Shu* (II Shui Mín) also has five: penalties, force, strength, awe, virtue. *MWD* Shíliù-Jing (Lùn) has ten stages: strength, awe, magnanimity, governance, stillness, fairness, tranquillity, simplicity, essence, divinity.

xv. STUDY PROBLEMS (Xuéwèn 學問第十五)

Héguan Zî, taking on himself the role of guru to the future messianic Sage, here outlines a program of 'nine ways, a check and to-do list for the coming messiah. He draws on Sun Zî's *Art of War* (IV) for their culmination, thus re-inventing the strategist's 'nine grounds'. In addition, 'six laws' of ritual propriety, music, humanity, justice, loyalty and good faith are given with 'music' added to the five virtues expounded above (ii). The excavated Guodiàn Six Virtues (ca. 300) text has sagacity and wisdom in place of ritual and music but identical last four (GD: 187). Ritual and Music are two of the Confucian Six Arts along with archery, charioteering, writing and counting.[314]

The reference to the six laws as a hexagram (guà) implies a metaphor of divination by combinations of six lines (yáng unbroken and yin broken) in the *Yìjing 'Book of Change'*. The use here of nine and six for 'ways' and 'laws' (Dàofâ) echoes *Yìjing* numerology's use of nine yáng numbers nd six for yin numbers. *Héguanzî* (xix-a) condemns reliance on "milfoil oracle or tortoise-shell augury" of which the former was the *Yìjing*'s foundation. Instead, he argues, destiny is to be determined, not by an inscrutable fate, but from compliance with the six moral 'laws'.

a) Nine Ways
Páng Zî asked Héguan Zî saying:
龐子問鶡冠子曰：
> The Sage Man in studying problems, submits to his teacher.
> 聖人學問服師也.
> Does this indeed have an end and a beginning?[315]
> 亦有終始乎?
> Or, do recital and memorization
> 　抑其拾誦記辭
> only after closing the coffin-lid stop?[316]
> 闔棺而止乎?

---

[314] *Guodiàn Chûmù Zhújiân* 1998: Liù-Dé 187. Jiâ Yì: *Xinshu* (VIII Liù-Shu, Dàodé shuo) 59- 60 on six principles of virtue: Way, virtue, human-nature, spirits, illumination, mandate.

[315] *Xúnzî* (I Quànxué) 9: begin with reciting the classics, end in reading ritual propriety... This is called Way and virtue's ultimate.

[316] *Shangjun Shu* (XVII Shângxíng 'Rewards and Punishments') 63: People's love of wealth and ennoblement only after closing the coffin ends. *Hánshi Wàizhuàn* (VIII) 348 credits this saying to Confucius: Study never ceases. Only after closing the coffin does it end.

Héguan Zî said:

鶡冠子曰:

> It begins at the first question,
>
> 始於初問,
>
> ad ends at the Nine Ways. (cf. viii-c)
>
> 終於九道.
>
> Not having heard the Nine Ways explained,
>
> 若不聞九道之解,
>
> even if your recital and memorization
>
> 拾誦記辭
>
> only at the closing of your coffin lid were to stop,
>
> 闔棺而止,
>
> how could it be settled?
>
> 以何定乎?

Páng Zî said:

龐子曰:

> What is meant by 'Nine Ways'?
>
> 何謂九道?

Héguan Zî said:

鶡冠子曰:

> First is Way and Virtue;
>
> 一曰道德;
>
> second are shade and sunlight; (*yinyáng*)
>
> 二曰陰陽;
>
> third are law and edicts;
>
> 三曰法令;
>
> fourth are heavenly bodies;
>
> 四曰天官;
>
> fifth are divine portents;
>
> 五曰神徵;
>
> sixth are skills and arts;
>
> 六曰伎藝;
>
> seventh is human reality;
>
> 七曰人情;
>
> eighth are tools and weapons;
>
> 八曰械器;
>
> ninth is management of arms.
>
> 九曰處兵.

Páng Zî said:

龐子曰:

> I wish to hear of the Nine Ways' operations.
>
> 願聞九道之事.

Héguan Zî said:

鶡冠子曰:

1) Way and virtue restrain conduct to make it habitual.
道德者操行所以爲素也.

2) Shade and sunlight's division and numbering in the calendar
陰陽者分數

are the means to observe energy's alterations.
所以觀氣變也.

3) Law and edicts are the ruler's Way,
法令者主道,

the order or disorder of a nation's mandate.
治亂國之命也.

4) Heavenly bodies signal auguries
天官者表儀祥兆

that below elicit responses.
下之應也.

5) Divine portents are phenomena of
神徵者風采

lights and glimmerings that herald calamities.
光景所以序怪也.

6) Skills and arts are to excel those of the same task
伎藝者如勝同任

to invent from nothing something uniquely different.
所以出無獨異也.

7) Human reality is the small and great,
人情者小大,

foolish and wise, worthy and unworthy,
愚知賢不肖,

brave ace and valiant hero in mutual pairing.
(Cf. i-b; xviii-c)
雄俊豪英相萬(=偶)也.

8) Tools and weapons are to use chariots and horses
械器者假乘焉[=馬]

in the generation's employment for national defence.
世用國備也.

9) Management of arms is the awesome lever:
處兵者威柄:

he who grasps it 'stands on invincible ground'.[317]
所持立不敗之地也.

---

[317] *Sunzî Bingfâ* (IV Xíng): stand on invincible ground.

Nine Ways forming the mind
九道形心
means spiritual efficacity.
謂之有靈.

Then you can observe revolutions and mandate them,
后能見變而命之,
adapt to what they contrive and settle them.
因其所爲而定之.
A mind without form's spiritual efficacity,
若心無形靈,
With language though of wide learning and concision,
辭雖搏[=博]捆,
will not know where to go.
不知所之.

When mind is master,
彼心爲主,
the internal will command the external.
則內將使外.
If internally you lack marvellous portents,[318]
內無巧驗,
the near at hand will not be reached,
近則不及,
the far off will not arrive.
遠則不至.

b) Six Attainments

Páng Zî said:
龐子曰:
    Ritual and music,
    禮樂,
    humanity and righteousness,
    仁義,
    loyalty and goodfaith:
    忠信:

    I wish to hear how they combine with technique.
    願聞其合之於數.

---

[318] MWD (Jingfǎ: Dàofǎ) 43: When the Under-Heaven has operations, there must be marvellous portents.

Héguan Zî said:

鶡冠子曰：

Ritual propriety means not to offend;

所謂禮者不犯者也；

Musical enjoyment means no harm.

所謂樂者無菑者也.

Benevolent humanity means to share in loving good;

所謂仁者同好者也；

Justice means to share in hating wrong.

所謂義者同惡者也.

Loyalty means ever more a friend;

所謂忠者久愈親者也；

Goodfaith means not being duplicitous.

所謂信者無二響者也.

The Sage Man by these six

聖人以此六者

makes hexagrams (guà) of a generation's

卦世

gains or losses, disobedience and obedience's warps[319]

得失逆順之經.

Now, apart from the Way, contrary to numbers,

夫離道非數

you may not connect to your starting principle.

不可以緒端.

Now the essential of the six laws is that[320]

不[=夫]要元[=六]法

you may not sever heart from limbs.

不可以劍心體.

He who has external technique, but an internal source,

表術,裏原,

though shallow, will not be exhausted.

雖淺,不窮.

---

[319] This is either metaphorical, or a long-lost tradition, for the six lines of yin-yáng combinations from the sixty-four hexagrams in the *Yìjing* used to predict fortunes.

[320] In accord with the preceding list, I read 'six laws' liù-fâ 六法, for the received text's 'prime law' yuánfâ 元法. Qín's First Emperor made the number 'six' (divisible by both two and three) his basic numbering unit. (*Shǐjì* VI, year 26, 42a)

He who is internally void and externally wide-ranging,
中虛外博,
though wide-ranging, will necessarily be voided.
雖博必虛.

Páng Zî twice bowed and said:
龐子再拜曰：
Your questioner has been admonished!
有問戒哉!
Though unlike this,[321]
雖毋如是,
his benighted talent will hereby be strengthened.
冥材乃健.
If he did not study it who would be capable of it?
弗學孰能?

This is the Under-Heaven's ultimate Way,
此天下至道,
yet this generation's masters have abandoned it. Why?
而世主廢之. 何哉?

Héguan Zî said:
鶡冠子曰：
Do not carry life in the wrong vessel
不提生於弗器
or cheapen life in the useless.
賤生於無所用.

In the middle of the Yellow River, having lost your boat,
中河失船,
one float is worth a thousand pieces of gold.
一壺千金.
Value and cheapness are inconstant:
貴賤無常:
times cause things to be so.
時使物然.

They who constantly recognize excellence as excellence
常知善善
have a succession over generations unchanged
昭繆不易 that may be at once verified up to the present.
一揆至今.

---

[321] Defoort 1997: 96. I prefer the Zîhuì's (1577) 'this' shì 是 to the Dàozàng edition's 'dark' míng 冥.

If they do not recognise excellence as excellence,
不知善善,
there will be men dead and nations doomed,
故有身死國亡,
interrupted sacrifices, extinguished lineages.
絕祀滅宗.

Small men still being such
細人猶然
cannot protect their longevity.
不能保壽.
Justice then is self-shaping.
義則自況.

xvi. GENERATIONS OF WORTHIES
(Shìxián 世賢第十六)

King Diàoxiang (卓=悼襄 of Zhào, r. 244-236) 'the Afflicted', asks strategist Páng Xuan whether he needs to be pro-active (yôuweí), implying that as ruler he should rest in stately 'non-contrivance.' The answer is that employment of worthies to act in good time will produce results but make it seem as if nothing was done. Páng Xuan makes the case for employment of worthies, a major theme of *Héguanzî*, from instances of advisers who helped a ruler recover his throne, become hegemon or overthrow a tyrant and found a dynasty.

The allegory of doctor for political adviser was also used by *Hánfeizî* to illustrate this tag from *Lâozî*: "Contrive it in the still non-existent..."[322] The message is that good government is not spectacular. Yet in the case of Shen Baoxu's rescue of King Zhao, this was already a last ditch effort.

The first case relates to King Hélyû of Wú's invasion of Chû in 506, forcing its King Zhao to flee to the small state of Suí. Zhao sent his premier Shen Baoxu to seek aid from Qín. As a result of Shen's diplomacy, Qín sent five hundred chariots, enabling Chû next year to rout Wú and recover its territory, though not the hegemony (as here).

The critical situation of Chû in this episode mirrors that then prevailing in Zhào, for which Páng Xuan will command the last coalition againt Qín and may here be fishing for that appointment. After the failure of their anti-Qín coalition in 241 and death of the king in 236, this piece might be presented as a funeral drama or satire to re-galvanize the nation. An up-beat piece of patriotic retrospective theatre may be seen for King Wûlíng (xix-b). Yet in 222, Qín finally annexed the kingdom of Zhào.

Worthies as 'Doctors of Medicine'

King Diàoxiang asked [General] Páng Xuan, saying:
卓襄王問龐煖曰:
> Now should the lord of men also have to contrive for the nation?
> 夫君人者亦有爲其國乎?

Páng Xuan said:
龐煖曰:
> Has the King alone not heard of Yúfù's contrivance in medicine?
> 王獨不聞俞跗之爲醫乎?

---

[322] *Hánfeizî* (XXI Yù Lâo) 118-19. *Lâozî* (LXXIV; LXXI).

The already healthy were necessarily cured.
已成必治.
Demons and gods shunned them.
鬼神避之.

King Zhao of Chû (r. 515-489, regained the throne)
楚王臨朝
with Suí (*and Qín's*) arms.[323] (*thanks to Shen Baoxu's diplomacy*)
爲隨兵.
So, just as with Yáo's appointment of men,
故,若堯之任人也,
he did not employ personal relatives,
不用親戚,
and necessarily employed the able.
而必使能.

To govern his 'sickness,'
其治病也
he did not appoint his beloved
不任所愛
but necessarily employed an experienced 'doctor.'
必使舊醫.

The King of Chû, having heard of his reputation,
楚王聞傳,
On the eve of 'sickness' in his person,
暮害在身,
necessarily depended on a Yúfù.
必待俞跗.

King Diàoxiang said:
卓襄王曰:
　Excellent.
　善.

Páng Xuan said: Has the King forgotten?
龐煖曰:王其忘乎?
　Formerly Yi Yîn doctored King Tang of Shang,
　昔伊尹醫殷,
　Taìgong doctored King Wû of Zhou.
　太公醫周武王.

---

[323] The story given here is incomplete and suppresses mention of Qín. *Shǐjì* (XL Chû Shìjia) dì-280c; (LXVI Lièzhuàn Wú Zîxu) dì-361b, c. This event occurred in 505. Cf. Defoort 1997: 82.

Baîlî Xi doctored Duke Mù of Qín,
百里醫秦,
Shen Biao (Baoxu) doctored King Zhao of Chû,
申鷈醫郢,
Yuán Jì (*Zhào Shuai*) doctored Duke Wén of Jìn (*Weì*),
原季(=趙衰)醫晉,
Fàn Lî doctored King Goujiàn of Yuè,
范蠡醫越,
Guân Zhòng doctored Duke Huán of Qí.
管仲醫齊.

So these five nations in turn got the hegemony.
而五國霸.
Their excellences were one,
其善一也,
yet their Ways did not share the same techniques.
然道不同數.

King Diàoxiang said:
卓襄王曰
> I wish to hear about their techniques.
> 願聞其數.

Páng Xuan said:
煖曰:
> Has the King alone not heard of
> 王獨不聞
> Duke Wén of Weì's questions to Biânquè?[324]
> 魏文侯之問扁鵲耶?
> He said: Of you three brothers,
> 曰:子昆弟三人,
> who is the most excellent in doctoring?
> 其孰最善爲醫?

Biânquè said:
扁鵲曰:
> My elder brother is the most excellent,
> 長兄最善,
> the middle brother is second,
> 中兄次之,
> I, Biânquè, am the lowest.
> 扁鵲最爲下.

---

[324] *Hánfeizî* (XXI Yù Lâo) 118 on doctor Biânquè and Duke Huán of Caì.

Duke Wén said:
魏文侯曰:
> May I get to hear about this?
> 可得聞邪?

Biânquè said:
扁鵲曰:
> My elder brother in sickness observes its spirit
> 長兄於病視神
> while it is still unformed and excises it.
> 未有形而除之.
> So, his name does not go beyond his household.
> 故名不出於家.
> The middle brother governs sickness in the down and hairs,
> 中兄治病其在毫毛,
> so his name does not go beyond his village.
> 故名不出於閭.
> As for me, Biânquè, I puncture blood and veins,
> 若扁鵲者鑱血脈,
> ply drugs and medicines, cut into flesh and skin's gap,
> 投毒藥,副肌膚,
> and my name goes forth and is heard by all the barons.
> 閒而名出聞於諸侯.

Duke Wén of Weì said:
魏文侯曰:
> 善.
> Excellent.

[Páng Xuan said:
爰曰]:
> Had Guân Zî practiced doctoring technique in Biânquè's Way,
> 使管子行醫術以扁鵲之道,
> I say would not Duke Huán have just about
> 曰桓公幾
> been able to complete his hegemony (*instead of being deposed*)?
> 能成其霸乎?
> All these did not take 'sickness as sickness.'[325]
> 凡此者不病病.
> They governed it in the unnamed, acted on it in the unformed.
> 治之無名, 使之無形.
> "They achieved success and finished the job.
> 至功之成.

---

[325] 'Sickness' (bìng 病) can also mean 'fault.' *Láozî* (LXXI): The sage is not faulty because he finds fault with faults. (LXIV): Contrive it in the still non-existent. *Hánfeizî* (XXI Yù Lâo) 118 on 'doctoring'. Cf. Guodiàn Chûmù Zhújiân: Weí Lî-zhi Dào (167, A37) 44-45.

To subordinates it seemed spontaneous."[326]
其下謂之自然.
So, good doctors reform you,
故良醫化之,
unskilled doctors destroy you.
拙醫敗之.
Though perchance you do not die,
雖幸不死,
they will wound and stretch your limbs and sinews.
創伸股維.

King Diàoxiang said:
卓襄王曰:
Excellent! As the Loner,
善.寡人,
though I cannot be unwounded,
雖不能無創
who can add a wisp of autumn hair
孰能加秋毫
onto this Lone Man's top?
寡人之上哉?

---

[326] Spontaneous/natural/self-so, zìrán 自然. *Lâozî* (XVII). Cf. iii-b, xi-a.

xvii. HEAVEN'S BALANCE
(Tianquán 天權第十七)

The mysterious opening may refer to Grand Unity as rotator (huán), flying like a shaman pacing the Dipper through the universe, or to the Dipper itself turning with the passing hours in the night sky. In an echo to *Lâozî* (I): "The name that may be named is not the constant name," it appears to delineate an unmoved mover, an un-named namer of ineffable godhead, light of the world.

Unity is defined in five cognitive qualities: space, time, virtue, the Way and things. The criticism of the limitations of sense perception parallels the caveats by Xún Zî and Lyû Bùweí.[327] There are five failures of cognition and action. Music unifies troops but must be in harmony with Heaven. The ruler at the centre can motivate untrained multitudes by virtue to fight as if bursting from a dyke. *Sunzî Bingfâ* (V). had compared tactics to varying combinations of musical notes and dynamics to the onrush of pent-up water.

Shèn Dào (**28** Yinxún) had urged adaptation to the dynamics of situations. Small can defeat big. Deception is a weapon. Mencius had declared his faith in ordinary people, through the Heaven-Earth-Man trilogy (Iib-1.1. cf. HGZ xiv-a). 'Driving townsfolk to fight' (xii-d) was the strategy used in 205 against a resurgent Zhào by Hàn general Hán Xìn (*Shîjì* XCII Lièzhuàn, dì-438b), perhaps quoting *Héguanzî*.

a) Space-Time
He who lifts up Heaven and Earth to travel
挈天地而能遊者
is called the rotator.
謂之遷[=環?].
He names but is not circumscribed by names.
名而不遷於名.
This man's brilliance shines light.
之人明照光.
Shining cannot shine on itself.
照不能照己.
His brilliance is governance.[328]
之明是[=正?]也.

---

[327] *Xúnzî* (XXI Jiêbì): 443. *Lyûshì Chunqiu* (Jì XXIII 3.5 Yôngsài): 7b-10b.
[328] Here I read 'this/right' 是 shì as 'governance' 正 zhèng.

Alone reforming from start to finish, (lit. 'finish to start')
獨化終始,

according to abilities in precedence he orders.
隨能序致.

Alone he sets up space and time without fief boundaries,
獨立宇宙無封,

he is called the Augustan of Heaven and Earth.
謂之皇天地.

He floats in suspension Heaven and Earth's luminaries.
浮懸天地之明.

He deputizes mandates in sub-divisions called seasons.
委命相鬲謂之時.

His communication and separation is called the Way.
通而鬲謂之道.

He connects the myriad things to lead Heaven and Earth.
連萬物領天地.

He joins up and rounds out those with common roots.
合膊同根.

His mandate is called space and time.
命曰宇宙.

He knows space, so nothing is unaccommodated.
知宇故無不容也.

He knows time, so nothing is insufficient.
知宙故無不足也.

He knows virtue, so nothing is unsettled.
知德,故無不安也.

He knows the Way, so nothing is unheard.
知道,故無不聽也.

He knows things, so nothing is not so.
知物,故無不然也.

b) Cognition and Sense Perception

If you know Unity, yet do not know the Way,
知一,而不知道,

you cannot yet internalize it.
故未能裏也.

Arms face death to seize life,
兵者涉死而取生,

cross danger to seize safety.
陵危而取安.

For this reason, when speech is such, the Way corresponds.
是故,言而然,道而當.

(*I move this paragraph up from after 'weight is wounded deeply'.*)

Formerly those who went, not knowing what they were going to seek,
昔行,不知所如往而求者,
were necessarily confused;
則必惑,
searching for what they did not know to find its image,
索所不知求之象者,
they necessarily did not get it.
則必弗得.

So, among men, none but are
故人者莫不
deceived in what they do not see,
蔽於其所不見,
prejudiced by what they do not hear,
鬲[=隔]於其所不聞,
obstructed by what they do not open,
塞於其所不開,
suppressed in what they cannot do,
詘於其所不能,
controlled by what they do not conquer.
制於其所不勝.

The generation's vulgar crowds are
世俗之眾
encaged by these five and do not penetrate them.
籠乎此五也而不通此.
They are not yet seen, yet have forms.
未見,而有形.

So, it is said: 'Without armies there are arms.
故曰:'有無軍之兵.
Without mourning there are funerals.'
有無服之喪.'
Men making light of death and life is the cause.[329]
人之輕死生之故也.

---

[329] Lâozî (LXIX, LXXV): People make light of death because their superiors seek life's luxuries ('thickness' hòu). Huaínánzî (II Chùzhen) 7a, as here (see below), has a gnat soaring in the ravine in its next stanza. Cf. vii-b.

Now, a mosquito or gnat,
夫,蚊虻,
falling down a thousand fathom ravine,
墜乎千仞之谿,
only then begins to soar and complete its form.
乃始翱翔而成其容.
Oxen and horses fall into it,
牛馬墜焉,
and are smashed into formlessness.
碎而無形.

From this one observes that (*cf. ix-g; xiii-b. Shèn Dào. Zhuangzî XVII*)
由是觀之
Size is inconvenient,
則大者不便,
weight is wounded deeply.
重者創深.

So, if one flea drills into your skin,
故一蚋鑽(?)膚,
you will not sleep till dawn.
不寐至旦.
If half a husk enters your eye,
半糠入目,
the four directions will be undiscerned.[330]
四方弗治.

This is what is meant by:
所謂:
'deception, how is it necessarily from
'蔽者豈必
the obstruction of curtains or
障於帷簾
concealment by hanging blinds?'
隱於帷薄哉!'
When horizons are level, not seeing is called deception.
周平,弗見之謂蔽.

---

[330] *Zhuangzî* (XIV Tianyùn) 522 attributes a variant of this stanza to Lâo Dan speaking to Confucius on limitations of knowledge, with 'mosquito' wén 蚊 in place of 'flea.' *Huaínánzî* (II Chùzhen) 12b. 'From this one observes' yóucî guan-zhi 由是/此觀之 is a trope of Shèn Dào (**8, 13, 49**), Thompson 1979: 233, 236, 260. *Zhuangzî* (XVII Qiushuî) 580. Ix-g, xiiii-b. The message is that the dynamics of situations (shì) vary. Small may defeat big.

So, with defective vision the eyes do not see,
故,病視而目弗見,
with defective hearing the ears do not hear.
疾聽而耳弗聞.
Ignorance is when knowledge's ability
蒙故知能[331]
in what is seen or heard is entirely exhausted.
與其所聞見俱盡.
Ineptitude is when settlement of tasks and conduct of operations
鬲[=隔]故奠務行事
in deployment of force is entirely exhausted.
與其任力俱終.
Obstruction is when orders to the four directions from headquarters
塞故四發上統
are interrupted and vanish.
而不續而消亡.

c) Setting Goals

Now, the Way must have responses to be effective.
夫道者必有應而後至.
Operations must have virtue to succeed.
事者必有德而後成.
Now, virtuous knowledge is
夫德知
that whereby operations succeed.
事之所成.
Success is what is got to then say:
成之所得而後曰:
'I can succeed.'
'我能成之.'
If success is not contrived,
成無爲,
if getting does not come,
得無來,
carefully examine its Way.
詳察其道.
Whence is it so?
何由然哉?
If misled about the past to observe the present,
迷往以觀今,
from this you know you will be unable.
是以知其未能.

---

[331] 'Ignorance' méng 蒙 is exchanged here for 'deception' bì 蔽, above.

He who sets a target to aim at will not be confused.
彼立表而望者不惑.
He who accords with law in apportionments will not be doubted[332]
按法而割者不疑.
Indeed, words are the means of announcing it.
固言有以希[= 布?]之也.
Now, if you aim without a target,
夫望而無表,
apportion without law,
割無法,
you will have confusion as a consequence!
其惑之屬耶!

d) Orientation

What is meant by confusion
所謂惑者
is not lack of sun and moon's illumination,
非無日月之明
the four seasons' sequence,
四時之序,
planets and constellations' motions.[333]
星辰之行也.

If you adapt to the contrary of these
因乎反茲
you will have confusion.
而之惑也.
Bewildered, you will strain to see yet become more disoriented
惑故疾視愈亂
and inadvertently change direction.
悖而易方.

The military have tallies,
兵有符,
the Way has proofs.
而道有驗.
Defences are necessarily in advance prepared,
備必豫具,
cogitations are necessarily beforehand settled.
慮必蚤定

---

[332] MWD Shíliù-jing (Cheng 81) 144a-b: If you rely on targets in aiming, you will not be confused; if you depend on law to rule, there will be no disorder.

[333] 'Planets and constellations' xingchén 星辰, literally 'stars and constellations'.

Below, adapt to Earthly profit,
下因地利,
control by the five agents:
制以五行:
to your left wood (east),
左木,
to your right metal (west),
右金,
to your front fire (south),
前火,
to your back water (north),
後水,
at the centre is soil.[334]
中土.

When encamping the army and deploying troops,
營軍陳士,
don't neglect contingencies.
不失其宜.
Once these five degrees are correct,
五度既正,
no operation will be unperformable.
無事不舉.
The Dipper's Beckoner star being above, [335]
招搖在上,
preparations are made below.
繕者作下.

Take Law from Heaven, (*with its four directional images for E, S, W, N*) 取
法於天,
at the four seasons seek their images:
四時求象:

---

[334] In practical terms, these may refer to the use of the five agents as symbols displayed on banners by the five divisions of an army. In later times, the eight trigrams served the same military purpose.

[335] *Ritual Record, Lǐjì* (I Qŭlǐ-shàng) 43-44 describes chariot banners with: Red Bird in front (south), Dark Warrior behind (north), Green Dragon on the left (east), White Tiger on the right (west), Beckoner above. The Dipper by its apparent annual rotation signals positions of the months as in *Huáinánzǐ* V. *Guānzǐ* (XLII Shì, 'Dynamics') 253: If you search but do not find, seek it beneath the Beckoner. *Wénzǐ* (IX Xiàdé) 79: Beckoner is the material sustainer of the myriad beings. *Shuìhǔdì Qínmù Zhújiǎn* 1990: Rìshu divinatory almanac, Dark Battle-axe (Xuán'gé) 187-188: Beckoner (Zhaoyáo) points to…"

In springtime use the Grey Dragon,
春用蒼龍,
in summer use the Red Bird,
夏用赤鳥,
in autumn use the White Tiger,
秋用白虎,
in winter use the Dark Warrior.[336]
冬用元[=玄]武.

When Heaven and Earth have been obtained,
天地已得,
what things may not be commanded?
何物不可宰?
Where rational principle resides is called Earth,
理之所居謂之地,
what divinities form is called Heaven.
神之所形謂之天.

He knows Heaven so he can
知天故能
by one undertaking get fourfold results,
一舉而四致,
when two together arise he alone will win.
並起而獨成.
His bird chariot races on,
鳥乘隨隨,
his colts fly draped in radiance.
駒(?)蜚垂耿(?).

So, formerly those who excelled at archery[337]
故昔善討[=射?]者
did not seek to profit,
非以求利,
except by enlightenment in the art.
將以明數.

Formerly they who excelled at war
昔善戰者
did not seek conquest,
非以求勝,
except by enlightenment to conquer.
將以明勝.

---

[336] *Lǐjì* (I Qulǐ-shàng; VI). Dark Warrior of the north is traditionally equated with Snake and Tortoise, perhaps for swift attack and defensive armour.
[337] I read 'archery' shè 射 for 'demand' tâo 討.

Have you alone not seen a conjurer?
獨不見夫隱者乎?
He sets you up by causing you to 'know it'
設使知之
so that your knowledge is confounded.
其知之者屈.
Your already 'knowing it'!
已知之矣!
Is as if you did not know.
若其弗知者.

Even though a teacher were to explain,
雖師而說,
you still will not understand.
尚不曉也. It is pitiful! 悲乎!
Deceived, ignorant, prejudiced, and obstructed,
夫蔽,象(=?蒙),鬲,塞,
these men, undefeated, will collapse.
之人,未敗,而崩.
If not dead they will be taken prisoner.
未死而禽.

e) Unification
By dynamics of arms to take a nation
設[=勢]兵取國
is martial prowess.
武之美也.
By not moving to capture a nation
不動取國
is culture's glory.
文之華也.

Knights eulogize the martial,
士益武人
they do not eulogize culture.
不益文.
Unity is little loved
一者寡愛
but cannot be exhaustively discussed.
不可勝論.

Ears can hear tuned sound
耳者可以聽調聲
but cannot contrive tuned sound.
而不能爲調聲.
Eyes can see outstanding forms
目者可以視異形
but cannot contrive outstanding form.
而不能爲異形.
Mouths can speak of divine illuminations
口者可以道神明
but cannot contrive divine illumination.
而不能爲神明.

So, the first kings submitted to teachers' techniques
故先王之服師術者
to summon the departed, educate the ignorant,
呼往,發蒙,
explain contracts and analyse tablets,
釋約解刺[=箾?],
penetrate gloom and open lights
達昏開明
to summarise knowledge from them.
而且[=具?]知焉.
So, they were able to theorize appropriately, assess dangers,
故能說適計險,
and successively surpass the vulgar.
歷越踰俗.
They superseded class, transcending ranks.
軼倫越等.
Their knowledge of strategic vision
知略之見
excelled the multitude of men.
遺跋眾人.

They sought out the isolated, connected the distant.
求絕,紹遠.
Difficulties in front they were able to confront,
難之在前者能當之,
difficulty behind they were able to ward off.
難之在後者能章[=障?]之.
The essential was to lead the Under-Heaven
要領天下
so none were neglected.
而無疏.

Far from enemy nations' control,
遠乎敵國之制,
they fought and conquered, attacked and captured.
戰勝,攻取.
Their Way responded to things endlessly.
之道應物而不窮.

By unity they commanded myriads
以一宰萬
Yet were not of the general species.
而不總類.
In the species of life's splendour
類生之耀
their name is present.
名之所在.

They plumbed worth and ability's alterations,
究賢能之變,
exhausted contradictions' ('spear and shield'?) mysteries.
極蕭[=矛?]楯之元[=玄?].
Theirs is called a locationless tradition,
謂之無方之傳,
manifested in borderless space.
著乎無封之宇.

In control of operations, internally, you cannot plumb their forms.
制事,內不能究其形者;
In use of arms, externally, you cannot fill their successes.
用兵, 外不能充其功.

f) Heavenly Arms
Their arms had Heaven, had men, had Earth.[338]
彼兵者有天,有人,有地.
Arms excel through men,
兵極人,
Men excel through Earth,
人極地,
Earth excels through Heaven.
地極天.

---

[338] *Mèngzǐ* (II) 1. *Guóyǔ* (XXI) 1-2. *MWD* Jing fǎ Liù-fen 49, 28b. Shíliù-jing (Bingróng): 71, 116b. cf. iv-e fn 117; x-a, 246; xiv-a, fn 113.

Heaven has conquests,
天有勝,
Earth has protection,
地有維,
mankind has successes.
人有成.

So, he who is expert at using arms
故,善用兵者
takes care by Heaven to conquer,
慎以天勝,
by Earth to protect,
以地維,
by mankind to succeed.
以人成.
When these three are illumined clearly,
王[=三?]者明白,
what establishments may not be envisaged?
何設不可圖?

What is meant by 'Heaven'
所謂天者,
is it not in imperceptibly having conquests?
非以無驗有勝?
Is it not in the sun's dynamic of growth
非以日勢之長
and in what the myriad things receive and submit to?
而萬物之所受服者邪?

Heaven generates things,
彼天生物,
yet is not a thing.[339]
而不物者.
It is the origin of shade and sunshine,
其原陰陽也,
the four seasons' birth, growth, harvest and storage,
四時生長收藏,
that do not lose sequence.
而不失序者.

---

[339] *MWD* Jiŭ-Zhŭ 29, 361: Heaven… generates things but is not a thing. Tian… sheng wù bù-wù. 天 … 生物不物.

Its balance is in keynotes.
其權音也.
Keynotes reside in the untransmittable.
音在乎不可傳者.
Their feats are heroic.
其功英也.

So, to commence study of arms,
故,所肄學兵,
it is necessary to prioritise Heaven's balance.
必先天權.
Deploy troops by the five agents,
陳以五行,
battle by the five keynotes.
戰以五音.

On the left pair **do** (gong) with **mi** (jiâo), (*third interval*)
左倍宮角,
on the right link **re** (shang) to **la** (yû). (*fifth interval*)
右挾商羽.
Sol (zhi) as ruler (at centre) follows[340]
徵君爲[中?隨

to drum up untrained multitudes. (*cf. 'drives townsfolk' in xii-d*)
以鼓無素之眾.
On dry land he will submerge men,
陸溺溺人,
so he can go and come, like water from a breached dyke.
故能往來竇決.

A solitary weapon (metal) unconnected,
獨金而不連,
will sever the Way's cable,
絕道之紀,
disorder Heaven's design.
亂天之文.

---

[340] Cf. x-c: sol east, la south, re west, mi north and centre do. Here the pentatonic scale in military formation has sol at centre. Taking sol as G, C-E at the third interval are on the left, and D-G at fourth interval on the right.

'Clashing keynotes'[341] mean
干音之謂
offending things' emotive reality.
違物之情.
If to Heaven you are unconnected,
天之不綱,
you will be censured by severe misfortune.
其咎燥凶.

If you desire to be without disorder or rebellion,
欲無亂逆,
reverently serve the Heavenly Hero.
謹司天英.
Should the Heavenly Hero's name be lost,[342]
天英各(=名?)失,
the triple army will lack substance.
三軍無實.

Now, except for the hero who has its substance,
夫,不英而實,
who has such a thing?
孰有其物?
Constantly, the Sage's universal, past and present,
常聖博,古今,
return one day is what
復一日者
Heaven and Earth await to close!
天地之所待而闔耳!

So, Heaven's balance is divine melody's
故,天權神曲
five keynotes in the technique of arms.[343]
五音術兵.

---

[341] 'Clashing tones' (ganyin 干音) is an otherwise unknown term.

[342] I read 'name' míng 名 for the similar looking 'each' gè 各. Name and substance are standard pairs.

[343] Defoort 1997: 250 n6 accepts Lù Diàn's commentary in taking these terms as names of unknown books. They must refer to music's role in drilling troops, signalling their deployment and overriding moral purpose. Cf. 'Heavenly Melody' (ix-d); 'battle by key- notes' (xii-d, xvii-f).

The proverb says:

逸言曰：

 'It manifests disaster or good-fortune like fitting tally-sticks.'[344]

 '章以禍福若合符節.'

All operations are born from cogitation,

凡事者生於慮,

completed by effort, doomed by panic.[345]

成於務,失於驚.

---

[344] *MWD* Jiû-Zhû (29) 31n.7 has virtually the same line. Cf. *Mòzǐ* (XVI Jian'aì-xià) 73. *Mèngzǐ* (Ivb.1 Shùn sheng -yú Zhuféng) 148.

[345] *Guânzǐ* (V) 14: Operations are: born through cogitation, completed through effort, lost through arrogance.

xviii. ENABLING HEAVEN
(Néngtian 能天第十八)

This chapter lyrically celebrates human self-reliance and rational understanding of dynamics. Its rejection of 'search by inspections' may, by context, be a rejection of superstitious prognostications. 'Getting' (dé), as a pun on 'virtue' in attainment of immortality through union with the Way, appears here, as in viii-c, *Zhuangzî* (VI, XII), *Guânzî* (XXXVI) and *Hánfeizî* (XX). It is apotheosis by self-effort and extraordinary merit of men to become gods with which they credit the Yellow Emperor among others, like Augustus *à la* Graeco-Roman mode.[346] It sounds like a description of the classic Daoist immortal, achieved by merit, not ingestion of a magic potion.

The Sage operates both through physical dynamics (shì 勢) and principle (lî 理). He is able to discern the truth beneath surface appearances. This Way is man-made. It echoes Confucius' dictum "man enlarges the Way, the Way does not enlarge man."[347] It is not a 'substance.' This is positive expectation of achievable destiny, not fatalism. Heaven is enabled through the human. Yet it has a transcendentalist link. (xi-b, xviii-b) The piece concludes with a throwback to Wide Selection (i-b; xv-c 7), 'Ace-Valiant-Hero' grading.

a) Song of the Primal Sage
(cf. viii-c The Sage Messiah)
The primal Sage's mental activity[348]
原聖心之作:-
from reality's invisible subtleties only then arises.
情隱微而後起.
He spreads to the infinite and seeks to oversee it.
散無方而求監[臨?]焉.
He transcends primal marvels and only then finishes.
軼元眇而后[=後]無.
He sails[349] the limpid depths
杭澄幽
and contemplates carefully there.
而思謹焉.

---

[346] *Zhuangzî* (VI) 247; *Hánfeizî* (XX) 108: Starting from Heaven, Earth and the Dipper, ending with the Yellow Emperor Xuanyuán, the hermit Red Pine Master and the sages. Horace: Odes (Carmina 3.3, lines 9-12) "In this manner, Pollux and the wanderer Hercules by striving attained the fiery heights among which is Augustus."

[347] Lúnyû (XV) 28.

[348] 'Punctuation mark' jù (句), apparently equivalent to semi-colon.

[349] I read 'sail' (236ati 航) for 'resist' (kàng 抗) here.

He cuts through the six co-ordinates unhindered.
截六際而不絞.
He observes the who and who-not,
觀乎孰莫,
listens in non-negation,
聽乎無罔,
excels at the untrammeled,
極乎無係,
discourses in mystic obscurity.
論乎窈冥.

He is translucent, not confused or entangled.
湛不亂紛.
So he can break through dusty defilements
故能絕塵埃
and stand in Grand Purity.[350]
而立乎太清.

He goes without companion,
往無與俱,
comes without escort.
來無與偕.
He has scant provisions, few followers.
希備寡屬.
Solitary, he has no equal,
孤,而不伴,
so he is without blemish.
所以無疵.

Infant-like,[351] he will alone arrive
保然獨至
to transmit the future that will be so
傳未有之將然
and lead its headless sequence.
領無首之即次.
He reckons by tens or fives in application to operations,
度十五而用事,
measures past and present in their fall and rise.
量往來而廢興.

---

[350] Guânzî (XXXVII Xinshù-xià) 223: Great purity is viewed in great brilliance; (XLIX Neiyè) 271: He is mirrored in great purity. Cf. viii-c, fn 202.

[351] I read 'bâo' (褓) as of an infant in swaddling clothes.

He adapts to motion and stillness to conclude life,
因動靜而結生,
enables Heaven and Earth to promote and set down.
能天地而舉措.

The self-such is form,
自然形也,
it may not be altered.
不可改也.
Odd and even are numbered,
奇耦數也,
they may not be increased or diminished.
不可增減也.

Victory and defeat are presaged,
成敗兆也,
they do not randomly[352] develop.
非而長也.
So he who gets the Way to stand,[353]
故其得道以立者,
Earth enables him to stand.
地能立之.

He who gets the Way to topple,
其得道以仆者,
Earth does not enable to stand.
地弗能立也.

He who gets the Way to be secure,
其得道以安者,
Earth enables to be secure.
地能安之.
He who gets the Way to be endangered,
其得道以危者,
Earth does not enable to be secure.
地弗能安也.

[352] I read 'randomly' êr 爾 for 'and' ér 而 here.

[353] This chapter takes a rationalist approach, adducing 'dynamics' (shì 勢). Cf. fn 355, below. He uses 'getting' (dé), a homonym for 'virtue', with the Way. *Zhuangzǐ* (VI Dà Zongshi; XII Tiandì) 247, 424; *Guânzǐ* (XXXVI Xinshù-shàng) 220-221; *Hánfeizǐ* (XX Jiê Lâo) 108: on gods, nature, including the Dipper stars (Weídôu 維斗), and men 'getting the Way' to live or die.

238

He who gets the Way to live,
其得道以生者,
Heaven enables him to live.
天能生之.
He who gets the Way to die,
其得道以死者,
Heaven does not enable him to live.
天弗能生也.

He who gets the Way to survive,
其得道以存者,
Heaven enables him to survive.
天能存之.
He who gets the Way to perish,
其得道以亡者,
Heaven does not enable to survive.
天弗能存也.

His security or danger is in dynamics.
彼安危埶[=勢]也.
Survival or perishing is by rational principle.
存亡理也.
How may it be blamed on Heaven's Way?
何可責於天道?
Demons and gods, how are they involved?
鬼神,奚與?
Unity is virtue's worthy,
一者德之賢也,
the Sage is the worthy's love.
聖者賢之愛也.

The Way is what the Sage employs.
道者聖之所吏也.
It is ultimately what is gotten to arrive.
至之所得也以至.

Documents may not record him,
圖弗能載,
names may not raise him.
名弗能舉.
Mouths may not convey his ideas,
口不可以致其意,
portraits may not set up his appearance.
貌不可以立其狀.

Like the Way in the image of
若道之象
gates and doors he is.
門戶是也.
Worthy and unworthy, foolish and wise
賢不肖愚知
by them enter and exit and do not differ.
由焉出入而弗異也.

b) Immortality and the Dynamic of Self

The Way is what opens up things
道者開物者也
it does not equalize things.[354]
非齊物者也.
So, the Sage is the Way,
故,聖道也,
the Way is not the Sage.[355]
道非聖也.

The Way inter-connects things,
道者通物者也,
the Sage sequences things.
聖者序物者也.

So there is the 'First Kings' Way'
是以有先王之道
but not 'the Way's First Kings.'
而無道之先王.

So, the Sage Man after Heaven and Earth is born, (cf. xi-b)
故,聖人者後天地而生,
yet knows Heaven and Earth's beginning.
而知天地之始.
He is before Heaven and Earth in perishing
先天地而亡
yet knows Heaven and Earth's end.
而知天地之終.
His strength does not compare with Heaven and Earth
力不若天地
yet he knows Heaven and Earth's duties.
而知天地之任.

---

[354] 'Equalizing Things' is the title of chapter Zhuangzǐ (II).

[355] Confucius: Lúnyǔ (XV) 28: Man expands the Way, the Way does not expand man.

His energy does not compare with shade and sunshine
氣不若陰陽
yet he can contrive to be their warp.
而能爲之經.
He does not compare with the myriad things in quantity
不若萬物多
yet he can contrive their governance.
而能爲之正.

He does not compare with the multitude in beauteous splendour,
不若眾美麗
yet he can promote good and point out faults.
而能舉善指過焉.
He does not compare with the Way and virtue in richness
不若道德富
yet he can contrive to honor them.
而能爲之崇.
He does not compare with Divine Luminaries in shining
不若神明照
yet he can contrive to master them.
而能爲之主.
He does not compare with demons and gods in concealment,
不若鬼神潛,
yet he can manifest their souls.
而能著其靈.

He does not compare with metal and stone in solidity
不若金石固
yet he can forge their strength.
而能燒其勁.
He does not compare with square and circle in symmetry[356]
不若方圓治
yet he can deploy their forms.
而能陳其形.

Formerly those who got the Way to be established
昔之得道以立
until the present unshifting are
至今不遷者
the four seasons and Grand Mountain[357]
四時太山是也.

---

[356] On the use of the circle and square, cf. ix-e and xi-a.
[357] This lyrical interlude may be compared to *Zhuangzǐ* (VI Dàzong Shi) 247 on human immortality as nature gods, including mountains and heavenly bodies and *Hánfeizǐ* XX: 108.

Those who got the Way of danger
其得道以危
until the present insecure are
至今不可安者
lichened peaks and misty streams,
苓蠻堙谿,
rotten trees that fall in the wind.
槀[=蠹?]木降風是也.

Those who got the Way to live
其得道以生
until the present unperishing are
至今不亡者
sun and moon, planets and constellations.
日月星辰是也.

Those who got the Way to perish
其得道以亡
until the present unviable are
至今不可存者
tender leaves meeting frost,
苓葉遇霜,
morning dew meeting the sun.
朝露遭日是也.

So, the Sage Man takes it from dynamics
故聖人者取之於埶[=勢]
and does not search by investigation.[358]
而弗索於察.
Dynamics are concentrated and at the self.
埶者其專而在己者也.
Investigations are scattered and go to things.
察者其散而之物者也.
Things as things, fragmented and divided,
物乎物芬芬份份,
which of them does not from unity issue
孰不從一出
and into unity change?
至一易?

---

[358] *Hánfeizǐ* (XX Jiě Lǎo) 108 which includes 'Grand Mountain', also *HGZ* iv-d.
Lǎozǐ (LVIII): When government is investigative, people are impoverished, qí-zhèng cháchá qí-mín quèquè 其政察察其民缺缺. 'Investigative' implies Legalism. Dynamics is taken as integrative. Shíliù-jing (Guan) 62, 86a undertaking operations don't intrusively investigate. Jǔshì wù yángchá 舉事毋陽察. Jing fǎ (Guócì) 45, 12a, b: wù yángqiè 毋陽竊.

So settle judgements in men,
故定審於人,
observe transformations in things.
觀變於物.

c) Knowing Words

The mouth is the means of expressing the mind's sincere ideas.
口者所以抒心誠意也.
Some cannot receive instruction or deeply understand.
或不能俞受究曉.
In promoting their meaning
揚其所謂
some exceed their substance.
或過其實.

So those whose actions differ condemn each other.
故行異者相非.
Those whose Ways differ do violence to each other.
道異者相戾.
Slanderous words distort things:
詖辭者革物者也:
the Sage knows where they diverge.
聖人知其所離.

Exaggerated words are based on things:
淫辭者因物者也:
the Sage knows to what they equate.
聖人知其所合.

Deceitful words confuse things:
詐辭者沮物者也:
the Sage knows what they disguise.
聖人知其所飾.

Evasive words [distort] the reality of things:
遁辭者[歪?]請(=情?)物者也:
the Sage knows their limits.[359]
聖人知其所極.

---

[359] *Mèngzǐ* (II) 39 on 'knowing speech' is very close to this: Evasive words, I know where they are deficient. Dùncí zhi qí suǒ qióng 遁辭知其所窮. Cf. *Guǐguzǐ* (IX Quán, 'Assesments') on speech.

Correct words empathize with things:
正辭者惠物者也:
the Sage knows on what they stand.
聖人知其所立.

He who stands can put into effect the knowable.
立者能效其所可知也.
None can speak of what they have not attained.
莫能道其所不及.

If you clearly comprehend the external and internal
明論外內
then you can bring stability to men.
後能定人.

Unity is there but may not be seen,
一在而不可見,
the Way is there but may not be monopolized.
道在而不可專.

It is exactly comparable to the abyss (ocean),
切譬于淵,
its depths are unfathomable.
其深不測.
It surges on placidly,
淩淩乎泳,
its waves are inexhaustible.
澹波而不竭.

Only the Ultimate Man,
彼雖[=唯?]至人,
can train his essential spirit,
能以練其精神,
cultivate his ears and eyes,
修其耳目,
adjust and adorn his body.
整飾其身.

Like the joining of matching tallies,
若合符節,
small and big details are controlled
小大曲制
without omission or error.
無所遺失.

Far and near, crooked and straight,
遠近邪直,
there is nowhere he does not reach.
無所不及.

So, he who does good by virtue to a myriad men
是以德萬人者
is called 'ace',
謂之俊,
he who does good by virtue to a thousand men is called 'valiant',
德千人者謂之豪,
he who does good by virtue to a hundred men is called 'hero.'[360]
德百人者謂之英.

Therefore, the Sage's words are universal.
故聖者言之凡也.

---

[360] i-a has 'Ace' jùn 雋, here written 俊; xv-b.

xix. KING WÛLÍNG (Wûlíng Wáng 武靈王第十九)

King Wûlíng 'Martial Spirit' (r. 325-299) of Zhào is celebrated for in 307 adopting Hunnish jackets and trousers to clad his mounted archers. He later turned this new cavalry against the 'barbarian' Xianyú kingdom of Zhongshan, leading to its absorption by Zhào in 296.[361] Yet his last years following abdication to his son were calamitous. This is the swan song of a failed state, the epilogue for a once proud nation.

Military advice on how to defeat an enemy of superior force placed in the mouth of Páng Huàn is addressed to King Wûlíng. The latter serves as a surrogate for his doomed descendent King Qian, confronted with the prospect of conquest by all powerful Qín. This came to pass in 228 with the installment of puppet King Fa, and Zhào's final annexation in 222.

This is the only chapter to break the book's 'two-word title' rule to follow the three-word mould of the 'inner chapters' of *Zhuangzî*. Though set with protagonists of the earliest date in the entire work, it is a piece of historical fiction. It functions as a fitting conclusion and retrospection to earlier themes like that of the night walker (iii) resumed here. It opportunistically combines the adaptative with the operative without the remaining three of the Five Governances defined by Héguan Zî (viii-c, d).

As in the medical examples (xvi), true success is not spectacular. The best results are obtained without overt use of force. This strategy reflects Sun Zî's *Art of War* which is quoted without attribution. The examples of the ultimate triumphs of King Goujiàn of Yuè over Wú, with that of Hán Xuan Zî, Weì Huán and Zhào Xiang over Zhì Bó, are also cited by Hán Fei Zî in his petition to the future First Emperor, urging him to become hegemon king of the Under-Heaven, and in his 'Parables of *Lâozî.*'[362]

Another interesting point of contact is the descriptive battle couplet "stiff corpses in millions, spilling blood a thousand lî," virtually verbatim to that used by Qín's First Emperor, as the young king, to describe the after-effects of a Son of Heaven's wrath (*Zhànguó Cè* XXV, Weìcè 4).

a) The Night Walker
King Wûlîng asked Páng Huàn, saying:
武靈王問龐煥曰：
> I, the Lone Man, have heard a current saying that:
> 寡人聞飛語流傳曰：

---

[361] *Shǐjì* (XLIII) dì-297c, 298a, b, c: Wûlíng 19ª year.

[362] *Hánfeizǐ* (I: Chujiàn Qín) 7-8; (XXI Yú Lâo) 122-123.

'In one hundred battles to conquer
百戰而勝
'is not the best of best.
非善之善者也.
'Not to fight yet conquer
不戰而勝
is the best of best.'[363]
善之善者也.
I would like to hear it explained.
願聞其解.

Páng Huàn said:
龐煥曰：
The skilled value having no contest.
工者貴無與爭.
So the great superior uses strategic planning.
故大[=太]上用計謀.
The next adapts to human operations.
其次因人事.
The next battles to prevail[364]
其下戰克.

He who employs strategy
用計謀者
beguiles and confuses the enemy nation's lord.
熒惑敵國之主.

He causes him by change and alteration
使變更
to corrupt morality so that
　淫俗
profligate sycophancy and arrogance are indulged
哆恭憍恣
and he will be lacking in the Sage Man's techniques.
而無聖人之數.
Men he loves I given favour,
愛人而與,

---

[363] *Sunzǐ Bīngfǎ* (III Móugong 'Debating Attacks').

[364] This pattern occurs in *Lǎozǐ* (XVII) on gradations of trust in rulers: the grand superior… the next…
the next… the next… The classic example of this was that of Goujiàn of Yuè who, having lost his
kingdom to King Fuchai (d. 473) of Wú (Jiangsu), endured years as a captive. Goujiàn finally
conquered Wú by strategy, aided by adviser Fàn Lǐ's covert work to corrupt and undermine it,
regained his throne and became hegemon of the states.

Those without merit will be enfiefed,
愛人而與,
those who do not labour will be rewarded.
未勞而賞.

When glad, he will pardon criminals,
喜則釋罪,
when angry, he will wantonly kill.
怒則妄殺.
If law-abiding people just look out for themselves,
法民而自慎,
few men will voluntarily arrive.
少人而自至.

There will be proliferation of the useless,
繁無用,
addiction to tortoise-shell oracles.
嗜龜占.
High justice will be debased to suit
高義下合
his fancy's favourites.
意內之人.

Therefore Goujiàn (of Yuè) employed this (*strategy*)
因句踐用此
and (his enemy) Wú nation was doomed.[365]
而吳國亡.

What is meant by 'adaptation to human operations' is
所謂因人事者
his amassing of wealth and use of valuables
結幣帛用貨財
to close off intimates and stop their mouths,
閉近人之[=而?]復[=覆?]其口,
to cause what they call right to be all wrong,
使其所謂是者盡非也,
and what they call wrong to be all right.
所謂非者盡是也.

---

[365] I move this line up from section's end to show its connection to the first example of 'he who employs strategy'. It could happen that when books were written on bamboo strips that their thongs broke and their order became confused. For the story of Goujiàn, see vii-b, fn 169, and xii-d.

So he will be divorced from the ruler's realm,
離君之際,
from the employment of loyal ministers' road.
用忠臣之路.
(King Líng of) Chû employed this,
楚用此而陳蔡舉,
so Chén and Caì were taken[366]

What is meant by 'battling to prevail'
所謂戰克者
is only after a nation is already inherently broken
其國已素破
should you let your troops attack it.
兵從而攻之. The three houses (*of Jìn*) used this
三家用此
and Zhì Bó was doomed.
而智氏亡.
Hán Xuan Zî used this and Jìn was divided in three.[367]
韓用此而東[=晉?]分.

In the present generation speaking of arms,
今世之言兵也,
all say the strong and great necessarily conquer,
皆強大者必勝,
the small and weak are necessarily annihilated.
小弱者必滅.
If this were always so, small nations' rulers
是,則小國之君
would have had no hegemonies or kingships,
無霸王者,
and myriad chariot lords
而萬乘之主
would never have destruction and doom.
無破亡也.

---

[366] I move this line up to show its connection to the second example of 'adaptation to human operations'. Historically, King Líng of Chû was enabled to annex the smaller states of Chén and Caì by a process of intrigue and subversion in 533-531.

[367] I read 'Jìn' 晉 for 'east' (dong 東). Usurper Zhì Bó (Yáo) was besieged at Jìnyáng (in Shanxi) in 453 by armies of Zhào, Weì and Hán under Hán Xiangzî who diverted the river Fen against him. The break-up of Jìn into three kingdoms followed Zhì Bó's defeat and death. *Zhànguó Cè* (Zhào Cè I-2).

Originally, the lands of Xià were broad
昔,夏廣
and those of Tang (Shang founder) narrow.
而湯狹.
Shang-Yin great but Zhou small,
殷大而周小,
Yuè weak but Wú strong.
越弱而吳強.
(Yet Shang overcame Xià, Zhou overcame Shang and
Yuè overcame Wú because the latter became corrupt.)

This is what is meant by:
此所謂不戰而勝
'By not fighting to conquer is best of best.' [368]
善之善者也.

This is Shady Warp's law,[369]
此陰經之法,
the Night Walker's Way,
夜行之道,
Heavenly warrior's ilk.
天武之類也.

Now some make stiff corpses in millions,
今或僵尸百萬,
spilling blood a thousand li[370]
流血千里.
(This recalls Qín's slaughter of Zhào's army in 260 at Chángpíng. Cf.
vii-b.)

Yet victory still undecided,
而勝未決也,
they reckon it a success
以爲功
and that there is nobody like them.
計之每已不若.

---

[368] *Sunzĭ Bingfă* (III Móugong).

[369] *Gŭigŭzĭ* (XIII Bênjing Yinfú) 95 uses this term 'shady warp' yinjing. Defoort 1997: 250 n6 follows Lù Diàn who identifies it as an unknown work by the Yellow Emperor. For 'Night Walker', see iii-b.

[370] *Zhànguócè* (XXV Weìcè: Qínwáng shĭrén weì Anlíng Jun) 4: Fúshi baîwàn liuxuè qian-lĭ 伏尸百萬 流血千里. *Huaínánzĭ* (VIII) 11b. Weingarten 2020: 218-222.

b) Virtue's Triumph

For this reason, the Sage Man in splendid solitude cogitates,
是故,聖人昭然獨思,
happily in solitude rejoices.
忻然獨喜.
His ear may hear gongs and drums' sounds,
若夫耳聞金鼓之聲,
yet he has few feats.
而希功.
His eyes may see flags and pennants' colours,
目見旌旗之色,
yet he has few deployments.
而希陳.
His hand grasps a bladed weapon's handle,
手握兵刃之枋
yet he has few battles.
而希戰.

He goes forth advancing into close combat,
出進合鬥,
yet has few victories.
而希勝.
This was how Lord Xiang of Zhào defeated doom.[371]
是襄主之所破亡也.
(*Xiang defeated tyrant Zhì Bó by diplomatic strategy
and divided Jìn to found Zhào in 453.*)

King Wûlíng was moved and sighed, saying:
武靈慨然歎曰:
'Preservation or doom are in the person.
'存亡在身.
'Subtle indeed is that which generates good-fortune!
'微乎哉福之所生!
'I, the Lone Man, having heard this,
'寡人聞此,
'daily and monthly have the means of self-contemplation.'
'日月有以自觀.'

---

[371] *Mòzǐ* (XVIII) 87-88. *Zhànguó Cè* (XVIII) 1; 2. Xiang Zî Wûxu (r. 457-425), Lord of Zhào, routed Zhì Bó at the siege of Jìnyáng in 453, after Zhang Mèngtán's secret diplomacy won over Hán and Wei, Zhì Bó's erstwhile allies. Defoort 1997: 111 reversed this: "Páng Xuan explains to the king of Zhào that the defeat of his ancestor, King Xiang (r. 457- 425), was caused entirely by the king's own fondness for warfare." Lî 2003: 21.

From of old, those of ability and virtue
昔克德者
never distorted their mandate.
不詭命.
To get its essentials the words are not numerous.
得要者其言不眾.

FINIS

Postscript 1: Jiâ Yì's Owl Rhapsody
(Fúniâo Fù 鵩鳥賦)

Jiâ Yì (201-169) was adviser to Emperor Wén of Hàn. Critical of Qín's 'excesses', Jiâ was no Confucian conservative. Jiâ's patron, Wú Gong 吳公, had been a student of Qín premier Lî Si. His support for reform antagonized the hereditary peerage and he was exiled to Chángsha. In this prosperous but remote region of the old southern kingdom of Chû, he tutored the son of the King of Chángsha, descendant of Wú Ruì (241-201), ex-Qín prefect who joined the Hàn revolution. Its aged premier Marquis Daì was shortly to be interred, with his *Lâozî* and 'Yellow Emperor Classics' of Way's Law ideology, in the grand Mâwángdui tumulus.

Finding semi-tropical humidity did not suit him, Jiâ Yì found consolation in local culture. Five years before his death, Jiâ composed this 'frustration rhapsody' (fù) in emulation of Chû's classic poet Qu Yuán, an exile like himself. (*Zhaomíng Wénxuân* XIII: 181-183, Fúniâo Fù. Defoort 1997: 107-10). Qu had been dismissed by King Qîngxiang (r. 298-263) for criticizing policies of appeasement. These had earlier resulted in the death of King Huaí (d. 296) as prisoner in Qín. In despair, Qu drowned himself in the Mìluó river. (*Shîjì* LXXXIV, dì-415a-b, 417 Lièzhuàn. Hawkes 1959: 13-15).

Other early examples in this lyric style, characteristic of the southern state of Chû, were composed by Xún Zî (26: 533ff) and Dông Zhòngshu.[372] Pheasant Cap's rhapsody of the hero (xii-d), from which Jiâ seems to have borrowed, is by contrast robustly optimistic. Matching lines and phrases to *Héguanzî*'s 'Rhapsody of the Hero' (xii-d) are underlined below. As a progressive Confucian, Jiâ Yì is here satirizing superstition and a pseudo-science of prognostication. It is inconceivable that a serious work like *Héguanzî*, praised by Hán Yù (768-824), lifted lines from a parody such as this. [*pace* Liû Zongyuán (773-819); Defoort 2015: 281-282, 286] More likely is it that Jiâ Yì is also subtly making fun of *Héguanzî*, from among the books, that he tells us, he turned up.

> I was the King of Chángsha's tutor. After three years an owl flew into my lodging and perched on my chair's corner. It seemed like a bird of ill omen. I had been exiled to live in Chángsha and Chángsha is low-lying and damp. I lamented that my lifespan could not be long. So I made this rhapsody to relieve my spirits, as follows:
>
> 誼爲長沙王傅三年 有鵩鳥飛入誼舍 止於坐隅 鵩似鴞 不祥鳥也 誼以謫居長沙 長沙卑濕 誼自傷悼以爲壽不得長 乃爲賦以自廣 其辭曰

---

[372] *Xúnzî* (XXV Chéngxiàng; XXVI Fù). Pankenier 1990: 434-459.

It was the Jupiter Chán'è year (174 BC) oh! 單閼之歲兮
the fourth month in mid-summer, 四月孟夏
on gengzî day at sunset oh![373] 庚子日斜兮
an owl roosted in my lodging, 鵩集予舍
Perched on my chair's corner oh! 止於坐隅兮
looking most relaxed. 貌甚閑暇

Strange things were occurring oh! 異物來萃兮
I wondered about their cause. 私怪其故
I looked up books to prognosticate it oh 發書占之兮
To divine its import. They said: 讖言其度　曰
"Wild owls enter the bedroom oh! 野鳥入室兮
Its owner will go." 主人將去

I enquired of the owl oh! Where will I go? 請問于鵩兮　予去何之
If it is good luck tell me, if bad say the worst. 吉呼告我　凶言其災
Will it be later or sooner? Make an estimate oh! 淹速之度兮
Tell me its timing. 語予其期

The owl then sighed, 鵩乃嘆息
Raised its head and shook its wings. 舉首奮翼
Its mouth could not speak. 口不能言
I asked it to answer through intuition. 請對以臆

Myriad Things transform oh! 萬物變化兮
they certainly never cease. 固無休息
Their girations flow and shift oh! 斡流而遷兮
Some one pushes them to and fro. 或推而還

Form and energy spiral continuously oh! 形氣轉續兮
Transmogrified they hatch out anew. 變化而蟺
Their subtle depths inexhaustible oh! 沕穆無窮兮
cannot be fully described. 胡可勝言

---

[373] Jupiter year (Chan'è), was the sixth year of Western Hàn dynasty Emperor Wéndì. Gengzî is the thirty-seventh day in the sexagenary cycle. Jiâ Yì supplies all this official- sounding documentation with sardonic intent.

'Disaster is what good-fortune leans on. 禍兮福所倚
Good-fortune is where disaster lurks in ambush.' 福兮禍所伏
(*Lâozî* LVIII)
Grief and joy assemble at the gate oh! 憂喜聚門兮
Good-fortune and disasters share the same territory. 吉凶同域

That Wú was strong and great oh! 彼吳強大兮
Fuchai was still defeated there. 夫差以敗
Yuè perched at Kuaìji oh! 越栖會稽兮
Goujiàn became hegemon of his generation. 勾踐霸世

Lî Si roamed around and finally succeeded oh! 斯游遂成
(as premier of Qín)
He died by the Five Punishments. 卒被五刑
Fù Yuè was a convict breaking rocks oh! 傅説胥靡兮
then premier to Wû Dîng 乃相武丁
(Martial King of Shang r. 1324-1266 BC).

Now disasters and good-fortune, 夫禍之與福兮
how do they differ? Both are intertwined. 何異糾纏
Mandates are inexplicable oh! 命不可說兮
Who knows their limit? 孰知其極
(*Lâozî* LVIII)

'Water shot forth goes dry oh! 水激則旱兮
Arrows shot forth go far.'[374] 矢激則遠
Myriad things turn and twist, 萬物回薄兮
Shaken and stirred they spin around; 振蕩相轉
Clouds steam up, rains fall oh! 雲蒸雨降兮
Intermingled and mutually entangled. 糾錯相紛

The Great Equalizer disperses things oh! 大鈞播物兮
Knocks and pounds (yang-ya) ceaselessly.[375] 坱圠無垠

---

[374] *Lyûshì Chunqiu* (XXV, 4-7 Quyóu) 16b against uncontrolled anger has the same couplet in reverse order. *Wénzî* (IX Xiàdé) 75: So when water is agitated, waves arise. When energy is disorderly, wisdom becomes clouded.... *Huaínánzî* (VIII Bênjing) 11a: energy agitated explodes in anger. (XV Binglyuè) 11b as in HGZ xii-d.

[375] Cf. xii-d: Yang-ya without end, Who hammers it out? 坱圠無(?)垠, 孰錘(?)得之? *Chûcí* (XII: Zhao Yînshì, 'Summoning a Recluse'): The cicada cries oh! 'yang oh ya'. Huìgu míng xi, yang-xi ya, 蟪蛄 鳴兮坱兮圠.

Heaven may not be anticipated oh![376] 天不可預慮兮
The Way may not be pre-planned. 道不可預謀
Later and sooner have their mandates oh!, 遲速有命兮
Who knows their timing? 焉識其時

Now Heaven and Earth are a furnace oh! 且夫天地爲爐兮
Creation is their work. 造化爲工
Shade and sunshine are their charcoal oh! 陰陽爲碳兮
The myriad things are their bronze. 萬物爲銅

They combine and scatter, oh! 合散消息兮
Where is their constant model? 安有常則
A thousand changes, a myriad metamorphoses oh! 千變萬化兮
They have never begun to have an ultimate. 未始有極

Suddenly they are made humans oh! 忽然爲人兮
How is it worth wrestling over?[377] 何足控搏[=搏]
They will be transformed into different things oh! 化爲異物兮
How is it worth considering it a catastrophe? 又何足患

Small knowledge is selfish oh! 小智自私兮
to devalue others, value myself. 賤彼貴我
The penetrating man has a big view oh! 達人大觀兮
Among things nothing is impossible for him. 物無不可

Greedy fellows sacrifice themselves for lucre oh! 貪夫殉財兮
Martyr knights sacrifice themselves for fame. 烈士殉名
(cf. *Zhuangzǐ* VIII)
Boasters sacrifice themselves for power oh! 夸者殉權兮
Commoners live for their own lives. 品庶每生

Fear oppressed fellows oh! 怵迫之徒兮
either flee east or west. 或趨東西
Great men are not crooked oh! 大人不曲兮
Their ideas evolve impartially. 意變齊同

---

[376] Here Jiâ Yì makes explicit his personal rejection of futurism, using the language of *Héguanzǐ*, perhaps sardonically to make fun of its messianic message.

[377] Lî Shàn, in *Zhāomíng Wénxuân* edition, glosses kòngtuán 控團 'loving life' (àisheng 愛生). *Héguanzǐ* xii-d writes it kòngbó 控搏 'wrestling'.

Foolish knights tied by vulgarity oh! 愚士繫俗兮
Are confined as if imprisoned. 窘若囚拘
The Ultimate Man abandons things oh! 至人遺物兮
Alone with the Way together. 獨與道同

The multitude of men are confused oh! 眾人惑惑兮
Loves and hatreds accumulate in millions. 好惡積億
The True Man is bland and quiet oh! 真人恬漠兮
Alone with the Way reposes. 獨與道息

He is free of knowledge and casts aside forms oh! 釋智遺形兮
Transcendentally bereaved of self. 超然自喪
In vacant desolation 寥廓忽荒兮
with the Way he soars. 與道翱翔

He rides the flow to depart oh! 乘流則逝兮
Gaining a landing he stops. 得坻則止
He loses his body, deputes his mandate oh! 縱軀委命兮
Unselfish he has no self. 不私與己

His life is like a float, 其生兮若浮
His death like a rest. 其死兮若休，
Lucid like a deep spring's tranquillity, 澹兮若深泉之靜
He sails away like an untied boat. 汎乎若不繫之舟
(*Zhuangzi* XXXII)

He does not for life's causes treasure himself oh! 不以生故自寶兮
He nourishes himself in emptiness and drifts. 養空而浮
The virtuous man has no encumbrances, 德人無纇
Knowing his mandate, he has no worries. 知命不憂

Minute causes and trifling chaff, 細故蔕芥
How are they sufficient to make him doubt? 何足以疑

Postscript II: Míng Emperor Yônglè's Revolution and *Héguanzî*'s Grand Record (xi)

Carine Defoort (1997: 84-91；2015: 286-287; Huáng Huáíxin 2014: 257) has pointed out an anomaly in the *Héguanzî* Grand Record chapter (xi Tàilù) of the hand-written copy from Míng Emperor Yônglè (r. 1404-1424)'s 1407 compendium of universal knowledge, Yônglè Dàdiân. This extraneous passage consists of 223 characters.

Editor-in-chief of this massive compilation was laicised Buddhist prelate Yáo Guângxiào 姚廣孝 (Dàoyàn 1335-1418), a monk of wide learning, both religious and secular. In addition to Buddhism and Confucianism, Yáo had studied Daoist yin-yáng theory which he believed foretold the imperial destiny of Zhu Dì 朱棣, future Yônglè Emperor.

Yáo thus became the future emperor's mentor, military adviser and loyal supporter in his bloody civil war of usurpation from his fief at Yànjing, which he was to recreate as Beîjing, 'North Capital'. He was instrumental in launching the campaign by which he secured the throne from his nephew enthroned at Nánjing, the 'South Capital'. It was said: Yáo Guângxiào advised Yônglè on the timing of rebellion after armed soldiers were seen in the sky under the Dark Emperor. (Seaman 1987, 26 quoting: Gao Dài 1557: Hóngyóu Lù 高岱鴻猷錄)

Empress Xú Xiàowén 徐孝文 (1362-1407)'s bond to Yônglè was also exceptionally close. She played an active role in his campaign and defence of Yànjing. Daughter of top general Xú Dá 徐達, she was a highly literate authoress and editor with Daoist and Buddhist leanings. In 1413, Yônglè began construction of Nánjing's world-renowned nine-storey octagonal porcelain pagoda, over 276 feet high, in her honour and that of the civil war dead. It was levelled by the mid-nineteenth century Tàipíng rebellion. (Goodrich/Fang eds. 1976: Chu Ti 363; Hsu, Empress 566-569.)

The Grand Record chapter of *Héguanzî* contains the most inflated paean to the messianic ruler, but Yônglè's insertion contains the only passage outrightly to condemn a ruler, in the personification of the 'Central Palace'. In the contemporary context, this could only refer to Zhu Dì's nephew Emperor Jiànwén (r. 1399-1403) against whom Zhu Dì rebelled in 1399 from his northern base at Yànjing with the Great Wall garrisons.

After three years' war, Nánjing was captured and the imperial palace burnt. The body of the deposed emperor was, it seems, never found. (Goodrich/Fang eds. 1976: Chu Ti 355-365; Yao Kuang-hsiao 1561-1564)

Following his accession, Yônglè was concerned to justify his actions in the eyes of scholars, even by attempting to re-write history. (Goodrich/Fang eds. 1976: Zhu Yun-wen 398, 403) Looking at the contents of his Heguanzî passage, apart from a few phrase copied from the original, the interpolation is clear.

The vocabulary of 'heavenly palace' tiangong and 'underworld mansions' dìfù is anachronistic for a work of the Warring States period.

We could take the interpolation as extraneous commentary, deliberately or inadvertently, copied into the original. It has the feel of a personal divine revelation, like those customarily communicated by Daoist mediums in 'spirit writing' fújì 扶乩 (cf. planchette). Yônglè's empress and helpmate, who died in the year before the encyclopaedia's completion, is a likely candidate, along with laicised Buddhist prelate Yáo Guângxiào, for its composition.

The Yônglè insertion starts from the third Chinese word, altered to 'not 不' from 'Earth 地' of the received text in chapter xi-b (fn 266 marks the spot):

In Heaven, when he was not a thing,
在天不物
The foolish did not believe in him.
愚莫信之
When on Earth he completed his form,
在地成形
The foolish then died by him.
愚故死之

The Sage Man pursues operations in the un-manifest,
聖人者從事乎未明
The foolish pursue operations in the already completed.
愚者從事於其已成也
Heaven and Earth strive for the plainstuff
天地者效素
To match the cultured principles of the Sage Man.
以同於文理於聖人者也

So his culture did not obliterate substance.
故文不滅質者
In all four directions there is blessed prosperity.
四通而祥利
His applications did not harm its root,
用不傷本者

Beauty is completed and good fortune arrives.
美成而福至
From this we fathom the Sage Man's interior.
以此角聖人之內

So Way's Virtue is valued,
故道德可貴

Degree and calculation may be taken as laws.
度數可法也

He understands the Way's Virtue's zenith
知道德之至

'Degree and calculation' mean
度數之謂者

He does not chase mental ideas' distractions,
則不從心意之所流

He does not follow ears and eyes' seductions.
不隨耳目之所淫

So, being able entirely to preserve their essence,
故能全粹

Myriad things all get to live.
萬物皆得其生

In this manner,
如是者

He does not borrow things to make a canopy,
不假物以爲蓋

He does not grasp Heaven or Earth to become great.
不持天地以爲大

At ease in himself he stays
自若以處

Yet myriad things are embraced by him.
而萬物包焉者

Of the Sage Man's attainments,
聖人之至也

Verbal descriptions are too crude,
以名與之則粗

Vocal expressions are surpassed.
以聲比之則外

When the Sage Man met what he hated,
至聖人之所惡

Deep was his subtlety,
深於微

Internal was his spirit.
內於神

So his exploits may be narrated
故其跡可道
But his feats may not be matched.
而功不可及也

When Law's Righteousness and Degree's Constitution
夫法義度制
Were obliterated in the Central Palace, [at *Nánjing?*]
滅於中宮
Flowers put forth their colours,
華發采出
To appear in Outer Encampments. [Yànjing?]
見於外營者也

As if in Heaven's Palace
若天宮者
His essential spirit was held in,
精神含焉
As if in the Underworld's mansions
若地府者
It grew in hibernation.
生長冬藏處焉

The 'Sage Man' is clearly the Emperor and the 'foolish' are those whom he slaughtered in order to wrest the throne from his Confucian enemy, enthroned in the early Míng capital at Nánjing. The flowers blooming outside in the 'camp' must refer to his military fief away to the north in the old Yuán dynasty capital at Dàdu, rear base of the Great Wall garrisons, where he would make his own capital, Beîjing.

When in Heaven's Palace his spirit was held in, suggests his soul, resident in a Buddhist paradise, awaiting reincarnation as emperor. His 'underworld' hibernation fits the period where he lay low, feigning sickness and madness to divert suspicions of his intent.

History's verdict on Yônglè is mixed. His manner of taking the throne and savage reprisals against those suspected of opposing him and their relatives are condemned. Yet, his achievements in consolidating the dynasty with Beîjing as its capital and great voyages under admiral Zhèng Hè to the Indian ocean, as far as Africa and Mecca, are generally applauded.

Appendix I: *Lâozî*, Six Works and 'Yellow Emperor' Scroll Concordances

1. *Lâozî* and Six Works' concurrences with *Héguanzî*

Lâozî is the biggest single source for *Héguanzî*, though their social policies disagree. We see here (below) a grand total of *Lâozî* **36x** concurrences, fairly evenly distributed through *Héguanzî*. This compares with a total of **66x** 'hits' from the nineteen Mâwángdui 'Yellow Emperor' scrolls altogether, mostly in *Héguanzî*'s earlier chapters. Of these, **33x** are from eight scrolls of 'Warp Law' Jing fâ, followed by **26x** from the fourteen scrolls of 'Sixteen Warps' Shíliù-Jing, with **7x** from 'Nine Rulers' Jiu-Zhû. If the earlier *Héguanzî* dates to the mid-third century BC, this provides a cut-off date for the 'Yellow Emperor' scrolls' composition. There are also **51x** evenly spread occurrences from other works, including Guânzî (14x), *Zhuangzî* (14x), *Hánfeizî* (5x) with three Qín (239 BC) and early Hàn commentary digests (18x). (see below)

Lâozî is celebrated above all for his doctrine of laissez-faire, 'non-contrivance' (LXIII-LXIV) as the ultimate rule, but also as a tactical tool: 'govern it before it is disordered.' *Héguanzî* (vi-a, xiii-a), like *Lâozî* (Guodiàn mss. XVIII, XXIX), blames 'mutually having-contrivance', with 'intelligence and cunning', for causing the conflicts that wrecked primeval 'Eden'.

The key to human empowerment, whether by an unseen divine or natural agency, lies in the word 'dynamics' (shì 勢). It is an inherent power, generated as if spontaneously from position, rather than by piecemeal legalistic interference. *Héguanzî* (xviii-b) warns the ruler 'to take it from dynamics, not to search for it by investigation', as if rejecting legalist methods, and that: dynamics are concentrated and at selfhood (執 者 其 專 而 在 己 者 也). Yet it also underlies all phenomena. *Lâozî* (LI, absent from Guodiàn *Lâozî*) has just one reference to dynamics in three-word line couplets:

The **Way** generates them, **Virtue** nourishes them. 道生之　德畜之
Things form them, **dynamics** complete them. 物形之　勢成之.

Héguanzî (v-d), as if writing an exposition in a four-word line quatrain, has:

From the **Way** of **Virtue**'s Law, 道德之法,
Myriad **things** take their enterprises: 萬物取業.
Lacking **form** but having divisions 無形有分,
It is called the Great **Dynamic**. 名曰大埶[=執/勢?].

Pre-imperial Qín's premier and regent Lyû Bùweí (*Lyûshì Chunqiu* IV Mèngxià 3, Zunshi 6b) applies this novel term, 'Great Dynamic', in an overtly political context, by adapting a *Lâozî* (XXXIX, 32-39) quote on unity, absent from *Héguanzî*:

He who has the **Great Dynamic**
may 'become Under-Heaven's governor!'
Yôu Dàshì kê'yî weí Tianxià zhèng'-yî!
有大勢可'以爲天下正'矣.

Writing in early Hàn, after the event of imperial unification, Liú An, Prince of Huaínán (*Huaínánzî* XIII Fànlùn 10b) paraphrases the same sentiment:

Rulers occupy a strong and **great dynamic** position.
Jun chû qiángdà shìweì 君處强大勢位.

Héguanzî (xvi), in answer to the question: do rulers 'have contrivance' (yôuweí) in their kingdoms, develops the metaphor of a doctor who at the highest level practises 'preventative medicine'. He cures disease before its symptoms become obvious without need for his professional intervention so that his 'cures' seem to happen of their own accord and he never achieves fame. While sharing many of *Lâozî*'s ideals, *Héguanzî* is committed to a pro- active agenda. It is anti-militarist but not pacifist. In answer to the question why Zhào's army has been crushed, Héguan Zî quotes two of *Lâozî*'s moral
strictures against warmongering. (vii-b; XXI, XLVI)

Unlike *Lâozî* which seems to spring from out of space and time, without the use of a single personal or place name, *Héguanzî* is filled with identifiable historical personages. *Lâozî* is rich in generalities, *Héguanzî* in specifics. Grand Unity (Taìyi) in *Héguanzî* (x-xi) is no abstraction but a divine being who speaks and answers questions. Nor is this presented as parable or parody, as in *Zhuangzî*, but as a revealed personage engaged in matters human, as well as divine.

This raises the question of ancient Chinese iconography and personalised deities. Whereas statuary of divinities are rife in most world cultures, and remained so in traditional China, they are largely absent in the early period. The Chinese word for 'image' xiàng 象 means literally 'elephant' or 'ivory', indicating perhaps that portrait images were made of this perishable material and have rarely survived.

Lâozî makes several references to images, notably the 'great image' (XXXV, XLI) and murky images that are hardly distinguishable (IV, XIV, XXI). To this idea, *Héguanzî* adds the concept of a 'Night Walker' (Yèxíng), equated by Guanzî with 'mental operations' (II, LXIV Xíngshì: xinxíng 心行). In x-b, where Grand Unity instructs Grand Augustan on rulership, the Great Image, like Prime Virtue, is something to be attained. *Lyûshì Chunqiu* (V-2 Dàyuè, 4a) directly equates *Lâozî*'s elusive presence with Grand Unity itself.

Here is a concordance tabulating *Héguanzî* distinctive phrases or lines corresponding to *Lâozî* and six texts of third to second century date. Occurences are counted equally, regardless of individual size. Chapters iii (7 x), viii (9 x) and xii (8 x) have the greatest number of matches. *Lâozî* is the most important source of parallels (37 x), followed by Guânzî (12 x) and *Zhuangzî* (12 x) on its themes in the grand total (82 x). This does not include numerous themes in Guânzî and others unrelated to *Lâozî*, which would require independent tabulations, not attempted here.

The largest single apparent quotation, from *Lâozî* XIV (absent from Guodiàn *Lâozî*) is in *Héguanzî* iii-b. It is not always clear which are primary sources, secondary sources or parallel branches from unknown sources. This tabulation is indicative rather than exhaustive. Other matches, not tabulated here for want of space, are in Confucian (Mèngzî, Xúnzî) and Legalist (Shang yang, Shèn Dào) classics, as well as militarist *Sunzî Bingfâ*.

n.b. *Square brackets indicate chapters absent from Guodiàn mss. Four Héguanzî chapters, namely i, iv, vi, and xv, have no matches.*

Graph 1a. *Lâozî* and Six Works' concurrences with *Héguanzî* by chapter

Héguanzî	ii	iii	v	vii	viii	ix	x	xi
Lâozî								
1x							[I]	
1x			II					
1x		[XIV]						
2x		XV					XV	
2x		XVII						XVII
2x		[XXI]				[XXI]		
1x		XXV						
2x				XXXI				
1x					XXXII			
2x							XXXV	XXXV
1x					XXXVII			
1x					[XXXIX]			
1x					XLV			
1x					[XLIX]			
1x			[LI]					
1x	LVII							
1x					[LVIII]			

1x						LIX		
1x					[LXVI]			
1x					[LXXIV]			
1x					[LXXX]			
Sub-total Lâozî 25x	1x	4x	3x	2x	7x	3x	3x	2x
Chunqiu Fánlù 3x		III-5			XVII-7			XIII
Guânzî 11x	XXXVI	II, LXIV	XI		XXXVI, -VII, -VIII, XLIX, LXXIII	XXIIx2		
Hánfeizî 2x					VI	VI		
Huaínánzî 3x		VI			VIII, XV			
Lyûshì Chunqiu 3x		V-2			V, XVII-7			
Zhuangzî 3x		XI, LXIV				LXXX		
Sub-total 25x	1x	7x	1x	0x	11x	4x	0x	1x

Graph 1b. *Lâozî* and Six Works' concurrences
with *Héguanzî* by chapter

xii	xiii	xiv	xvi	xvii	xviii	xix	Héguanzî
			XVII			XVII	2x
	[XXIX]						1x
[LVIII]					[LVIII]		2x
				LIX			1x
	LXIV		LXIV				2x
			[LXXI]				1x
				[LXXV]			1x
	[LXXX]						1x
1x	3x	0x	3x	2x	1x	1x	Sub-total = 11x; + 25 = 36x
							Chunqiu Fánlù: 0x; +3 = 3x
				V	XXXVII, XLIX		Guânzî: 3x; +11 = 14x

265

VIII			XXI		XX		*Hánfeizî:* 3x; +2 = <u>5x</u>
VIII, XV	XIII		II				*Huaínánzî:* 4x; +3 = <u>7x</u>
XXV, Lan XVI	VI-5			XXIII-3	III-4		*Lyûshì Chunqiu:* 5x; + 3 = <u>8x</u>
I, VIIIx2, X, XXXII	IX, XXVI, XXIX	XXV		XIV	VI		*Zhuangzî:* 11x; +3 = <u>14x</u>
10x	5x	1x	1x	4x	5x	0x	**Sub-total = 26x; + 25 = Total: <u>51x</u>**
							GRAND TOTAL: 36 + 51 = <u>87x</u>

2   Mâwángdui 'Yellow Emperor' Scroll concurrences

Héguanzî has matches from sixteen Mâwángdui, separately entitled, essay manuscripts. These matches are found in twelve, almost two thirds, of *Héguanzî*'s nineteen chapters (i-ii, iv-xii, xiv, xvii), all excepting six (iii, xiii, xv- xvi, xviii-xix). These minority chapters are more transcendentally Daoist (iii, xviii), or moralistically Confucian (xiii, xv-xvi, xix). The majority chapters, showing affinities to Mâwángdui scrolls, outline the messianic message of Way and Law and the Augustans.

Unlike those Mâwángdui scrolls (Shíliù-Jing), in which the Yellow Emperor appears, *Héguanzî* makes only one passing reference to the Yellow Emperor (xii-a), though it repeatedly acclaims his minister Cangjié for the invention of writing, calendar, bureaucracy and law. (vii-c, ix-g)

The matches between the two works are not random. Each contain programs for political unification with divine sanction. While each has its own integral construction, independent of the other, there are too many points in common to be coincidence. Both are close in time to the realisation of their projects of imperial unification, but the Mâwángdui 'Yellow Emperor' texts are explicit about the launch of a campaign of outright conquest.

To summarise, I here below present the main elements in common of the program of the relevant Mâwángdui texts with those of *Héguanzî*, side by side for ease of comparison under six topics.

I. Way's Law

First, both systems derive their Law from the Way. In quite a different sense, *Lâozî* had said "The Way makes a Law of (models itself on) the Natural." (xxv 82-85: 道自然) For *Lâozî*, the Way is Nature's law, superior even to

Heaven, whereas here human law is extrapolated from and sanctified by the Way of Nature and Heaven. It is to reject the selfish and quarrelling, but monopolised from one source, shared by fixed measures and names, a means of control and covert tactics.

a) **HGZ** xiv-b: the Way generates Law. 道生法; v-b: Only the Way's Law is impartial in governance and illumination. 唯道之法, 公政以明.
    MWD Jing fâ **Dàofâ** 43, 1a: The Way generates Law. 道生法. Cf. *Guóyû* xxi Yuèyû-xià 1-2.

b) **HGZ** vi-c: reject selfishness to establish the public. 廢私立公; vii-d: Law makes people reject selfishness for the sake of the public. 法者使 去私就公.
    MWD Jing fâ **Dàofâ** 43, 7b; **Sì-Dù** 51, 44a: reject the selfish to establish the public 去私而立公. Cf. *Hánfeizî* vi Yôudù: 22.

c) **HGZ** vi-c: good giving and not quarrelling. 善與不爭.
    MWD Shíliù-Jing **Cheng** 83, 166b: good giving and not quarrelling. 善予不爭.

d) **HGZ viii-c**: ordinances issue from one source. 令出一原.
    MWD Shíliù-Jing: **Chéngfâ** 72, 123b: all watch one hole. 皆閱一空. Cf. *Guânzî* LXXIII Guóxù 359: strong nations have one hole, lost nations four. Shang junshu III Nóngzhàn 10: people, seeing superior's profit from one hole issue, work as one. 民見上利從壹空出也則作壹. *Lyûshì Chunqiu* XVII.7 Bù'èr 16a: as if issuing from one aperture. 如出乎一穴者.

e) **HGZ** ix-g: Accumulated in a silo, grain whether in pecks or piculs distributed or in pints stored, has no loss. 積如倉粟斗石以陳升 委不失也. This implies multiplicity rather than monolithic unity.
    MWD Jing fâ **Dàofâ** 43, 5a: Operations like straight trees, many as a silo's grains, in bushels and pecks supplied, or in feet and inches laid out, have nowhere to escape with their spirit. 事如直木 多如倉粟斗 石已具 尺寸已陳 則無所逃其神.

f) **HGZ** ii-b: Regular and irregular have their places, Names and titles do not deviate from them. 端倚有位, 名號弗去.
    MWD Jing fâ **Dàofâ** 43, 7b: Regular and irregular have their positions, names and titles do not depart from them. 正奇有立 而名*弗去.
    Cf. *=lacuna. *Sunzî Bingfâ* V Bingshì: "irregular and regular are mutually generating" 奇正相生.
    HGZ iv-a: to see an opening and by asymmetries mutually control. 見閒則以奇相御.
    MWD Jing fâ **Dàofâ** 43, 7b: by assymetires mutually control 以奇相御.

h) **HGZ** xii-d: Ostensibly he contrives Law; the subtle Way is what he practises. 明者爲法, 微道是行.

MWD Shíliù-Jing 2x **Guan** 62, 82a; **Xìngzheng** 69, 109b: He ostensibly he contrives Law; the subtle Way is what he practises. 其明者爲法, 而微道是行. Cf. Xúnzî (XXI Jiêbì 439); Guóyû (XXI Yuèyû-xià): 明者爲法, 微道是行. Zhang Shùnhuì 1988: 40ff on 'forged' *Shàngshu*: Dà Yû mò: The Way's heart is subtle, men's hearts dangerous. 道心惟微人心惟危.

II. Unity

Unity here implies governance of the 'myriad things' or beings, wàn-wù, by heavenly balance and mandate. 'Things' wù therefore refer to all created phenomena, animal, vegetable and mineral which the divine ruler was to rule by Law in accordance with the heavenly Way. The astronomy in g), used to illustrate the model for Law from ix-a and x-a, is a near-repetition.

a) **HGZ** iv-a: If Heaven abandoned Unity, it would revert to being a thing. 天若離一, 反還爲物.

MWD **Jiû-Zhû:** 30, 378 "If a ruler is unlawful, he will revert to being a thing." 主不法則, 乃反爲物.

b) **HGZ** xvii-f: that Heaven generates things but is not a thing. 彼天生物而不物者.

MWD **Jiû-Zhû** 29, 361: Heaven's constitution…generates things but is not a thing 天乏[=範]生物不物.

c) **HGZ** viii-a: What I mean by 'Heaven' refers to its making the suchness of things and unconquerablity. 所謂天者, 言其然物 而無朕 =勝者也.

MWD **Jiû-Zhû** 30, 376: Yi Yîn said: "The Record says: 'Only Heaven conquers. All things are conquered.'" 志曰惟天勝 凡物有勝." Cf. *Huaínánzî* (XV Arms' Strategy) 3a: All things are conquered, only the Way is unconquered. 凡物有朕=勝 惟道無朕=勝.

d) **HGZ** iv-a: When subordinates are suppressed, superiors may be deceived. 下之所造 上之可蔽; vii-c, ix-e: suppressed subordinates deceive superiors 造下蔽上.

MWD **Jiû-Zhû** 29, 353: suppressed subordinates deceive superiors 造下蔽上.

e) **HGZ** iv-a; The leaders of energies is the seasons to generate and kill are its laws. 領氣時也生殺法也. x-a: Three seasons produce and grow, One season (winter) kills and punishes. The four seasons being fixed, Heaven and Earth are finished! 則萬物莫不至矣. 三時生長一時煞刑. 四時而定 天地盡矣.

MWD Jing fâ (**Lùnyue** 57, 66a): Three seasons to achieve successes; one season (winter) to penalise and kill: is Heaven and Earth's Way. The four seasons are fixed. 三時成功一時刑殺. 天地之道也 四時時而定.

f) **HGZ** ix-a: Heaven is illumination, stars are its signs: its constellations are not disorderly. Each in precedence moves. 天者明星其稽也列星不亂,各以序行; x-a: Constellations by not disordering their ranks, exchanging places but not encroaching, are position's signs. Heaven's illumination by three fixes unity. 列星不亂其行, 代而不干位之稽也. 天明三以定一. The sun sincerely comes out, sincerely goes in. At south and north it has its poles. So, none but take it as Law's model. Heaven is faithfulness, the moon is its form/penalties. The moon faithfully dies, faithfully is born. 日誠出誠入,南北有極,故莫弗以爲法則.天者信其月刑也月信死信生; x-a: The sun faithfully rising, faithfully setting, north and south having poles: are measure's signs. The moon faithfully dying, faithfully being born, advancing and retiring with constancy, are number's signs. 日信出入,南北有極度之稽也.月信死信生進退有常數之稽也.

MWD Jing fâ **Lùn** 53, 49b: Constellations by having numbers but not losing their ranks are goodfaith's sign. Heaven's illumination by three fixes duality. 列星有數而不失其行信之稽也. 天明三以定二.

g) **HGZ** x-a: Heaven illumines by three to fix unity. 天明三以定一.

MWD Jing fâ **Lùn**: 53, 49a-b: Heaven holds unity to illumine three: the sun faithfully coming out and going in, south and north having limits, is ********dying, advancing and retiring with constancy, is numbers' sign; 天執一以明三　日信出入　南北有極　********死　進退有常　數之稽.

h) **HGZ** iv-e: So, the Sage King Heavens it, Earths it, Man it. 故聖王天之地之人之; x-a: Heaven, Earth and human operations, these three return to unity. 天地人事　三者復一也. **xiv-a**: To implement arms Laws, Heaven them, Earth them, Man them. 用兵之法　天之地之人之; **xvii-f**: Its arms have Heaven, have Earth, have Man. 彼兵者有天有地有人.

MWD Shíliù-Jing **Bingróng** 71, 116a: form of Heaven... law of Earth... form and law of Man ...刑天... 法地... 刑法...人; Jing fâ **Liù- fen** 49, 28b: To be king of the Under-Heaven the Way has Heaven, has Earth, has Man 王天下之道　有天焉　有地焉　有人焉; **Mèngzî** (II-1) Heaven's timing, Earth's advantages, Human Harmony 天時　地利　人和.

III. Decisions and Dynamics

Three 'Yellow Emperor' texts give variants of a rhyme used by Fàn Lî in advice to Goujiàn on timing his campaign against Wú to recover the throne. The word 'cut' (duàn), meaning 'decide', rhymes with 'disorder' (luàn), as of tangled strands. The Six Satchels (Liù-Tao I.7), ascribed to Taìgong Wàng, GrandDuke of Zhou, warns: If you grasp a knife you must cut. If you hold an axe you must attack. (Sawyer 1993: 46)

269

The timing is that for the final battle. *Héguanzǐ*, which begins with 'Royal Axe', ends with a call for resolute action to implement its program, literally: No death, no birth. No decision, no completion (i-b). The remaining question is who to do it? The time is at hand.

a) **HGZ** xvii-e: He who establishes a target to aim at will not be confused. He who accords with Law in apportionments will not be doubted. 彼立表而望者不惑.按法而割者不疑.

   MWD Shíliù-Jing **Cheng** 81, 144a-b: If you rely on targets in aiming, you will not be confused; if you depend on Law to rule, there will be no disorder. 侍表而望則不惑案法而治則不亂.

b) **HGZ** i-b: No death, no life. 不死不生.

   MWD Shíliù-Jing **Zhengluàn** 67, 106b x2: No death, no life. 不死不生.

c) **HGZ** i-b: If you do not take decisions (cut), there will be no success. 不斷不成; iv-a: leader of energies is the seasons; to generate and kill are its laws. Compliance with degree in decisions is Heaven's rhythm. 領氣時也生殺法也循度以斷天之節也.

   MWD Shíliù Jing x2 **Guan**: 63, 90a: You must at Heaven's timing decide (cut). If what must be decided is undecided, you will get disorder. 當天時與之皆斷　當斷不斷將受其亂; **Bingróng** 71, 118b: 因天時與之皆斷　當斷不斷反受其亂…環受其殃. **Cheng** 81, 149b: Heaven has revolving penalties. You on the contrary will get its disasters. 天有環刑反受其殃).

   HGZ xii-d: Early or late, contracting or expanding, Opposites are mutually bred and born. 蚤晚紃嬴,反相殖生.

   MWD Shíliù Jing **Cheng** 82, 156b: Early or late, contracting or expanding, afterwards reversal will be applied. 蚤晚紃嬴,後將反施.

d) **HGZ** viii-b: By relying on dynamics (resorting to force) omens are generated. 人執=任勢(?) 兆生.

   MWD Jing fâ **Guócì** 45, 12a/13a-b x2: Don't fixate on dynamics…Let those who rely only dynamics be banished to the four quarters… He who relies on dynamics loses the people. 毋故執…人執=任勢(?)者流之四方…人執者失民; Shíliù-Jing **Guan** 62, 86b-87a x2: In employing people do not rely on dynamics. 使民毋人執.

e) **HGZ** xviii-b: So, the Sage Man takes it from dynamics and does not search by investigation. 故聖人者取之於執[=勢]而弗索於察.

   MWD Shíliù-Jing **Guan** 62, 86a: in undertaking operations, don't intrusively investigate. Jûshì wù yángchá 舉事毋陽察. Cf. Jing fâ Guócì; wù yáng qiè 毋陽竊. Cf. *Lâozǐ* (LVIII): When government is investigative, people are impoverished. Qí-zhèng cháchá qí-mín quèquè 其政察察　其民缺缺.

IV. Mandates

In the first example we see a complete reversal of the same concepts: HGZ harshly warns cultivating life will lead first to heavenly punishment or otherwise encounter human slaughter. On the other hand, *MWD* warns cultivating death will be condemned as perverse, leading to human slaughter or otherwise heavenly punishment. Curiously, the word iv-d uses for 'encounter' nì 逆 is used by *MWD* here as 'counter'.

a) **HGZ** ix-b x2,-d: This is how he with Heaven and Earth consummates. 此所以與天地總.

   MWD Jing fâ **Lùn** 53, 48a: When the eight coordinates are not lost then you are with Heaven and Earth consummated. Ba-zhèng bù-shi zé yû Tiandìzông 八正不失則與天地總.

b) **HGZ** iv-d: If you trust feelings to cultivate life, even though not by Heaven punished, you will encounter human slaughter. 信情修生非其天誅, 逆夫人僇.

   MWD Jing fâ **Lùnyuè** 57, 68a: If you nourish death to attack life, your mandate is counter to success. If there is no human slaughter, there will necessarily be heavenly punishment. 養死伐生 命曰逆成 不有人僇 必有天刑. **Mínglî** 58, 72a: nourish the means of death… 逆成養其所以死…

c) **HGZ** vii-b: He who employs men without selection is doomed (wáng). This is how 'counter rhythm' is generated. 用人而=無擇之者亡 逆節之所生.

   MWD Jing fâ **Wánglùn** 55, 60a-b: When 'counter rhythm' is finally complete, Heaven will not fulfil his mandate and make severe his punishment. 逆節果成 天將不盈其命 而重其刑. Cf. *Guóyû* XXI Yuèyû-xià: 1-5. Guânzî XLII Shì 'Dynamics': 252.

d) **HGZ** vii-a: For this reason, not killing men who have surrendered is what rulers of the Way extol. 是故不殺降人主道所高.

   MWD Jing fâ **Wánglùn**: 55, 60a: killing men who have surrendered, punishing the innocent: disaster will for all conversely reach himself. 戮降人 刑無罪 禍皆反自及也.

e) **HGZ** ix-a: To implement arms' laws you must Heaven them, Earth them, and Man (humanize) them.' Rewards urge to battle, punishments compel multitudes. 用兵之法 天之人之地之賞以勸戰 罰以必眾. xvii-f. Its arms have Heaven, have men, have Earth. 彼兵者有天有人有地.

   MWD Shíliù-Jing x2 **Lìmìng** 61, 78b x2: We receive mandate from Heaven, settle positions on Earth, complete names among Men. 吾受命於天 定位於地 成名於人. **Bingróng** 71, 116b: If arms are not formed by Heaven, arms may not move. If they do not take law from

Earth, arms may not be placed. If penalties and law are inhuman, arms may not win. 兵不刑天　兵不可動　不法地兵不可措　刑法不人兵不可成. Mèngzî IIb.1: Heaven's timing, Earth's advantages, Human cooperation. 天時地利人和.

f)　**HGZ** xii-d: Early or late, contraction or expansion, Opposites are mutually bred and born. 蚤晚絀贏, 反相殖生.

　　MWD Shíliù-Jing **Cheng** 82, 156b: "Expansion and contraction transform, later they will reverse." 贏絀變化後將反也.

g)　**HGZ** v-d: what is meant by the Way is necessity (unstoppable). 所謂道者無已者也. This may be better read as 'without self' 無己.

　　MWD Shíliù-Jing **Bênfá** 75, 129b: The Way's action is from necessity (-bùdéyî), from necessity so it is inexhaustible. 道之行也繇不得已　繇不得已則無窮. Cf. Lúnyû IX, 130: Confucius over a river said: "What is passing is like this, unceasing day or night." 子在川上曰　逝者如斯夫不捨晝夜. Jiâ Yì: *Xinshu* IX Xiuzhèngyû-shàng; The Yellow Emperor said: "The Way is like river-valley water issuing unceasingly (wuyî), its running is unstoppable/unstopping." 黃帝曰道若川谷之水其出無已其行無止.

h)　**HGZ** xvii-f: It is manifested in disaster and good-fortune like joined tally-sticks. 章以禍福若合符節.

　　MWD Jiû-Zhû 29, 356: preservation and doom are like joined tallies 存亡若會符.

V. Personal Embodiment and Recruitment

There appears to be a contradiction here between disembodied natural or 'spontaneous' (zìrán) forces and belief in invisible deities with human form. Deified ancestors, worshipped at memorial observances, would be impersonated by masked players and their parts performed quasi-shamanically by living 'corpses' (shi 尸). It likely included spirit-possession, a feature of traditional Daoism. (cf. Seaman 1987 12ff) *Zhuangzî* (VII: Ying Dìwáng, wúwéi míng shi 無爲名尸) uses the term 'to encorpse' as a verb to convey *Lâozî*'s ideal of non-contrivance by the ruler as simply a puppet.

This verb 'to encorpse' is used by *Héguanzî* for those whose name embodies each of 'five governances' (viii-c, d), as if interchangeably with 'to embody' (tî 體) for him of the Complete Ninth's system who 'with Divine Luminaries will embody governance' (ix-b, g). In a transmigrational context, one might be tempted to use the word 'incarnate', meaning made flesh from the Latin, or 'avatar' meaning spiritual descent in Sanskrit, to capture the full meaning of the original.

There is no doubt that the emperor was believed to incorporate government and hence divinity in his physical person. In this there is an almost perfect match between *Héguanzî* (vi-b) and the Yellow Emperor text (*MWD*) Shíliù-Jing **Wû-Zhèng** 65, 91a-91b) collated under 5.b, below) in the advice to 'promulgate the five governances', a term explained only in *Héguanzî* (viii-c, d).

a) **HGZ** i-b: Emperors with teachers associate, Kings with friends associate, Doomed lords with slaves associate. 故帝者與師處 王者與友處 亡主與徒處.

MWD Shíliù-Jing **Cheng** 81, 145b-46a: An emperor's ministers are called ministers, they are actually teachers. A king's ministers are called ministers, they are actually friends. A hegemon's ministers are called ministers, they are actually [guests. The endangered one's] ministers are called ministers, they are actually servants. The doomed one's ministers are called ministers, they are actually slaves. 帝者臣名臣實師也 王者臣名臣實友也霸者臣名臣實[賓也危者]臣名臣實庸也亡者臣名臣實虜也. Cf. *Shuoyuán*: Jundào.

b) **HGZ** vi-b: The unified nation's form is concentrated in his own body. Through his person he examines his generation. 一國之刑 具在於身. 以身老[=考]世;

MWD Shíliù-Jing **Wû-Zhèng** 65, 91a-91b of the Yellow Emperor: It begins in his body... The five governances being promulgated to serve the Five Luminaries... 始在於身 五正既佈以司五明.

c) **HGZ** viii-c: Heaven and Earth, shade and sunlight, take their signs from his body. So he will promulgate the Five Governances to serve the Five Luminaries. Ten transformations and Nine Ways, their signs from his body start...天地陰陽 取稽於身故布五正[=政]以司五明.十變九道稽從身始... (cf. iii-a; viii-c, d, cf. iv a-e).

d) **HGZ** xviii-c: So, the Sage Man establishes Heaven as father, founds Earth as mother. 故聖人立天爲父 建地爲母.

MWD Shíliù-Jing **Guôtóng** 66, 98a: By Heaven contrive fatherhood; by Earth contrive motherhood. 以天爲父 以地爲母.

e) **HGZ** vi-b: He may not be named so is called 'divine'. He attains divinity's zenith, manifesting it unerringly. 不可名故謂之神 至神之極 見之不忒.

MWD Jing fâ **Lùn** 53, 52a-b: Ultimate divinity's zenith will be manifested unambiguously. 至神之極 見知不惑; **Mínglî** 58,75a: 見知不惑 manifested unambiguously.

f) **HGZ** ix-g: If your Way is evil disaster will reach your person. 道惡禍及於其身.

MWD Jing fâ **Wánglùn** 62a: if danger is not overcome, disasters will reach your person. 危不朕=勝禍及於身; **Mínglî** 72a: so there are counter forms/penalties whose disasters will reach your person. 故有逆刑禍及其身.

g) **HGZ** xi-b: Shadow follows form, echo responds to sound. 影則隨形, 響則應聲.
   MWD Jing fâ **Mínglî** 58, 76a: Shadow follows form, echo follows sound. 影則隨形,響則應聲.

h) **HGZ** vi-d: without speaking he has goodfaith. 不言而信. *MWD* Jing fâ **Mínglî**, 58,70b: without speaking he has goodfaith. 不言而信.

VI. CONCORDANCES

Graph 2. Jiû-Zhû and Jingfâ concurrences by *Héguanzî* chapter

Jiû-Zhû 九主	Dàofâ 道法	Guóci 國次	Liù-Fen 六分	Sì-Dù 四度	Lùn 論	Wánglùn 亡論	Lùnyue 論約	Mínglî 名理	Totals
	ii-b								1
iv-a x2	iv-a		iv-e				iv-a,-d	iv-d	7
	-vi-c			vi-c	vi-b			vi-b,-d	5
vii-c						vii-b x2			3
	viii-d	viii-b x2							3
ix-e	ix-g				ix-b x4	ix-a; g x2	-	ix-g	10
					x-a x4				4
								xi-b	1
xii-f									1
xiii-a									1
	xiv-b		xiv-a						2
xvii-f		-	xvii-f		-		-	-	2
7	**6**	**2**	**3**	**1**	**9**	**5**	**2**	**5**	**40**

Graph 3. Shíliù-Jing concurrences by *Héguanzî* chapter

Lìmìng 立命	Guan 觀	Wû-Zheng 五正	Guôtóng 果童	Zhengluàn 正亂	Xingzheng 姓爭	Totals
-	i-b	-	-	i-b	-	2
-	-	vi-b	-	-	-	1
-	viii-b x2	viii-c x2	-	-	-	4
ix-a	-	-	-	-	-	1
-	xii-d x2	-	-	-	xii-d x2	4
-	xviii-b	-	xviii-c	-	-	2
1	**6**	**3**	**1**	**1**	**2**	**14**

Bingróng 兵容	Chéngfâ 成法	Cheng 稱	Bênfá 本伐	Totals
i-b		i-b		2
iv-e		iv-a		2
			v-d	1
	-	vi-c	-	1
	viii-c			1
ix-a				1
		ix-a		1
xiv-a	-	-	-	1
xvii-f	-	xvii-e	-	2
5	1	5	1	12
				+ 14 = 26

Graph 4. All Mâwángdui Scroll concurrences by *Héguanzî* chapter

Héguanzî	i	ii	iv	v	vi	vii	viii	ix	x	xi	xii	xiv	xvii	xviii	Ttl
Bênfá				1											1
Bingróng	1	1					1					1	1		5
Cheng	1		1								1		1		5
Chéngfâ							1								1
Dàofâ		1	1		1		1	1				1			6
Guan	1						2				2			1	6
Guócì							2								2
Guôtóng														1	1
Jiû-Zhû		2			1		1				1	1	1		7
Liù-Fen		1										1	1		3
Lìmìng							1								1
Lùn			1				4	4							9
Lùnyue		2													2
Mínglî		1		2			1		1						5
Sì-Dù			1												1
Wánglùn					2		3								5
Wû-Zheng			1		2										3
Xìngzheng											2				2
Zhengluàn	1														1
Total:	4	1	9	1	7	3	8	12	4	1	6	4	4	2	66

Appendix II: The Nine Augustans and their Dipper Stars

1. Identification of the Dipper's Nine Stars

a) The Northern Dipper, Ursa Major the 'Greater She-Bear', and Plough are some of the names by which the iconic constellation of seven stars is readily recognised all over the world. It has doubtless since prehistoric times aided mankind in direction finding by the alignment of its two right-hand stars with the North Pole.

In China it is known as the 'Bushel' (Dôu 斗) and its stars have formed the focus of much religious belief and superstition. Unusually, though its seven stars are generally accepted, a strong tradition in Daoism counts its stars as nine. When asked about the physical evidence for the existence of the additional two stars needed to complete this total, the reply is that these two stars are invisible or faint, and reside to the left of the seven clearly visible stars. If this is the case, it is hard to understand how such a concept could have originated.

Nine has long been an auspicious number in China and is a homonym for 'longlasting' or 'eternal' (jiû 久). Furthermore, nine (3 x 3) can form a square with a centre and is the highest single-digit odd (yáng) number, though ten was the highest single-digit (marked as a cross) before the invention of zero. These properties made nine a highly useful number for surveying space and was expressed in the sacred Luò River diagram of antiquity. It is therefore natural that the awkward number seven should be subsumed to it.

Yet it seems strange that the number nine should be imposed on the Dipper without more solid manifestation. Yet there is one ancient source that purports to possess such a thing, and added that source is the earlies documented case of a nine star Dipper. This is found only in the long neglected text labelled *Héguanzǐ*.

Its fourth chapter (iv-a) describes the Dipper, its handle, group of three and four stars with Pole (Jí 極) above, Horn (Jiâo 角) and long Halberd (Yuè 鉞) constellations to left and right, making nine. This is dramatically rounded picture without invisibleor conjectural accretions. Yet somehow it became forgotten.

The corollaries to this ninefold vision are not explicitly drawn by *Héguanzǐ*. Other chapters elaborate on a divine succession Nine Augustan rulers under the god Grand Unity and mention the shaman's 'limping step', but without drawing any mutual equivalence between these various elements. (iv-a, v-b, xvii-d) Nevertheless all found their integral place in future Daoist rituals of the Dipper. To what extent they were already linked is still unclear.

Recent years have seen important studies in English of the Dipper constellation and its relationship to ancient and traditional Chinese belief and astronomical theory. (Andersen 1989; Pankenier 2004, 213; Allred 2003/2004) Modern scholars have questioned *Héguanzǐ*'s knowledge of astronomy. (Defoort 1997: 190-191, 275 ns. 60-63; Williams 1987: 231 n. 203) It seems unlikely that the ancient author would be ignorant of knowledge so fundamental to his belief system which he has laid out in such unequivocal terms.

b) Early texts refer to the 'Beckoner' Zhaoyáo as synonymous with the Dipper whose annual rotation serves to mark seasons and months.[378] *Héguanzǐ* (xviii-a), echoing Lǐjì (I 43-44), refers to this pointer as the 'Dipper's handle' (dǒubǐng 斗柄). Thus, Simâ Qian says: the handle is what points to seasonal stations.[379] Simâ Qian, speaking of a seven-star Dipper, places Beckoner at the end of its handle. He says: the handle end has two stars, the one inside is the Spear- axe Beckoner.[380] A commentary by Simâ Zhen of Táng, citing the great Hàn *Shuowén Jiêzì* dictionary, simply equates the Dipper handle with Beckoner.[381]

c) Post-Hàn texts place the Beckoner as a barely visible star beyond the tail of the Dipper, hardly able to function as the hand of a seasonal clock. In Daoist scriptures, these stars have the alternative names 'no. 8, Cavern Brilliance, Outer Assistant' and 'no. 9 Hidden Light, Inner Deputy'. (Plate 2, End Plate 26) Allred cites Needham (1959: 250-251): "These two lost stars were probably the extension of the handle formed by the bright stars Zhaoyáo (gamma Boötis) and Dajiao (Arcturus)." (2003: 45-46 n.91) 'Beckoner' Zhaoyáo is now equated with Seginus, gamma, a dim star with magnitude of only 3.2 in inverse numbering, while 'Great Horn' Dàjiâo is Arcturus, alpha at -0.05 visual magnitude, in Boötes the Ox-driver constellation and the brightest star in the northern hemisphere.

---

[378] *Lǐjì* (I Qulǐ-shàng) 43-44. *Guânzǐ* (XLII Shì) 253. *Wénzǐ* (IX Xiàdé) 79. Shuîhûdì Qínmù Zhújiân 1990 (Rìshu almanac) 187-188. *Huaínánzǐ* (V) 12x. Major 2010 tr., *Huaínánzǐ* V, fn 1: Zhaoyao, "Far Flight" in Schafer's translation, is a bright star in the constellation Boötes. It wcas envisioned by the Chinese as the last star in the "handle" of the constellation beîidôu, "Northern Dipper" (usually called the "Big Dipper" in English). See Edward H. Schafer, Pacing the Void: T'ang Approaches to the Stars (Berkeley: University of California Press, 1977), 239.

[379] *Shǐjì* XXVII, dì-210c Dong Gong: biáo-suô zhî-yî jiànshí 杓所指以建時.

[380] *Shǐjì* XXVII, dì-210a Zhong Gong: biáo duan yôu liâng-xing, yi-nei weí máo Zhaoyáo 杓端有兩星一內爲矛招搖.

[381] *Shǐjì* XXVII, dì-211c Xi Gong: Suôyìn: Yòng hun jiànzhong-zhê biáo. *Shuowén* yún: Biáo Dôubîng, yin pì-yáo fân, jí Zhaoyáo.索隱: 用昏建中者杓. 説文云杓斗柄, 音匹遙反即招搖.

Simâ Qian states that the Dipper's handle connects to the Dragon's Horn.[383] This fits *Héguanzî*'s 'Horn' and the super bright star Arcturus, lying to the left (east) of the Dipper, in a direct line from its handle. Appropriately, in Latin, 'Arcturus' means 'Bear Guardian', that is guardian of the Dipper, the 'Great She-Bear', Ursa Major.

d) Simâ Qian locates 'Halberd' (i.e. Pole-axe) star (Yuè 鉞) to the right of the Dipper, as located by *Héguanzî*, saying: To the east, the 'Well' contrives water operations. On its west corner, the star is called 'Halberd'.[384] Astronomy identifies this Halberd as eta Gemini, a star of magnitude only 3.8, in the Well Mansion. This Halberd seems too dim and low in elevation compared to the Dipper to fit *Héguanzî*'s depiction.

At the right side of the Dipper, as if facing Arcturus, is Capella the she-goat, alpha in the constellation Auriga the charioteer. It is the third brightest star in the northern hemisphere, at +0.08 visual magnitude. In Chinese it is known as 'Pentagon Chariot, Two' (Wû-Che, èr) in the Net Mansion (Bìxiù 畢宿). This star would perfectly fit *Héguanzî*'s Halberd position and brightness.

Simâ Qian strangely misplaces Pentagon Chariot constellation at the end of his eastern section, overlapping into the western section. He remarks:[385]

Coach-house has Pentagon Chariot; Chariot star **Horn** seems to benefit the multitude. If not, don't install chariot horses.
庫有五車 車星角 若益眾 及不具 無處車馬

---

[382] Allred 2003: 145-148: on Zhaoyáo, 'The Roaming'. *Dàozàng Jíyào*: Dôují 2, *Beîdôu Yánsheng Jing* zhùjiê 60: no. 8. Beîdôu Dì-ba, Dòngmíng Waìfû Xingjun; no. 9. Beîdôu Dì-jiû, Yînguang Neîbì Xingjun. *Dàozàng Jíyào* 1906: Dôu-jí ii, 52-61, 2938-2942, *Beîdôu Yánshòu Jing*; Dôu-jí iii, 17ff, 2972ff: *Jiû-Huáng Xin Jing*. Werner 1922: 144-145. Mollier 2008: 135 on two auxiliary stars Fû and Bì to make the Dipper nine; 157; iv. Under Stellar Protection 134-173. Robinet 2008: on Beîdôu in Pregadio 2008: 225-226 cites Bù Tiangang Fei Dìjî Jing 步天綱飛地紀經 on two 'assistant stars', left and right: 4. Zuôfû, 5. Yòubì.

[383] *Shîjì* XXVII, dì-210a Zhong Gong: Biáo xí Lóng Jiâo 杓攜龍角.

[384] *Shîjì* XXVII Nán Gong: Jîng weî shuîshì. Qí xiqu xing yue Yuè 東井為水事其西曲星曰鉞. Cf. (Táng) Wáng Ximíng 王希明: Dan Yuánzî Bùtiange 丹元子步天歌 on 'Well Mansion' Jîng Xiù 井宿 supports Simâ Qian: One star called Halberd (Yuè) by the Well's side rests. Yi-xing míng yuè Jîng-bian'an 一星名鉞井邊安. Wáng also identifies Horn in Horn constellation, Pentagon Chariot in Net and a secondary 'Halberd' (Fuyuè 鈇鉞), 103 Aquarius, in the Encampment Mansion (Shixiù 室宿). Cf. official Qing dynasty Qin Tianjian's 欽天監 compilation by Ignaz Kogler (ca. 1750): Yíxiàng Kâochéng 儀象考成. Yi Shìtóng 伊世同 1981. 'Dark Halberd' Xuán'gé 玄戈, Bootes lamda, 'Dark Battle-axe'.

[385] *Shîjì* XXVII, dì-211c Dong Gong: Kù yôu Wû-che, Che xing jiâo, ruò yì zhòng, jí bú-jù, wú-chû chemâ.

'Chariot star **Horn**', would seem an error, except that he calls Arcturus 'Dragon's Horn', not simply 'Horn' to distinguish it. The constellation's Chinese name 'Pentagon Chariot', literally 'Five Chariot' (Wû-che), with its five-star shape, is an amazing coincidence with the same Greek constellation named after Auriga, the charioteer who held the she-goat Capella, whose horn, broken by infant Zeus, became Cornucopia, the horn of plenty.

This identity could explain Simâ Qian's comment on the Chariot star Horn 'benefitting the multitude'. It implies western influence, likely related to importation by Qín of chariot technology with war horses along the Silk Road from Central Asia (as done by Hàn's Martial Emperor), resulting in the replacement of indigenous nomenclature and the demotion of 'Halberd' to the Well. The importance of horses and the quadriga horse chariot to Qín is attested from the First Emperor's burial pits.

d) In conclusion, the evidence supports *Héguanzî*'s picture of a nine-star Dipper with two extra bright 'guardian' stars on either side of it, against the tradition of two inconspicuous or invisible stars tied to its handle. Bright star Arcturus as Horn on the Dipper's left perfectly matches *Héguanzî*'s description. Traditional Halberd's position in Well is on the correct side of the Dipper but lacks the elevation and brightness to balance Horn. This suggests Capella had a pre-Hàn identification with Halberd, lost to time except in *Héguanzî*'s identification.

2. Grand Unity and Pacing the Dipper

a) *Héguanzî* does not mention the traditional Daoist ritual of 'pacing the Dipper' (bùgang) by name, but implies it in mentioning the shaman's hop or 'limping step' (v-d), traditionally associated with it. Grand Unity (Taìyi) and Nine Augustans (Jiû-Huáng), also linked to later Daoist Dipper rituals, are both centre stage in *Héguanzî* (x-a, xi-a). Further chapters describe the astral travel (xii-d) and a 'rotator' (huán) in flight, activities linked with shamanic or at least symbolic Dipper-centric religious practices. (cf. Plate 10, Diagrams 1-4)

Indeed celestial flight by of a shamanic nature was already featured in many early Chû lyrics (e.g. *Chûcî*: Jiû Ge, Yuânyóu; *Zhuangzî* I: Xiaoyaoyóu), and with immortals as 'feathered men' yûrén depicted on the backs of magic bronze mirrors. All this is consistent with enaction of 'pacing the Dipper' (bùgang) the ritual practice, described as flying in post-Hàn Daoist texts, in which a priest is believed to incorporate the movement of Grand Unity, resident in the Little Dipper, through the cosmos. (Andersen 1989: 24, 38; 2008, 237–240).

According to *Wénzî*:"Lâo Zî said: 'The Emperor embodies Grand Unity…'" (IX Xiàdé, 82) The idea was elaborated in an encyclopaedic of Liú An, Prince of Huaínán (and uncle to Emperor Wû). His *Huaínánzî* tells us: The Purple Palace is Grand Unity's seat… the Purple Palace controls the Dipper's left rotation (i.e. anti-clockwise. III Tianwén 5a) The Five Emperors and Three Kings have separate tasks but the same aim… the Emperor embodies Grand Unity… He who grasps Grand Unity encages Heaven and Earth... he who embodies Grand Unity is illumined in Heaven and Earth's real-feelings... (VIII Bênjing 7a-7b) Liú An's own ambitions of embodiment in Grand Unity, revealed by his abortive revolt in 122 BC, were ended by imperially ordered suicide.

Grand Unity's essence communicates with Heaven's Way. (IX Zhûshù 1b) Uncreated yet creator of things he is called Grand Unity... the True Man is never divided from Grand Unity. (XIV Quányán 1a-b) No doubt the Prince of Huaínán considered himself such a person, to his ultimate detriment.

The importance of Grand Unity, in the imperial observances of early Hàn is covered in detail by Simâ Qian's contemporary accounts. In 110 BC (year one of Yuánfeng) Hàn Martial Emperor, in a bid to outdo Qín's First Emperor, ascended to worship Shandong's Grand Mountain, Taìshan. (*Shîjì* XII, Bênjì XXIV 83c)

Simâ Qian's Music Record states: The house of Hàn always on the eighth day of the First Month worships Grand Unity at Ganquán. Martial Emperor's hymn even thanked Grand Unity for the descent of 'heavenly horses' acquired from Central Asia. (*Shîjì* XXIV: Yuèshu 192b. Loewe 1979: 97ff) In the Central Palace the Heavenly Pole star is first in brightness. It is Grand Unity's constant residence. (XXVII Tian'guanshu 209c) He quotes Daoist Miù Jì: Grand Unity's assistants are the Five Emperor Gods... (XXVIII Fengshàn Shu, dì-226b)

In 1977, the 165 BC tomb of Rûyin Hóu of the early Hàn dynasty at Shuanggû Dui, Fùyáng (Anhui), was found to hold a 'Grand Unity Walking the Nine Palaces Divination Board' in Luò River map sequence.[386] In real life, the shaman or priest performing the ceremony was believed to embody the God Grand Unity. This divination board would appear to reproduce in portable form the same ritual enacted at shrines honouring the Dipper, as the master of fate and fortune. Its importance to the individual, in this case a baron of enormous wealth and power, is reflected in its accompaniment of him to the afterlife.

In the Six Dynasties period of disunion independent Daoism flourished. Exhaustive documentation has been preserved in Daoist compendia or recovered from Dunhuáng's cave library. Two main schools developed, namely the more individualist Shàngqing which paced the Dipper according to naturalistic star formations and orthodox Zhèngyi favoured by Emperor Huizong of Northern Sòng.

Andersen 2005: 29-30 cites Xuè Youxi (fl. 750): "Grand Unity is also the Grand Lord, Dàjun. Grand Lord is the most honoured of the hundred numinous forces in the body, the master of the ten thousand breaths. Therefore, he is called Grand Unity." In "Jiao" (Pregadio 2008: I, 542-543) Andersen cites the Suí History on Zhèngyi Daoist night ritual offered to the Heavenly Augustan of Grand Unity (Tianhuáng Taìyi) together with the five planet emperors.

---

[386] Taìyi Xíng Jiû-Gong` Zhanpán 太一行九宫占盤. Harper 1978-1979: 1-10. Da Dai Lìjì:Míngtáng. Needham 1959: 57. Andersen 1989: 25, 29-35. Kalinowski 1998-99: 125.

The Zhèngyi school follow the Luò River schema of 'The walk of Taiyi through the Nine Palaces' [Taìyi bù jiû-gong 太一步九宮] in quests for immortality, exorcism, protection of the nation, even in a dance for couples with neìdan 'inner circulations'. (Andersen 1989: 17–18, 24, 27, 38, 145. Dàozàng 1294: Shangqing huangshu guodu yi 上清黃書過度儀)

This Luò River 3 x 3 grid may be seen as idealised encapsulisation of the nine Dipper stars and the Nine Augustan rulers, believed to inhabit them or emanate from them.[387] As illustrated, in the Introduction to this work, the practice of 'pacing the Dipper' (bùgang 步罡) in the intricate pattern of the nine-fold grid survives to this day in Daoist observances and has influenced martial arts with its double-helix shaped movements. (Diagrams 1-3)

Ideas of extra-terrestial space travel and inter-galactic astral flight in spirit, as 'treading the Dipper' (bùgang tàdôu 步罡踏斗), limping 'steps of Yû' (Yûbù 禹步), and 'pacing the void' (bùxu 步虛) in circles with visualisation and invocation of goddesses and gods in each star by turn, proliferated. (Robinet 1997: 173-174, 239) 'Nine Monarchs' Jade Scripture on Flying' (Feixing jiuchen yujing 飛行九晨玉經) and other Shangqing revealed texts describe 'the way of the flying walk' (feibù-zhi dào 飛步之道):

> You ride a chariot yoked with flying dragons.
> The heaven of the Supreme Pole
> presents you with the fungus of immortality. The
> Jade Emperor gives you immortal lads.
> (Bù Tian'gang Jing 步天綱經, Dàozàng 1316, tr. Andersen 1989: 38)

To conclude, we find in Heguanzî the following discrete elements: **Dipper constellation + Nine Augustans + Grand Unity + shaman's limping step + cosmic flight**

which in combination, and conclusion, add up to nothing less than a precursor of received Daoist ritual practices on whose ultimate origins further researches is yet to discover.

---

[387] *Taìyi Shù Tôngzong Dàquán* 1780: iii 1-4 Jiû-Gong Guìshén Tôngxíng Biànxiàng Shù lists Nine Palaces in Luò River sequence, citing Guo Pú 郭璞 (276-324): *Líng yào Jing* 靈曜經 (ii-zé); iv: 17b lists the appropriate military prayer, troop deployment and sacrificial offerings for each.

3. Nine Augustan Stars and Dipper Mother Myths

a) The most widely read account of Daoist mythology, narrated in popular story-telling style for the general public, is the Romance of the Enfiefment of the Gods (Fengshén Yânyì 封神演義) by Xû Zhònglin 許仲琳, Lù Xixing 陸西星, published around 1601 in late Míng.

Here Chinese history, religion and folk beliefs are melded with Buddhist and Hindu elements in wars of the gods, echoing the drama of Hindu epics. Here humans are gods and gods human. As in Luó Guànzhòng's acclaimed Yuán dynasty *Water Margin* epic (*Shuihûzhuàn*), where at the grand finale 108 heroes are canonised as stars, stellar apotheosis is virtue's ultimate reward. Canonisation takes the form of feudal enfiefment whereby at the inauguration of a dynasty its leading henchmen would be rewarded by family land-grants, in this case a place in the stars.

Narrated as a 'crusade' by house of Zhou to overthrow the evil-doing last king of Shang, royal adviser of divine wisdom Jiang Zîyá plays a commanding role. He enfiefs the Holy Mother Gold Spirit (Jinlíng) as Dipper Mother, a deity unattested in Chinese classical literature but identified with Marîcî from Hinduism. (LXXXII 703-704; XCIX 862-863).

A century later in early Qing, Zhang Jìzong 張繼宗 (d. 1716), 54th Correct Unity Celestial Teacher, in his review of immortals, reveals that the Heavenly Mother, in one pregnancy begot nine sons as Human Augustans. Her ninth star son, named Péng 蓬, then went south to rule the world. (1701: Lìdai Shénxian Tong jiàn, 1701, I: 3b)

Like Mârîcî her "chariot is drawn by seven pigs. She is called the Way's Mother (Dàomû) in Primal Energy's Brahma Heaven Dipper, around whom all the stars revolve." (IV: 10b) "Human Augustans manage the Northern Dipper's nine stars. They are Jade True Immortal Souls and salute to Dipper Mother from their residences." (V: 10b)

This text, notwithstanding its obviously late date, displays some exact matches with *Héguanzî* (x-a, xi-a): Grand Unity (Taìyi) "can hold the Under-Heaven's Great Community (Dàtóng 大同) and modulate the universe's Great Expanse's energy (Dàhóng-zhi qì 大鴻之氣)." He ruled for four hundred years. (I: 4b).

b) On the nomenlature of Dipper stars, there is considerable divergence. The names in astromical surveys and maps (Zhang Ximíng of Táng; Suzhou Star Map dated 1434) differ radically from those of Daoism. (Chart I) Grand Unity Technique's Collated Lineages Great Completion (*Taìyî Shù Tôngzong Dàquán* 太乙數統宗大全, II: 2-3), published in 1780 with function of each, corresponds in nomenclature with that currently used in Phuket's 'Vegetarian Festival'. (Cheu Hock Tong 1993: 42-43): (Diagram 3, above. Chart I, column D).

D1. Heaven Hero, Tianying 天英; for governance, Heaven's Son, sunny (yáng) virtue.

D2. Heaven Deputy, Tianrèn 天 任; for law, shady (yin) penalties and female rulers.

D3. Heaven Pillar, Tianzhù 天柱; for commands and disasters.

D4. Heaven Heart, Tianxin 天心; kills, occupying the centre to kill criminals.

D5. Heaven Bird, Tianqín 天禽; attacks rebels against the Way.

D6. Heaven Assistant, Tianfû 天輔; for danger and granaries.

D7. Heaven Charge, Tianchong 天衝; for departments (bù), weapons and executions.

D8. Heaven Herb, Tianruî 天芮; 'Dark Battle-axe', Xuán'gé is for armed rebellions and bandits.

D9. 天 蓬 Heaven Bramble, Tianpéng; 'Heavenly Spear, Beckoner', Tianqiang Zhaoyáo is for violent disturbances and change.

Northern Dipper's Prolongation of Life Scripture (*Beîdôu Yánsheng Jing* Zhùjiê 北斗延生注解 in *Dàozàng Jíyào* 道藏集要, Dôují 斗集 II, assuming Dàozàng dated 1444) and Dipper Mother Prime Dignity's Nine Augustan Scripture (Dôumû Yuánzun: Jiû- Huáng Jing in *Sanfeng Quánjí*) give a very different version (column **E**), apparently representing the Complete Truth (Quánzhen) Daoist school, which echoes most of Zhang Jìzong's version (column **C**) but in different sequence:

E1. Sunny Bright, Ravenous **Wolf**, Grand Star Lord: (C**7**)
Yángmíng Tanláng Taì Xing jun 陽明貪狼太星君

E2. Shady Essence, **Vast Gate**, Prime Star Lord: (C**8**)
Yinjing Jùmén Yuán Xing jun 陰精巨門元星君

E3. True Man. Wealth Kept, True Star Lord: (C**9**?)
Zhenrén Lùcún Zhen Xing jun 真人錄存真星君

E4. Dark Brilliance, **Civil Tune**, Knot Star Lord: (C**2**)
Xuánmíng Wénqû Niû Xing jun 玄明文曲紐星君

E5. Cinnabar Pill, Modest True, Cable Star Lord: (C**1**?)
Danyuán Liánzhen Gâng Xing jun 丹元廉貞綱星君

E6. North Pole, **Martial Tune**, Thread Star Lord: (C**3**)
Beîjí Wûqû Jî Xing jun 北極武曲紀星君

E7. Heaven Pass, **Break Army**, Pass Star Lord: (C**6**)
Tianguan Pòjun Guan Xing jun 天闗破軍闗星君

E8. Cavern Brilliance, **Outer Support** Star Lord: (C**4**)
Dòngmíng Waìfû Xing jun 洞明外輔星君

E9. Hidden Light, **Inner Adjutant** Star Lord: (C**5**)
Yînguang Neìbì Xing jun. 隐光内弼星君

The above version (**E**) is that followed by the numbered plaques of the Nine Augustans in the Tianshuî shrine. However, the actual seating order is different and the plaques may no longer match their originally intended owners. The two end figures, clad in military 'chain mail' on the left of the Dipper Mother should be the guards **E8** and **E9**, but instead are labeled **E6** and **E8**. (Plate 14)

Chart I. Nine Dipper Stars Names Collated

A	B	C	D	E	F
Arabian/ Greek	(Táng) Wáng Ximíng	*Enfiefment of the Gods* (1601)	Correct Unity Daoism (1701, 1780)	*Nine Augustan Scripture* (pre 1444?)	*Héguanzî* iv-a
1. Dubhe/ alpha	Pivot, Shu 樞	Heaven's Steel Tiangang 天罡	Heaven's Hero Tianying 天英	Ravenous Wolf Tanláng 貪狼	Four Energies Sì-Qì 四氣
2. Merak/ beta	Roller, Xuán 璇	Civil Tune Wénqû 文曲	Heaven's Deputy Tianrèn 天任	Shady Essence Yinjing 陰精	"
3. Phecda/ gamma	Ball, Ji 璣	Martial Tune Wûqû 武曲	Heaven's Pillar Tianzhù 天柱	True Man Zhenrén 真人	"
4. Megrez,/ delta	Balance, Quán 權	Left Support Zuôfû 左輔	Heaven's Heart Tianxin 天心	Dark Brilliance 玄明/冥	"
5. Alioth/ epsilon	Jade Measure, Yùhéng 玉衡	Right Adjutant Yòubì 右弼	Heaven's Bird Tianqín 天禽	Elixir Pill Danyuán 丹元	Central Three Zhongsan 中參
6. Mizar/ zeta	Open Sunny, Kaiyáng 開陽	Break Army Pòjun 破軍	Heaven's Support Tianfû 天輔	North Pole Beîjí 北極	"
7. Alkaid/ eta	Waving Light, Yáoguang 搖光	Heaven's Wolf Tianláng 天狼	Heaven's Charge Tianchong 天冲/衝	Heaven's Gate Tianguan 天關	"
8. Alcor 80	Three Heavenly Spears San-Tianqiang 三天槍	Great Gate Jùmén 巨門	Heaven's Herb/ Dark Battle-axe; Tianruî 天芮/ Xuán'gé 玄戈	Cavern Brilliance, Outer Support Dòngmíng Waìfû 洞明外輔	Horn Jiâo 角 = Arcturus?
9. n.a.	n.a.	Beckoner Zhaoyáo 招摇	Heaven's Bramble/ Spear; Tianpéng 天蓬/ qiang 槍	Hidden Light, Inner Adjutant Yînguang Neìbì 隐光内弼	Halberd Yuè 鉞 = Capella?

End Plate 26. North Dipper, Star No. 9, Hidden Light Yǐnguang, **Inner Adjutant** Star Lord (Beǐdǒu Yánsheng Jing Zhùjiê 北斗延生注解 in Dàozàng Jíyào 道藏集要, Dôují 斗集 II)

Bibliography

I. Primary Sources, Original Texts

Baopuzi 抱朴子. Ge Hung 葛洪 (283-343). DZ no. 1185. Ban Gu, see Hanshu, 'Han History'.

Beidou Yansheng Jing Zhujie 北斗延生經注解, in Daozang Jiyao 道藏集要, Dôují 斗集 II.

Chunqiu Fanlu 春秋繁露. (Han) Dong Zhongshu 董仲舒. Zhuzi Baijia congshu 諸子百家叢. 1989: Guji Chubanshe, Shanghai.

Confucius, Kongzi 孔子, see Kongzi Jiayu, Lunyu.

Csikszentmihalyi, Mark 2008. "Shangqing huangshu guodu yi 上清黃書過度 儀 'Liturgy of Passage of the Yellow Writ of Highest Clarity'"", in The Encyclopedia of Taoism, ed. by Fabrizio Pregadio. Routledge, 868–869.

Dadai Liji jinzhu jinyi. 大戴禮記今註今議. (Han) Gao Ming 高明 ed. 1975: Taiwan Shangwu Yinshuguan, Taipei.

Daodejing 道德經 in 81 verses. Qiu Xigui 裘錫圭 ed. In Mawangdui Hanmu boshu 馬王堆漢墓帛書. 1980: Wenwu Chubanshe, Beijing.

DZ = Daozang 道藏. Numbering system, see: Schipper and Verellen 2004.

Daozang: DZ220, IV: 10a11a (Yuan); DZ221, IV: 129b130b (Nan Song) Yutang Zhengzong Gaoben Neijing Yushu; DZ751: XVII: 53a54b.

Daozang Jiyao 道藏輯要 1906: Dou-ji II, 52-61, 2938-2942, Beidou Yanshou Jing; Dou-ji III, 17ff, 2972ff: Jiu-Huang Xin Jing. Erhxian An, Chengdu. Dong Zhongshu. See: Chunqiu Fanlu.

Doumu Yuanzun Jiu-Huang Jing, see Jiu-Huang Jing.

Fengshen yanyi. 封神演義. Xu Zhonglin 許仲琳, Lu Xixing 陸西星, 1601. 1979: Wenyuan Shuju, Taipei.

Guanzi 管子. (Tang) Yin Zhizhang 尹知章, (Qing) Dai Wang 戴望 ed. Yang Jialuo 楊家駱 ed. with Shang junshu 商君書. Zhong guo sixiang mingzhu 中國思想名著 no. 13. 1981: Shijie shuju, Taipei.

Guiguzi 鬼谷子, 無字天書 'Demon Valley Master'. Qin Wei 秦偉 ed. 1992.1. Guangxi Shifan Daxue, Nanning. Cf. Cleary tr. 1994; Thunder in the Sky.

Guodian Chumu Zhujian 郭店楚墓竹簡. Qiu Xigui 裘錫圭 ed. 1998: Wenwu Chubanshe, Beijing.

Guoyu. 國語. (Wu 吳) Wei Zhao 韋昭 ed. Sibu beiyao 四部備要. 1975: Zhonghua shuju, Taipei.

Han Fei Zi. 韓非子集解. Wang Xianshen 王先慎 ed. 1881. Yang Jialuo 楊家駱 ed. Zhong guo sixiang mingzhu 中國思想名著 no. 14. 1986: Shijie Shuju, Taipei.

Hanshi Waizhuan jinzhu jinyi 韓詩外傳今註註今譯. Lai Yanyuan 賴炎元 ed. 1972: Shangwu Yinshuguan, Taipei.

Hanshu 漢書. (Han) Ban Gu 班固 (CE 32-92) and sister Ban Zhao 班昭 (ca. 45-116). 1977: Zhonghua Shuju, Beijing.

Han Yu 韓愈. Han Changli ji 韓昌黎記.

HGZ = Heguanzi 鶡冠子. (Song) Lu Dian 陸佃 ed. ca. 1100. Sibu beiyao 四部備要. 1970: Zhonghua Shuju, Taipei.

Heguanzi zihui 子彙. Zhou Ziyi 周子義 (1529-1587) ed. Wanyou Wenku 萬有文庫. 1966-1973: Shangwu yinshuguan, Taipei.

Heguanzi 鶡冠子評註. 鶡冠子撰; 陸佃 Lu Dian 解; 王宇 Wang Yu 評; 汪明際 Wang Mingji, 朱養純 Zhu Yangchun 參評; 朱養和 Zhu Yanghe 訂. Hangzhou, 1625 Huazhai (with Guanzi). Hong Kong Library, Hong Kong.

Heguanzi. Huijiao Jizhu. Huang Huaixin ed. 2004; 2014, see in 'Secondary Studies'.

Huainanzi 淮南子. Liu An 劉安 (179-122 BCE). (Han) Gao You 高誘 ed. (Sibubeiyao 四部備要). 1974: Zhonghua shuju, Taipei. See: Major, John et al. tr., ed.

Huangdi Neijing Lingshu 黃帝內經靈樞. Fu Jinghua 傅景華 ed. 1997: Zhongyi Guji, Beijing.

Jia Yi 賈誼 (201-169 BC): *Xinshu* 新書. Xin Yan 辛妍 ed. Wuyingdian Juzhenban 武英殿聚珍版. Zhuzi baijia congshu. 諸子百家叢書.1989: Guji Chubanshe, Shanghai.

Jiu-Huang Jing, Doumu Yuan zun, 斗姆元尊: 九皇經, (Yuan/Ming) Zhang Sanfeng 張三丰; Li Xiyue 李西月, Cai Congzhe 蔡聰哲 2003 ed., in Sanfeng Quanji vii, 403-414, qv.

Jiu-Huang Xin Jing 九皇新經, see: Dàozàng Jíyào.

Kongzi Jiayu 孔子家語. Wang Su 王肅 ed. Sibu beiyao 四部備要. 1976: Taiwan Zhonghua shuju, Taipei.

Laozi, see Daodejing; Mawangdui Hanmu Boshu; Levi 2009/2011; Star 2001.

Lidai Shenxian Tong jian 歷代神仙通鑑. Zhang Jizong 張繼宗 (1701). 1976: Zhonghua shijie ziliao gongying, Taipei.

Liezi jishi 列子集釋, Yang Bojun 1987. Huazheng chubanshe, Taibei.

Liji jinzhu jinyi 禮記今注今譯. Wang Meng'ou 王夢鷗 ed. 1984: Shangwu yinshuguan, Taipei.

Liu-Tao 六韜, 'Six Satchels', attr. Jiang Taigong 姜太公, see Sawyer 1993.

Liu Zongyuan 柳宗元 (773-819): Liu hedong ji 柳河東集. (Tang). Sibu beiyao 四部備要. 1975: Zhonghua shuju, Taipei.

Lunyu huijian 論語會箋. Xu Ying 徐英 ed. 1981: Zhengzhong shuju, Taipei. Luo Bi 羅泌 pref. 1170: Lushi 路史. Sibu beiyao 四部備要. 1976: Taiwan Zhonghua shuju, Taipei.

Lyushi Chunqiu/ Lüshi Chunqiu 呂氏春秋. (Qin) Lü Buwei 呂不韋. (Han) Gao You 高誘ed. (Qing) Bi Yuan 畢沅 ed. Sibu beiyao 四部備要. 1982: Zhonghua shuju, Taipei.

Lu Shi, see: Luo Bi.

Lyu Buwei/ Lü Buwei, see: Lyushi Chunqiu/ Lüshi Chunqiu.

Mawangdui Hanmu Boshu (1). 馬王堆漢墓帛書(壹). Qiu Xigui 裘錫圭 ed. 1980. Incl. 'Yellow Emperor Classics' and Laozi. 1980: Wenwu chubanshe, Beijing.

Mawangdui Hanmu Yishu jiaoshi 馬王堆漢墓醫書校釋. Wei Qipeng 魏啓鵬, Hu Xianghua 胡翔驊. 1992: Chengdu chubanshe, Chengdu.

Mengzi. 孟子, 'Mencius'. (Han) Zhao Qi 趙岐 ed. Wen Jincheng 温晉城 ed. 1970: Zhengzhong shuju, Taipei.

Mozi jiangu 墨子間詁. (Qing) Sun Yirang 孫詒讓 ed. (Zhuzi jicheng 諸子集成). 1986: Shanghai Shudian, Shanghai.

MWD see Mâwángdui.

Sanfeng Quanji 三丰全集 attr. (Yuan/Ming) Zhang Sanfeng. Huang Xinyang 黃信陽, Cai Congzhe 蔡聰哲 2003, (Qing) Li Hanxu 李涵虛 1844, (Mengjiu) Wang Xiling (夢九) 汪錫齡 1723, eds., Zhongguo Daojiao Dandao Xiulian Xilie Congshu, ISBN 978-7-80254-651-4, Zongjiao Chubanshe, Beijing.

Sanguo Yanyi 三國演義, 'Romance of the Three Kingdoms'. (Yuan) Shi Nai'an 施耐菴. 1995: Zhonghua shuju, Beijing.

Shanhai Jing jianshu 山海經箋疏. Guo Pu 郭璞. Ruan Yuan 阮元 pref. 1799. Sibu beiyao. 1979: Taiwan Zhonghua shuju, Taipei.

Shang jun Shu jiegu dingben. 商君書解詁定本. Zhu Shizhe 朱師轍 ed. (with Guanzi, Zhong guo sixiang mingzhu 中國思想名著 no. 13). 1981: Shijie shuju, Taipei.

Shangshu zheng yi 尚書正義. (Tang) Kong Yingda 孔穎達. 1990. Xinhua shudian, Beijing.

Shen Dao, see Thompson, John. 1979.

Shiji 史記. (Han) Simâ Qian 司馬遷. (Liu-Song) Pei Yin 沛殷, (Tang) Sima Zhen 司馬貞, (Tang) Zhang Shoujie 張守節 ed. Guoxue jiben congshu 國學基本叢書 1974, Wenhua tushu gongsi, Taipei.

Sima Qian: see Shiji.

Shizi 尸子 (Huhailou kanben). 1989 with Shang jun Shu. Zhuzi baijia congshu. Shanghai: Guji chubanshe.

Shuihudi Qinmu zhujian 睡虎地秦墓竹簡. Wu Tiemei 吳鐵梅 ed. 1990. Wenwu chubanshe, Beijing.

Suishu 隋書. 1977. Zhonghua shuju, Beijing.

Sun Bin Bing fa 孫賓兵法. 1975, Yinqueshan hanmu zhujian 銀雀山漢墓竹簡. Wenwu chubanshe, Beijing.

Suzhou Star Map, 1434, Húntian Yi-tông Xingxiàng Quántú.

Taiping Yulan 太平御覽. Li Fang 李昉 (925-996). Sibu congkan 四部叢刊 no. 3.

Taìshàng Dòngyuan Shénzhòu Jing 太上洞淵神咒經, ref. Seidel 1969-1970.

Taiyi Shu Tongzong Daquan 太乙數统宗大全. Luo Jifu 羅集福 1780 ed., Li Ziming 李自明 pref. 1795, in Sanfeng Quánjí: Jiù-Huáng Jing. 1966. Zhenshanmei, Taipei.

T= Tripitaka Dàzàng 大藏. (Yuán) T21: 1307 Foshuo Beidou Qixing Yanshou Jing. Wang Ximing 王希明 (Tang) Danyuan Zi Butian Ge 丹元子步天歌.

Wenxin Diaolong 文心彫龍. (Jìn) Liu Xie 劉勰. (Qing) Huang Shulin 黃叔琳 ed. 1975. (Guoxue congshu 國學叢書). Dafang, Taipei.

Wenzi yuanyi 文子原義. (Song) Du Daojian 杜道堅 ed. Wuyingdian juzhenban 武英殿聚珍版. 1989. Zhuzi baijia congshu. 諸子百家叢書. Shanghai: Guji chubanshe.

Xiao Yuncong chimu 蕭雲從尺木: Lisao quantu 離騷全圖 (1638). Siku quanshu 四庫全書. 1978. Sancai, Taipei.

Xu Zizhi Tong jian Changbian 續資治通鑑長編. (Southern Song) Li Tao 李燾 (1114- 1183). 1979. Zhonghua shuju, Beijing.

Xunzi jinzhu jinyi 荀子今注今議. Xiong Gongzhe 熊公哲 ed. 1984. Shangwu yinshuguan, Beijing.

'Yellow Emperor Classics', in Mawangdui Hanmu Boshu. Yì Jing, Changes Classic, Wilhelm 1967.

Yiwei 易緯. Siku quanshu 四庫全書 ed. 1978. Sancai, Taipei.

Yinwenzi 尹文子 (c. 200 AD?). (Qing) Ma Guohan 馬國翰 ed. Wang Qixiang 王啟湘 ed. 1914. In Sibu kanyao 四部刊要. Fajia yishu jiben qizhong 法家佚書輯本七種. 1985. Shijie shuju, Taipei.

Yixiang Kaocheng 儀象考成. (Qing) Qin Tianjian's 欽天監 astronomical compilation by Ignaz Kogler (ca. 1750. Ref. Yi Shitong 伊世同 1981.

Yongle Dadian. 永樂大典 1408. Vol. 10,287 Zi references HGZ chs. 1-15, but only Vol. 19,743 Lu, with HGZ ch. 11, is extant. 1977: Shijie Shuju, Taipei.

Zhang Jizong, see Lidai Shenxian Tong jian. Zhang Sanfeng, see Sanfeng Quanji; Jiu-Huang Jing.

Zhang Sanfeng, see: Jiû-Huáng Jing.

Zhanguoce 戰國策. Wang Fuhan 王扶漢, Meng Ming 孟明 ed. 1993. Zhongyang Minzu Xueyuan, Beijing. Zhang Sanfeng, see Sanfeng Quanji.

Zhaomíng Wénxuân 昭明文選, (Liáng) Zhaomíng Taìzî; (Táng) Lî Shàn zhù. (Sòng) Chúnxi bên. 1979, Wénhuà Túshu Gongsi, Taîbeî.

Zhouli 周禮. Ed. Lin Yin 林尹. 1972. Taipei: Shangwu yinshuguan.

Zhuangzi jishi 莊子集釋. Guo Qingfan 郭慶藩 ed. 1961: Zhonghua shuju, Beijing.

2. Secondary Studies

Allan, Sarah. 1981; (expanded) 2016. The Heir and the Sage: Dynastic Legend in Ancient China. China Materials Centre, San Francisco; State University of New York.

Allan, Sarah. 1984. "Drought, Human Sacrifice and the Mandate of Heaven in a Lost Text from the Shang shu." Bulletin of the School of Oriental and African Studies 47: 523-39.

Allan, Sarah. 2003. "The Great One, Water and the Daodejing, new light from Guodian." T'oung Pao 89.4: 237-285.

Allan, Sarah. 2010. "Abdication and Utopian Vision in the Bamboo Slip Manuscript Rongchengshi." Journal of Chinese Philosophy 37: 67-84.

Allred, David T. 2003/2004: The Circumpolar Stars of Ancient China, UMI 1417379, Indiana University.

Ames, Roger T. 1983. The Art of Rulership. University of Hawai'i, Honolulu.

Andersen, Poul. 1989-90. "The Practice of Bugang." Persée. Cahiers d' Extreme Asie 55: 15-53.

Andersen, Poul. 1991. Taoist ritual texts and traditions with special reference to the practice of bugang, the cosmic dance. Faculty of Humanities, University of Copenhagen, Copenhagen.

Andersen, Poul. 2005. "Scriptural Traditions West and East: Foundation of Belief versus Frameworks for the Transmission of Methods." In Scriptures, Schools and Forms of Practice in Daoism: A Berlin Symposium, edited by Poul Andersen and Florian C. Reiter, 13-32. Wiesbaden: Harrassowitz.

Andersen, Poul (2008), "Bugang", in The Encyclopedia of Taoism 237–240, ed. by Fabrizio Pregadio. Routledge.,

Bauer, Wolfgang. 1956. "Der Herr vom gelben Stein." Oriens Extremus 3: 137-52. Bauer, Wolfgang. 1976. China and the Search for Happiness. Tr. Michael Shaw. Sanctuary, New York.

Bodde, Derk. 1975. Festivals in Classical China: New Year and Other Annual Observances during the Han Dynasty 206 B.C. – A.D. 220. Princeton University, Princeton.

Boretz, Avron A. 1995: "Martial Gods and Magic Swords: Identity, Myth and Violence in Popular Chinese Religion," Journal Of Popular Culture 29-1: 93-109, Wiley-Blackwell USA.

Bray, Francesca, Vera Dorofeeva-Lichtmann, Georges Métaillié ed. 2007. Graphics and Text in the Production of Technical Knowledge in China, The Warp and the Weft. Leiden: Brill.

Brown, Fred R. 1922: Superstitions Common in Kiangsi, New China Review, 4(6) 493- 504, New China Review Office, Shanghai.

Caldwell, Ernest 2014. "Promoting Action in Warring States Political Philosophy: A First Look at the Chu Manuscript Cao Mie's Battle Arrays." Early China (2014) Vol. 37. 259-289.

Campbell, Joseph. 1962. Oriental Mytholog y. Viking Compass, New York. Campbell, Joseph. 1968/1970. The Masks of God: Creative Mytholog y. New York:

Viking Compass, New York.

Carrozza, Paola. 2002. "A Critical Review of the Principal Studies on the Four Manuscripts Preceding the B-version of the Mawangdui Daodejing." Asian Review 13: 49-69.

Chamberlain, Jonathan. 1983. Chinese Gods. Long Island Publishers, New York.Chan, David B. 1976. The Usurpation of the Prince of Yen, 1398-1402. Chinese Materials Centre, San Francisco.

Chan, Wing-tsit. 1963. A Source Book in Chinese Philosophy. Princeton University, Princeton.

Chang, K.C. 1976. Early Chinese Civilization, Anthropological Perspectives. Harvard: Harvard-Yenching Institute Monograph Series 23.

Chao, Shin-yi. 2010. Daoist Rituals, State Religion, and Popular Practices: Zhenwu Worship from Song to Ming (960-1644). Routledge, London.

Chen Guying 陳皷應, ed. 1994. Daojia wenhua yanjiu 道家文化研究. 5 vols. Guji, Shanghai.

Chen Yunchao 陳云超 2012: "Heguanzi Preparation for War thinking in regard to Enterprise Management Crisis's Insights" 鶡冠子備戰思想對企業管理危機的啟示. Shayang shifan gaodeng zhuanke xuexiao xuebao 沙陽高等專科學校學報 13.1: 103-04.

Chen Zhengming 陳正明, ed. 1997. Yonglegong bihua quanji 永樂宮壁畫全集. Tianjin: Tianjin Renmin Meishu chubanshe.

Cheng Yifan. 2007. "Guodian 'Laozi'de shuxie shixu. 郭店老子書寫時序" In Chudi jianbo sixiang yanjiu 楚地簡帛思想研究. Edited by Ding Sixin 丁四新, 526-544. Hubei Jiaoyu, Wuhan.

Cheu Hock Tong 1993. "The Festival of the Nine Emperor Gods in Peninsular Southeast Asia" in ed. Chinese Beliefs and Practices in Southeast Asia. ISBN 967 978 452 5: Pelanduk Publications, Selangor Darul Ehsan, Malaysia.

Childs-Johnson, Elizabeth, July/August 2020: "Who is that Human at Shimao? China's Ancient Belief in Metamorphic Power," Orientations, Volume 51, Number 4.

Chong, Kim-chong. 2010. "Zhuangzi and Hui Shi on Qing." Qinghua Journal of Chinese Studies 40.1:21-45.

Chu Kunliang 1991: Les aspects rituels du théâtre Chinois, College de France, Paris.

Cleary, Thomas tr.. 1992. The Secret of the Golden Flower: The Classic Chinese Book of Life. Harper, San Francisco.

Cleary, Thomas tr. 1994. Thunder in the Sky (Guiguzi). Shambhala, Boston.

Cohen, Erik. 2001: The Chinese Vegetarian Festival in Phuket, ISBN 9747534894, White Lotus, Bangkok.

Cook, Scott. Dec. 2002: "The 'Lüshi chunqiu' and the Resolution of Philosophical Dissonance," Harvard Journal of Asiatic Studies, vol. 62, no. 2, 307-345, DOI: 10,2307/4126601, Harvard Yenching Institute.

Covell, Alan Carter. 1984. Shamanist Folk Paintings: Korea's Eternal Spirits. Hollym International Corporation, Seoul.

Creel, Herrlee Glessner. 1961. "The fa jia: 'Legalists' or 'Adminstrators'?" 92- 120 In Creel 1970.

Creel, Herrlee Glessner. 1974. Shen Pu-hai: A Chinese Political Philosopher of the FourthCentury B.C. University of Chicago, Chicago.

Creel, Herrlee Glessner. 1970. What is Taoism? and Other Studies in Chinese Cultural History. University of Chicago, Chicago.

Csikszent Mihalyi, Mark. 2002. "Traditional Taxonomies and Revealed Texts in the Han." See Kohn 2002.

Davis, Edward L. 2002. "Arms and the Dao, 2: The Xu Brothers in Tea Country." In Daoist Identity: History, Lineage, and Ritual, ed. Livia Kohn, Harold D. Roth, 149-64. University of Hawai'i, Honolulu.

Dean, Kenneth. 1998. Lord of the Three in One, The Spread of a Cult in Southeast China, Princeton.

De Groot, J. J. M. (1892-1910). The Religious System of China. 6 vols. Leiden: Brill.

Defoort, Carine. 1997. The Pheasant Cap Master (Heguanzi): A Rhetorical Reading. Reproduces the 1557 woodblock Zihui 子彙 edition of the HGZ text. State University of New York, Albany.

Defoort, Carine. 2004. "Mohist and Yangist Blood in Confucian Flesh: The Middle Position of the Guodian Text 'Tangyu zhi Dao' 唐虞之道." Bulletin of the Museum of Far Eastern Antiquities 76: 44-70.

Defoort, Carine 2015: "Pheasant Cap Master" 281-306 in Dao Companion to Daoist Philosophy, ed. Xiaogan Liu, University of Hong Kong.

Despeux, Catherine, and Livia Kohn. 2003. Women in Daoism. Three Pines Cambridge, Mass..

Ding Sixin 丁四新. 2007 ed. Chudi jianbo sixiang yanjiu 楚地簡帛思想研究. Hubei Jiaoyu, Wuhan.

Duan Yu 段渝. 1996. Hushi liuhezhi shi: Fajia yu guojia tong yi 虎視六合之勢法家與國家統一. Sichuan Renmin, Chengdu.

Dudbridge, Glen. 1970. The Hsi-yu-chi: A Study of Antecedents to the Sixteenth Century Novel. Cambridge University, Cambridge.

Eberhard, Wolfram. 1952. Chinese Festivals. Henry Schuman, New York.

Ebrey, Patricia. 2000. "Taoism and Art at the Court of Song Huizong." in Daoism and the Arts of China, ed. Stephen Little and Shawn Eichman, 95-111. University of California, Berkeley.

Eliade, Mircia. 1971. The Myth of the Eternal Return: Cosmos and History. Princeton University, Princeton.

Elliott, Alan J.A.. 1955. Chinese Spirit-Medium Cults in Singapore. Anthropology Department, The London School of Economics and Political Science. Republished by Southern Materials Center, Inc., Taipei.

Ess, Hans von. 2014. "Emperor Wu of the Han and the First August Emperor of Qin in Sima Qian's Shiji" 239-257 in Pines et al. 2014.

Fang Suzhen 方素真 2002. "Taiyi shengshui yu Zhouyi cantongqi de guanxi" 太一生水 與《周易參同契》的關係. Chengda Zong jiao yu Wenhua xuebao 成大宗教與文化學報 2: 117-42.

Feuchtwang, Stephan. 2001. Popular Religion in China: The Imperial Metaphor. Routledge Curzon, London.

Frazer, Sir James. 1922. The Golden Bough. Macmillan, New York.

Gao Huaping 高華平. 2007. "Dui Chujian Daodejing ji Laozi qishu qiren de zairenshi" 對楚簡老子及老子其書其人的再認識. In Chudi Jianbo Sixiang yanjiu 楚地簡帛思想研究, Ding Sixin 丁四新 ed., 509-25. Hubei Jiaoyu, Wuhan.

292

Gao Min. 1979. "Lun Lyu-zhong d' Sefu yi-guan," Yunmeng Qinjian chutan 185-200, Zhonghua Shuju, Beijing.

Geaney, Jane. 2002. On the Epistemolog y of the Senses in Early Chinese Thought. University of Hawai'i, Honolulu.

Gentz, Joachim. 2005. "The Past as a Messianic Vision: Historical Thought and Strategies of Sacralization in the Early Gongyang Tradition" 227-254 in Historical Truth, Historical Criticism, and Ideology: Chinese Historiography and Historical Culture from a New Comparative Perspective, Brill.

Gesterkamp, Lennert. 2011. The Court of Heaven. Leiden: Brill.

Giles, Lionel. 1910. Sun Tzu on the Art of War. Luzacs, London.

Girard, René N.T. 1978. Les choses cachés depuis la foundation du monde. Grasset, Paris. Girard, René N.T. 1979. La violence et le sacré. Grasset, Paris.

Goldin, Paul R. 2011. "Persistent Misconceptions about Chinese 'Legalism.'"Journal of Chinese Philosophy 38.1: 88-104.

Goodrich, L. Carrington; Chaoying Fang eds.: 1976. Dictionary of Ming Biography. Columbia University, New York.

Gottschang, Karen Turner. 1983. "Chinese Despotism Reconsidered: Monarchy and Its Critics in the Ch'in and Early Han Empires." PhD Diss., University of Michigan, Ann Arbor.

Gould, Thomas. 1990. The Ancient Quarrel between Poetry and Philosophy. Princeton University, Princeton.

Graham, A.C. 1978. Later Mohist Logic, Ethics and Science. Chinese University, Hong Kong.

Graham, A. C. 1989. Disputers of the Tao: Philosophical Argument in Ancient China.
Open Court Publishing Company, La Salle, Ill..

Graham, A.C. 1989a. "A Neglected pre-Han Philosophical Text: Ho-kuan-tzu." In Bulletin of the School of Oriental and African Studies 52.3: 497-523.

Graham, A. C. 1990. "The Origins of the Legend of Lao Tan." In Studies in Chinese Philosophy and Philosophical Literature, Graham ed.: 111-24. State University of New York, Albany.

Graham, A.C. 1993. "The Way and the One in Ho-kuan-tzu." In Lenk and Paul 1993: 31-43. State University of New York, Albany.

Gu Zhizhong. 1993. Creation of the Gods. New World, Beijing.

Hall, David, and Ames, T. Roger. 1998. Thinking from the Han: Self, Truth and Transcendence in Chinese and Western Culture. State University of New York, Albany.

Hall, David, and Roger T. Ames. 1987. Thinking through Confucius. State University of New York, Albany.

Hansen, Chad. 1983. Language and Logic in Ancient China. University of Michigan, Ann Arbor.

Hansen, Chad. 1993. "Term-Belief in Action." In Lenk and Paul 1993: 45-68. State University of New York, Albany.

Hansen, Chad. 1995. "Qing (Emotions) in Pre-Buddhist Chinese Thought." In Emotions in Asian Thought: A Dialogue in Comparative Philosophy, Joel Marks and Roger T. Ames ed.: 181-212. State University of New York, Albany.

Harbsmeier, Christoph, and Kenneth Robinson. 1998. Science and Civilisation in China VII.1: Language and Logic. Cambridge University, Cambridge.

Harbsmeier, Christoph. 1991. "The Mass Noun Hypothesis and the Part-Whole Analysis of the White Horse Dialogue." In Chinese Texts and Philosophical Contexts: Essays Dedicated to Angus C. Graham edited by Henry Rosemont, Jr., 49-66. Open Court Publishing, La Salle, Ill..

Harbsmeier, Christoph. 1993. "Conceptions of Knowledge in Ancient China." In Epistemological Issues in Classical Chinese Philosophy, edited by Hank Lenk and Gregor Paul, 11-33. State University of New York, Albany.

Harbsmeier, Christoph. 2004. "The Semantics of Qing in Pre-Buddhist Chinese." In Love and Emotions in Traditional Chinese Literature, edited by Halvor Eifring, 69-149 Leiden: Brill.

Harper, Donald 2007: "Communication by Design: Two Silk Manuscripts of Diagrams (Tu) from Mawangdui Tomb Three." In Graphics and Text in the Production of Technical Knowledge in China, The Warp and the Weft, ed. Francesca Bray, Vera Dorofeeva-Lichtmann, Georges Métaillié. Leiden: Brill.

Harper, Donald. 1978. "The Han Cosmic Board." Early China 4: 1-10.

Harper, Donald. 1980. "The Han Cosmic Board: A Response to Christopher Cullen." Early China 6: 47-56.

Harper, Donald. 2001. "The Nature of Taiyi in the Guodian manuscript Taiyi sheng shui – Abstract Cosmic Principle or Supreme Deity?" Chūgoku shutsudo shiryō kenkyū 中国出土資料研究 5: 1-23.

Hawkes, David. 1959. Ch'u Tz'u: The Songs of the South: An Ancient Chinese Anthology. Oxford University, Oxford.

Hay, John. 1994. Boundaries in China. Reaktion Books, London.

Hendrischke, Barbara. 2006. The Scripture on Great Peace: The Taiping jing and the Beginnings of Daoism. University of California, Berkeley.

Henricks, Robert. 1989. Lao-Tzu: Te-Tao ching. New York: Ballantine.

Hong Shidi 洪世滌. 1972. Qin Shihuang. Shanghai Renmin Chubanshe, Shanghai.

Hope, Richard. 1961. Aristotle's Physics. Lincoln: University of Nebraska, Lincoln.

Hou Wailu 侯外廬. 1957. Zhong guo Sixiang Tongshi 中國思想通史. Renmin, Beijing.

Hsing I-tien 2014: "Qin-Han Census and Tax and Corvée Adminisration", in Pines et al. 2014.

Huang Huaixin 黃懷信. 2014. Heguanzi jiaozhu. 鶡冠子校注. Zhonghua Shuju, Beijing.

Huang Huaixin 黃懷信. 2002/2004. Heguanzi huijiao jizhu. 鶡冠子彙校輯注. Zhonghua Shuju, Beijing.

Huang, Shih-shan Susan. 2001. "Summoning the Gods: Paintings of Three Officials of Heaven, Earth and Water and Their Association with Daoist Ritual Performance in the Southern Song Period (1127-1279)." Artibus Asiae 61.1:5-52.

Huang, Shih-shan Susan. 2010. "Daoist Imagery of Body and Cosmos, Part 1: Body Gods and Starry Travel." Journal of Daoist Studies 3: 57-90.

Huang, Shih-shan Susan. 2012. Daoist Visual Culture in Traditional China. Harvard University, Centre for Chinese Studies, Cambridge, Mass.

Huhm, Halla Pai. 1980. Kut Korean Shamanist R ituals. Elizabeth, NJ: Hollym International Corporation, Seoul.

Ingo Wandlet. 1993: "The Cult of Surya Kencana in Jakarta: New-Style Peranakan Chinese Spirit-Mediumship" in Cheu Hock Tong 1993.

Jaang, Li; Sun, Zhouyong; Shao, Jing; Li, Min. 22 August 2018: "When Peripheries were centres: a preliminary study of the Shimao-centered polity in the loess highland, China," Antiquity 92, issue 364, 1002-1022. Cambridge University.

Jia, Jinhua. 2009. "Religious Origins of the Terms Dao and De and their Signification in the Laozi," Journal of the Royal Asiatic Society, Series 3, 19.4, 459-488, London.

Jordan, David K. 1972. Gods, Ghosts and Ancestors: Folk Religion in a Taiwanese Village. University of California, Berkeley.

Jowett, B. 1892. The Dialogues of Plato, Random House, New York.

Jullien, Francois. 1995. The Propensity of Things: Toward a History of Efficacy in China. tr. Janet Lloyd. Zone Books, New York.

Kalinowski, Marc. 2006. "The Use of the Twenty-eight Xiu as a Day-Count in Early China." Chinese Science 13: 55-81.

Kalinowski, Marc & Phyllis Brooks. 1998-99: The Xingde Texts from Mawangdui, Early China 23/24, 125-202.

Kang Li 康立, Wei Jin 衛今 et al., eds. 1976. Jing fa Mawangdui hanmu boshu 經法馬王堆漢墓帛書. Wenwu, Beijing.

Kern, Martin. 2000. The Stele Inscriptions of Ch'in Shih-Huang: Text and Ritual in Early Chinese Imperial Representation. American Oriental Society, New Haven.

Ki, Sunu. 1985. The Canon of Acupuncture: Huangti Nei Ching Ling Shu. Yuin University, Los Angeles.

Kirkland, Russell. 2004. Taoism: The Enduring Tradition. Routledge, New York.

Klein, E. 2010. "Were there 'Inner Chapters' in the Warring States? A New Examination of Evidence about the Zhuangzi." T'oung Pao 96.4-5: 299-369.

Kohn, Livia. 1998. God of the Dao: Lord Lao in History and Myth. University of Michigan, Centre for Chinese Studies, Ann Arbor.

Kohn, Livia. 2000. "Doumu: The Mother of the Dipper." Ming Qing yanjiu 8: 149-95.

Kohn, Livia ed. 2000. Daoism Handbook. Brill, Leiden.

Kohn, Livia and Harold D. Roth, eds. 2002. Daoist Identity, History, Lineage and Ritual. University of Hawai'i, Honolulu.

Kohn, Livia 2014: Zhuangzi Text and Context, Three Pines Press, St Petersburg, Florida.

Lagerwey, John, and Marc Kalinowski, eds. 2008. Early Chinese Religion, Part One, Shang through Han (1250 BC - 220 AD). Leiden: Brill.

Lagerwey, John, and Peng Zhilü, eds. 2009. Early Chinese Religion, Part Two, The Period of Disunion (220-589 AD). Leiden: Brill.

Lagerwey, John. 2010. A Religious State. Hong Kong University, Hong Kong. Lai, Guolong 來國龍 2014. "The Mawangdui Diagram of the Taiyi

Incantation 馬王堆太一祝圖考" Zhejiang University Journal of Art and Archaeology I, Zhejiang University.

Lai, Guolong 2015. Excavating the Afterlife, the Archaeolog y of Early Chinese Religion, University of Washington.Lau, D. C. 1973. "Review of Creel, What is Taoism?" Asia Major 18: 122-23.

Lee, Yong-yun. 2010. "A Naturalistic Understanding of Taiyi sheng shui 太一生水 Cosmology."http://cccp.uchicago.archive/2010 Creel Luce Paleography Workshop/ong-yun Lee.

Lenk, Hank, and Gregor Paul, eds. 1993. Epistemological Issues in Classical Chinese Philosophy. State University of New York, Albany.

Levi, Jean. tr. 2008: Le Ho-Kouan-Tseu, Precis d Domination, Allia, Paris.

Levi, Jean. 2008. "The Rite, the Norm and the Dao, philosophy of sacrifice and transcendence of power in ancient China." In Lagerwey and Kalinowski 2008: 645-692. Leiden: Brill.

Levi, Jean. tr. Jody Gladding. 2009/2011: The Complete Tao Te Ching with The Four Canons of the Yellow Emperor, Inner Traditions, Rochester, Vermont.

Lewis, Mark Edward. 1990. Sanctioned Violence in Early China. State University of New York, Albany.

Lewis, Mark Edward. 2007. History of Imperial China. Harvard University, Cambridge, Mass..

Li Dingsheng 李丁生. 1994. "Wenzi fei weishu kao" 文子非偽書考. In Chen Guying 陳皷 ed. 1994: 462-473. Guji, Shanghai.

Li Hong 李紅, ed. 1997. Zhong guo huihua daquan 中國繪畫大全. Wenhua, Beijing.

Li Hongchun 1982: Jingju Chang Tan, Zhongguo Chubanshe, Beijing.

Li Ling 李零. 1991. "Mawangdui Hanmu shen zhi tu yingshu bibing tu" 馬王堆漢墓神之圖應屬避兵圖." Kaogu 1991.10: 940-942.

Li, Ling. 1995. "An Archaeological Study of Taiyi (Grand One) Worship." Early Medieval China 2: 1-39.

Li Xueqin 李學勤. 1983. "Mawangdui boshu yu Heguanzi" 馬王堆帛書與鶡冠子. Jiangnan Kaogu 江南考古 2: 51-56.

Li Yiyan 李怡嚴. 2003. "Heguanzide zuojian wenti" 鶡冠子的错简問題. Zhong guo shi yanjiu 中國史研究 2003.1: 19-28.

Liao Ping 廖 頻 ed. 1985. The Yongle Palace Murals. Foreign Languages Press, Beijing.

Lin Xiurong 林秀蓉. 2011. "Lijao yu Qingjiao – Feng Menglong 'Li Xiuqing yijie Huang Zhennü' banzhuang yihan tanxi" 禮教與情教—馮夢龍〈李秀卿義結黃貞女〉扮裝意涵探析. Gaoxiong Shida Xuebao 30, 65-80. Kaohsiung.

Lin Suying 林素英. 2007. "Zhongni yanju, Kongzi xianju yu lunli zuanji-zhi bijiao" 仲尼燕居孔子閒居與論理篆辑之比較. In Ding Sixin 2007: 284-315. Hubei Jiaoyu, Wuhan.

Little, Stephen, with Shawn Eichman. 2000. Taoism and the Arts of China. University of California, Berkeley.

Liu, Cary Y., Naomi Noble R ichard et al, eds. 2005. Recarving China's Past: Art, Archaeology, and Architecture of the Wu Family Shrines. Princeton University.

Liu, Fu-shih 2008. "Image and Status of Shamans." In Lagerwey and Kalinowski 2008: 397-458.

Loewe, Michael. 1979. Ways to Paradise: The Chinese Quest for Immortality. George Allen and Unwin, London.

Lu Shuguo 祿書果 2008. "Heguanzi 'yinfu chenghao shuo' kaobian" 鶡冠子因服 成號說考辨. Yuwen Zhishi語文知識.

Lü Simian 呂思勉 1985. Xianqin Gailun 先秦學概論. Zhongguo Dabaike Quanshu, Shanghai.

Luo Genze 羅根則. 1930. 1981. Guanzi Tanyuan 管子探源. Taipei: Liren shuju, Taipei.

Lupke, Christopher, ed. 2005. The Magnitude of Ming: Command, Allotment, and Fate in Chinese Culture. University of Hawai'i, Honolulu.

Lyu Yufei, Sun Zhouyong, Shao Jing 2018/2019: "The Alignment of the East Outer City Gate at the Ancient Chinese City of Shimao" 481-527 in

W. Orchiston et al. eds.: The Growth and Development of Astronomy and Astrophysics in India and the Asia-Pacific Region, Astrophysics and Space Science Proceedings 54, Hindustan Book Company 2018, Springer Nature Singapore Pte Ltd.

Major, John S. 1993. Heaven and Earth in Early Han Thought: chapters three, four and five of the Huainanzi. State University of New York, Albany.

Major, John S. et al. tr., ed. 2010: The Huainanzi, A guide to the theory and practice of government in early Han China, Columbia University Press.

Mak, Michael Y. and Albert T. So 2015: Scientific Feng Shui for the Built Environment, City University of Hong Kong.

Makeham, John. 1991. "Names, Actualities, and the Emergence of Essentialist Theories of Naming in Classical Chinese Thought." Philosophy East & West. 41.3: 341-363.

Makeham, John. 1994. Name and Actuality in Early Chinese Thought. State University of New York, Albany.

Mawangdui Hanmu Boshu, see above: *MWD*, under Primary Sources.

Mi Jing 米靖. 2002. "Heguanzi Jiaoyu Sixiang Qianxi" 鶡冠子教育思想淺析. Zhong guo daojiao 中國道教 7: 110-12.

Middendorf, Ulrike 2008: "Again on Qing with a translation of the Guodian Xing zi ming chu." Oriens Extremus 47: 97-159.

Mollier, Christine. 2008. Buddhism and Taoism Face to Face: Scripture, Ritual and Iconographic Exchange in Medieval China. Honolulu: University of Hawai'i.

Mori, Yuria. 2002. "Identity and Lineage: The Taiyi Jinhua Zongzhi and the Spirit-Writing Cult to Patriarch Lü in Qing China." In Kohn and Roth: 165-84.

Mroz, Daniel 2011: The Dancing Word, Consciousness, Literature and the Arts 30, Rodofi, Amsterdam and New York.

Nadler, Steven. 2012 "Baruch Spinoza." In Stanford Encyclopedia of Philosophy, http://plato.stanford.edu/archives/fall 2012/entries/spinoza/.

Nakajima Ryuzo 中島隆藏 2007: "Guodian Chujian 'Xing zi Ming chu" 郭店楚簡 '性自命出' 篇小考, 416-447, in Chudi Jianbo Sixiang yanjiu 3, Hubei Jiaoyu Chubanshe.

Naqin, Susan. 1976. Millennarian Rebellion in China. Yale University, New Haven.

Needham, Joseph et al. 1956. Science and Civilisation in China, vol. II: History of Scientific Thought; 1959 vol. III: Mathematics and the Sciences of the Heavens and the Earth; 1980, vol Vd Chemistry. Cambridge University.

Neugebauer, Klaus Kral. 1986: Hoh-kuan-tsi: Eine Untersuchung der dialogischen Kapitel (mit Übersetzung und Annotationen). Peter Lang, Frankfurt.

Opitz, Peter J. 1993. "The Birth of 'History'." In Lenk and Paul 1993: 137-158.

Pankenier, David W. 1990: "'The Scholar's Frustration' Reconsidered: Melancholia or Credo?" Journal of the American Oriental Society 110.3: 434-459.

Pankenier, David W. 2004: "A Brief History of Beiji: (Northern Culmen) With an Excursus on the Origin of the Character di." Journal of the American Oriental Society 124.2: 211-236.

Pankenier, David W. 2013: Astronomy and Cosmolog y in Early China, Conforming Earth to Heaven. Cambridge University, Cambridge.

Peerenboom, Randall P. 1991. "Heguanzi and Huang-Lao thought." Early China 16: 169-86.

Peerenboom, Randall P. 1993. Law and Morality in Ancient China: The Silk Manuscripts of Huang-Lao. State University of New York, Albany.Phillips, Scott, Park. 2016. Possible Origins: A Cultural History of Chinese Martial Arts, Theater, and Religion. Baby Books, Colorado.

Pines, Yuri. 2010. "Political My thology and Dynastic Legitimacy in the Rongchengshi Manuscript." Bulletin of the School of Oriental and African Studies 73.3: 503-29.

Pines, Yuri 2014 with Lothar von Falkenhausen; Gideon Shelach, Robin D. Yates eds.: Birth of an Empire, The State of Qin Revisited Global, Area and International Archive, University of California Press.

298

Poo Mu-chou. 2014: "Religion and Religious Life of the Qin," 187-205, in Pines et al. eds. 2014 Birth of an Empire.

Porter, Bill. 1993. Road to Heaven: Encounters with Chinese Hermits. Mercury House, San Francisco.

Pregadio, Fabrizio, ed. 2008. The Encyclopedia of Taoism. 2 vols. Routledge, London.

Puett, Michael J. 2002. To Become a God: Cosmology, Sacrifice, and Self-Divinization in Early China. Cambridge, Mass.: Harvard University, Asia Centre Publications.

Puett, Michael J. 2004. "The Ethics of Responding Properly: The Notion of Qing in Early Chinese Thought." in Love and Emotions in Traditional Chinese Literature, edited by Halvor Eifring, 37-68. Leiden: Brill.

Qian Mu 錢穆. 1986 [1935]. Xianqin zhuzi xinian 先秦諸子繫年. Dongda, Taipei.

Qiu Xigui, see above 'Primary Sources' *MWD* 1980; Guodian chumu zhujian 1998. Qiu Xigui 1981: "Sèfu Chutàn" in Yunmeng Qinjian Yanjiutan 226-302, Zhonghua Shuju, Beijing.

Rand, Christopher. 1980. "Chinese Military Thought and Philosophical Taoism." Monumenta Serica 34: 171-218.

Ritchie, Jennifer Lundin. 2012. "The Guodian Daodejing and Taiyi shengshui: A Cognitive Science Reading." Journal of Daoist Studies 5: 1-30.

Robinet, Isabelle 1997: Taoism: Growth of a Religion, tr. by Phyllis Brooks, Stanford University Press.

Robinet, Isabelle 2008: on "Beidou" in Pregadio 2008: 225-226.

Rosemont, Henry, Jr., ed. 1991. Chinese Texts and Philosophical Contexts: Essays Dedicated to Angus C. Graham. Open Court Publishing, La Salle, Ill..

Roth, Harold D. 1994. "Redaction Criticism and the Early History of Taoism." Early China 19: 191-46.

Roth, Harold D. 1999. Original Tao: Inward Training (Nei-yeh) and the Foundations of Taoist Mysticisim. Columbia University, New York.

Ryden, Edmund. 1997. The Yellow Emperor's Four Canons: A Literary Study of the Text from Mawangdui. Guangqi, Taipei.

Sakade, Yoshinobu. 2000. "Divination as Daoist Practice." In Daoism Handbook, edited by Livia Kohn, 541-66. Leiden: Brill.

Saso, Michael R. 1972. Taoism and the Rite of Cosmic Renewal. Washington State University Press.

Sawyer, Ralph D. 1993. Six Satchels (Liu-Tao) in:The Seven Militar y Classics of Ancient China. Westview, Boulder.

Schafer, Edward H. 1951. "Ritual Exposure in Ancient China." Harvard Journal of Asiatic Studies 14: 130-84.

Schafer, Edward H. 1977. Pacing the Void, T'ang Approaches to the Stars. University of California Press, Berkeley.

Shaughnessy, Edward L. 2005, Dec.: The Guodian Manuscripts and their place in Twentieth-Century Historiography on the Laozi, Harvard JAS Vol. 65, No. 2, 417- 457, Harvard-Yenching Institute.

Schipper, Kristofer 2000: "Taoism: The Story of the Way" in Little 2000. Schipper, Kristofer, and Franciscus Verellen, eds. 2004. The Taoist Canon: A Historical Companion to the Daozang. 3 vols. University of Chicago, Chicago.

Schwartz, Benjamin. 1985. The World of Thought in Ancient China. Harvard University, Cambridge, Mass..

Seaman, Gary. 1987. Journey to the North: An Ethnohistorical Analysis and Annotated Translation of the Chinese Folk Novel Pei-yu-chi. University of California, Berkeley.

Seidel, Anna, K. Nov. 1969 – Feb 1970. "Perfect Ruler in Early Taoist Messianism, Lao Tzu and Li Hung" 216-247 in History of Religions 9.

Seidel, Anna. 1983. "Imperial Treasures and Taoist Sacraments: Taoist Roots in the Apocrypha" in Tantric and Taoist Studies 291-371, Michel Strickman ed. Institut Belge des Hautes Etudes Chinoises, Brussels.

Seidel, Anna. 1984, Dec. "Taoist Messianism" in Numen, vol. 31, fasc. 2, 161-174, Brill.

Sellmann, James D. 1999: "The Origin and role of the state according to the Lüshi chunqiu," Asian Philosophy, 9.3: 193-218, Routledge, Taylor and Francis Group.

Sellmann, James D. 2006. "On the Origin of Shang and Zhou Law." Asian Philosophy 16.1: 49-64.

Shen Pingshan 沈平山. 1979. Zhong guo shenming gailun. 中國神明概論. Xinwenfeng, Taipei.

Shuîhûdì Qínmù Zhújiân 1990, Wénwù Chubânshè, Beîjing.

Slingerland, Edward. 2001. Effortless Action: Wuwei as Conceptual Metaphor and Spiritual ideal in Early China. Oxford University, New York.

Smith, K idder. 2003. "Sima Tan and the Invention of Daoism, 'Legalism, etc." Journal of Asian Studies 62.1: 122-56.

Star, Jonathan 2001: Tao Te Ching, the definitive editition, Tarcher, Penguin.

Steavu-Balint, Dominic Emanuel. 2010. "The Three Sovereigns Tradition: Talismans, Elixirs, and Meditation in Early Medieval China." Ph. D. Diss. Stanford University, Stanford.

Steinhardt, Nancy Shatzman. 1998. "The Temple to the Northern Peak in Quyang." Artibus Asiae 58: 69-90.

Strickmann, Michel. 1978. "The Longest Taoist Scripture." History of Religions 17: 331-54.

Sun Fuquan (Lutang) 孫福泉　祿堂　1924. Quanyi Shuzhen 拳意述真, Paul Brennan tr. 2015: Authentic Explanations of Martial Arts Concepts, WordPress.com.

Sun Fuxi. 孫福喜　2000. "Lun Heguanzi yu boshu Huangdi sijing yufa weti bijiao yanjiu" 論鶡冠子與帛書黃帝四經語法文體比較研究. Xibei daxue xuebao zhexue shehui kexue ban西北大學學報哲學社會科學班　3: 38-41.

Sun Fuxi. 孫福喜 2000. "Lun Heguanzi de benyuan yuzhou guan" 論鶡冠子的本原宇宙觀. Xibei daxue xuebao ziran kexueban 西北大學學報自然科學班4: 363-365.

Sun Fuxi. 孫福喜 2002. Heguan Yanjiu 鶡冠子研究. Shaanxi Renmin, Xi'an.

Sun Lìqún 孫立群 2007: Jiedu Da Qin zhengtan shuangxing Lyu Buwei yu Li Si 解讀大秦政壇雙星 呂不韋與李斯, Zhonghua Shuju, Beijing.

Sun Zhouyong 孫周勇 2013.09.01: "Shimao: A Stone-Walled Settlement of the 2ⁿᵈ Millennium BC in Northern China". Institute of Archaeology, Chinese Academy of Social Sciences., Shaanxi Provincial Institute of Archaeology, Chinese Archaeology.

Sun, Z., J. Shao, N. Di, N. Kang, Y. Zhao, A. Shao & N. Xia. 2017 (7): 46-56. "Shaanxi Shenmuxian Shimao chengzhi Huangchengtai didian." Kaogu, Beijing.

Sutton, Donald S. 2003. Steps of Perfection: Exorcistic Performers and Chinese Religion in Twentieth Century Taiwan, Harvard Asia Centre.

Tan Jiajian 譚家健. 1986. "Heguanzi shilun" 鶡冠子試論. Jianghan luntan 江漢論壇1986.2: 57-62.

Tang, Yijie. 2003. "Emotion in Pre-Qin Ruist Moral Theory: Dao Begins in Qing." tr. Brian Bruya and Wen Haiming. Philosophy East & West 53.2:271-81.

Thompson, Paul M. 1979. The Shen Tzu Fragments, 慎子逸文 [Shèn Dào 慎到]. Oxford University.

Tourism Authority of Thailand, Phuket Office 2015: Phuket Vegetarian Festival. Phuketemagazine.com.

Tseng, Lillian Lan-ying. 2011. Picturing Heaven in Early China. Harvard University Asia Centre Cambridge, Mass..

Tsuchiya, Masaaki. 2002. "Confession of Sins and Awareness of Self in the Taiping jing." In Kohn and Roth 2002.

Turner, Karen. 1989. "The Theory of Law in the Ching-fa." Early China 14: 55-76.
Vankeerberghen, Griet. 2001. The Huainanzi and Liu An's claim to Moral Authority, State University of New York.

Wang Pei 王沛 2005. "Heguanzi yu zhanguo shiqi fade guannian" 鶡冠子與戰國時期'法'的觀念. Faxue luntan法學論壇43: 83-89.

Wang, R.G. 2012. The Ming Prince and Daoism, institutional patronage of an elite. Oxford University, Oxford.

Wang, Robin R. 2012: Yinyang, The Way of Heaven and Earth in Chinese Thought and Culture, Cambridge University, Cambridge.

Weingarten, Oliver, 2020: "Intertexuality and Memory in Early Chinese Writings" 201-236 Early China 42, Cambridge University Press.

Wei Qipeng 1992 see: Mawangdui hanmu yishu jiaoshi, above.

Welch, Holmes 1957. Taoism: The Parting of the Way. Beacon, Boston.

Wells, Marnix St.J. 2001. "Shi: Dynamics of Cognition and Causation." Ph. D. Diss., SOAS, London University, London.

Wells, Marnix. 2004. "Pheasant Cap Master: Predicting Unification." Paper presented at the Second Annual Hawai'i International Conference on Arts & Humanities, Honolulu.

Wells, Marnix. 2005. Scholar Boxer, Chang Naizhou's theory of internal martial arts and the evolution of taijiquan. North Atlantic Books, Berkeley Ca..

Wells, Marnix. 2007. "'Pheasant Cap Master' Heguan Zi and the 'End of History.'" Paper presented at the 17th International Society for Chinese Philosophy annual conference at Wuhan University.

Wells, Marnix 2013: The Pheasant Cap Master and the End of History, Three Pines Press, St Petersburg, Florida.

Werner, E. T. C. 1922. Myths and Legends of China. Harrap, London.

Werner, E.T.C. 1932. Dictionary of Chinese Mythology, Shanghai.

White, William C. 1940. Chinese Temple Frescoes. Royal Ontario Museum, Toronto. Wilhelm, Richard; tr. Carl F. Baynes 1967: The I Ching or Book of Changes. Bollingen Series XIX. Princeton University Press.

Wilhelm, Richard. 1931, 1962. The Secret of the Golden Flower. Routledge & Kegan Paul, London.

Williams, Bruce. 1987. "Ho-kuan-tzu: Authenticity, Textual History and Analysis, together with an Annotated Translation of Chapters 1 through 4." M.A. Thesis, University of California, Berkeley.

Wong, Siu-kit 1969: Ch'ing [情] in Chinese Literary Criticism, PhD thesis, OxfordUniversity.

Wu Guang 吳光. 1985. Huanglao zhi xue tonglun 黃老之學通論. Hangzhou: Zhejiang Renmin.

Wu, Jing-Nuan. 1993. Ling Shu or The Spiritual Pivot. Washington, D.C.: The Taoist Centre.

Wu Xiansheng, Wang Jingchun 吳憲生, 王經春ed. 2001.1. Zhong guo Lidai Ming jia Jifa Jicui, Renwu juan. 中國歷代名家技法集萃, 人物卷. Shandong Meishu Chubanshe, Jinan.

Xiao Hanming 蕭漢明. 2005.7. "Heguanzi de yuchou lun yu Suhuang neidi zhi fa" 鶡冠子的宇宙論與素皇內帝之法. In Ji Xianlin 季羨林 ed.:

INDEX

G

N

O

Lightning Source UK Ltd.
Milton Keynes UK
UKHW010711260722
406385UK00001B/44